THE BEATLES AND THEIR REVOLUTIONARY BASS PLAYER

Dennis Alstrand

The Larry Czerwonka Company, LLC
Hilo, Hawai'i

First Edition – April 2014

All trademarks are the property of their respective companies.

Published by: The Larry Czerwonka Company, LLC
http://thelarryczerwonkacompany.com

Printed in the United States of America

ISBN: 0615995349
ISBN-13: 978-0615995342

To Sandi

Cover design by Roxana Anderson

Contents

Acknowledgements

The creation of what became this book began in the late 1990s. Here I am in 2014 finishing the book. I now know first-hand why authors always thank their spouses so thanks to **Sandi Alstrand**. For one thing, this entire book was written on our one shared computer. She was ever enthusiastic about this project, even when I was down. Love you.

William Anderson is the guy who talked me into turning my website into a book. Little did he know that I'd spend four years doing it.

Wanting to lend an air of actual sophistication and scholastic musical understanding to the proceedings, I asked musicologist **Dr. Alan W. Pollack** (PhD from University of Pennsylvania in Music Theory and Composition) if I could quote him extensively and he gave me the go-ahead.

Ken Michaels has been in the Beatle business for many years and offered immediate enthusiasm.

Beatle author **Joel Benjamin** offered some darned good correspondence regarding the Beatles.

My ever-Canadian friend **Don Monson** provided editing tips and reminding me to think about using a spell checker.

My cousin **Jerry Dicey** and I have spent years discussing what being a bass player means. After reading initial drafts, he talking me into cleaning this up and making it more professional than it originally was.

Rainer Toschke deserves a special mention here. He lives in Germany and, upon initial publication of this information as a website, he wrote me to ask what "kick ass" means. Did it mean to put one's foot in a donkey? Not only did I learn (from him) to try to refrain from idiomatic speech, but a strong friendship was struck up and my family visited his in a truly memorable visit to his homeland. In fact, the amount of friends I made from this book is incredible to me and, for that reason alone, I place it as my most valuable writing ever.

Big Island publisher/businessman **Larry Czerwonka** is a man who pays his success forward. He makes writing and publishing a book like this one possible. There's a lot to be learned from him.

To all of the Beatles authors, especially **Mark Lewisohn** and **Walter Everett**.

Introduction

How the hell did four guys, from a city on the Northwest Coast of England, come to rule the world? I can not imagine what life would have been like without them. Can you?

How would the current economic state or all of the sorrows of the world compare to going through life never hearing "She Loves You" or "A Day in the Life"? Instead, we were able to live vicariously through a story that would make a great novel (if someone ever chose to write it as such). It has everything you need: desire, early failures, bleak moments, heartbreak, love affairs, dragon women and helpless maidens, martyrs, incredible characters—some dark and some light—coming and going just when they were most needed, insecurity and loyalty, triumph against all odds, the world held in the sway of four men who changed it all, a breakup that was viewed with more despair than Charles and Diana and—finally—four figures, four separate Phoenixes, stumbling to their feet and learning for the first time how to stand up without their three mates at their side.

The intention of this book is to capture some of that story with a focus on the evolution of the bass playing of Paul McCartney. The book's genesis was a website devoted to his bass guitar work (still online at www.alstrand.com) but it became clear that any discussion of one aspect of the Beatles leaves the rest of the story wanting. For example, to talk only about McCartney's most famous bass line—the one in "Come Together"—ignores the innovative drumming of Ringo Starr, the swampiness of Paul's electric piano, the quality of John Lennon's voice, and the mere fact that he is saying "shoot me" at the start of each instrumental riff. To talk about one thing, you *have* to talk about it all.

Writing this book, I soon realized, was like riding on an emotional roller coaster. Pull out an old Beatles' chestnut and listen closely to it with the intention of explaining it to someone else and you'll see what I mean. In my case, maybe something about the structure of the arrangement would strike me as brilliant and I'd grapple for words to describe it. Words that did not make me sound like a wide-eyed, throat-gurgling, gob-smacked fanatic. Which I am, but I do try to hide it in these pages.

The songs that I had the most fun with were "She Loves You," "A Day in the Life," "Hey Jude," "Come Together" and "I Want You (She's So Heavy)." Each song presents itself as a well-orchestrated masterpiece, complete in every way. To me, the Beatles were such an incredible team—such a tight unit—that whatever an individual did had an impact on the larger unit. In the early days, the group would generally run their songs through what I call the Beatles Machine. A song would go in with chords and melody and come out a full-fledged Beatles song.

As for McCartney's bass playing, let better minds than mine tell it for me:

"Paul was one of the most innovative bass players ever. And half the stuff that is going on now is directly ripped off from his Beatles period."

~ John Lennon
(*The Playboy Interviews With John Lennon and Yoko Ono*, 1981)

I won't argue with John Lennon. As you go through this book, you will find that many of the foremost bass players of the world feel the same way. His bass playing was as influential to rock bass players as James Jameson's was to soul players and, dare I say, the incredible Charles Mingus' playing was to jazz players.

McCartney wasn't the fastest or the greatest technical player, but when it came to lifting a song up to a new level, he was (and remains) up there with the best of them. The difference between him and others is that McCartney was always at the forefront of innovative ways to cause his bass guitar to make noise. Consider the following: he was the first rock bass player to be a front man. He was the first rock bass player to use double stops (two finger chords). He was one of the first to combine a melodic and rhythmic approach to bass playing. And, in the end, he came to be a major influence on bass players with no less renown than Stanley Clarke, Will Lee, Sting and Billy Sheehan as well as me and a thousand others.

Like thousands of others, I took up bass playing in the late 1960s mainly because of Paul McCartney. He made it look like fun and played thundering bass lines to boot. I've gone through hero-worshipping phases: Jack Bruce and Chris Squire figured prominently in my development, but it always comes back to the man who started it all: Paul McCartney. In 1966, he switched exclusively to a Rickenbacker 4001 bass and started making the bass a crucial part of Beatles' recordings. But I suspect it was his playing style on the white album that is the most influential of all of his playing. I hear that style everywhere to this day.

What to Expect With This Book

The audience: The book is written with the lay listener in mind. If there are musical terms or phrases that you don't understand, then I haven't quite done my job. But I like to listen to what's going on behind the scenes in a song. If you like listening to the Beatles but don't normally dig into the underpinning of the recordings, this book might cause you to start listening in more detail.

Chapters: There is a chapter for every year of the Beatles (1961-69) and one for some of McCartney's post-Beatles work. At the start of each chapter, you'll find a breakdown of major events in the lives of the band during that year. This will be followed by a discussion of a selection of Beatles songs for that year. I won't go into every song; for example, you will find an at-length discussion of the song "Please Please Me," including what it must have meant to the Beatles to score their first number one hit. But there is almost nothing about their next release, "From Me to You." I just can't think of what to say about that one.

Features: The book is loaded with a *lot* facts and information that I think you'll find fascinating. How long did it take Paul McCartney to become an accomplished bass player? Read the chapter on 1961. When did McCartney and the Beatles develop the bass playing and recording style that would carry on through to Abbey Road? Read the chapter on 1965. What are the Beatles *actually* saying in "She Loves You"? How do you get to the crosswalk at Abbey Road? How did Paul do on John and George's songs? How, exactly, did Capitol Records mash up the Beatles' music? Read about these and more "Between the Chapters."

In various places, there are little sections entitled "Did You Hear That?!" This came from a weekly spot I've been doing for some years in Hawai'i on radio station B97 (Hilo) B93 (Kona) with the morning DJ, Darrin Carlson (DC). I'd hear a little piece of a song that wasn't obvious to the listener and call in and talk about it with him. It was always fun, so I've included some of those in this book as well.

The book should be fun to read. Thank you for picking it up!

ONE

In the Beginning
(1957-1960)

The chain of various incarnations, lineups and band name changes that eventually became the Beatles all began in 1956. Ring-leader John Lennon formed a band called the Quarrymen, named after Quarry Bank High School.

The band name came from the school song which had the line "Quarrymen, strong before our birth" (and you thought only pro wrestlers and leaders of Middle Eastern countries made outrageous claims). By the way, the Quarrymen as a band exist to this day, although most of the original members have died including, saddest of all those who have ever died, its founding father, John Lennon.

A huge day in the life: on July 6th, 1957, the Quarrymen were enlisted to play an outdoor party behind a church in Woolton, a suburb of Liverpool. Just after 4:00 p.m., they played their first set. It has been surmised somehow that the band was playing the Del-Vikings' hit "Come Go With Me" when Paul McCartney showed up. After their set, John's friend Ivan Vaughan introduced Paul to John and the rest of the Quarrymen.

Lennon was always famous for his inability to remember lyrics, and so when the two sat down after the set and Paul sang the lyrics to Eddie Cochrane's "Twenty Flight Rock," Lennon was impressed. In the next few days, Lennon realized he had a tough decision to make. Should he ask Paul to join the Quarrymen? It may seem to us now as the easiest decision in the world. After all, this young McCartney fellow knew how to play real guitar chords unlike the banjo style chords which were all that Lennon knew. Not only that, he could sing like a bird, and while he seemed to Lennon like a bit of a goody two-shoes, he had a certain aspect to him that showed he might be going places. Paul McCartney was talented.

But there was an enormous downside to letting Paul into the group. With a chip on his shoulder (yes, bigger than his feet) John had always been the leader with his friends and with the Quarrymen he was the unquestioned ruler. He sang all of the songs and he fancied himself the best musician of the lot. If he allowed the young upstart in, he would be trading total leadership for someone at his level. This would not be an easy thing for him to do. It took him weeks to come to the conclusion that the music of the Quarrymen was more valuable than his leadership of the group. McCartney wasn't invited to join until quite a bit later and he took his time in responding. As he remembered in his song "Here Today," both he and John were playing hard to get. However, to the immense satisfaction of music fans, record companies and book publishers for years to come, he finally joined and had his first appearance with the Quarrymen on October 18, 1957.

As the years sailed by, the Quarrymen changed lineups. Paul brought George Harrison into the band in 1958 and in 1960 John brought in his college friend, Stu Sutcliffe who was the first bass player in the Beatles' story.

As the original Quarry Bank High band members gradually left the band, the name Quarrymen made less and less sense. Between 1959 and 1960, the band tried out many names, but it was apparently Sutcliffe—and not a man on a flaming pie—who came up with the name Beatles (or Beatals as it was originally spelled).

The Beatles trudged through these formative years, picking up work when they could, being "let off leash" for the first time (as Paul later said) and wondering—quite often—if they had any hope of being anything but *working class for life*.

But these were truly the formative years. They listened to and copied from records, watched other bands, learned new chords and progressions, invented their own unique styles and personae, and competed with what ended up being hundreds of bands around their home town. It was this fierce competition that drove the Beatles in more ways than one. There were ground rules. If a song became identified with a certain group, the other groups would not perform it. Gerry Marsden remembers, though that some groups might trade songs. "If you let me play your 'Jambalaya,' I'll give you my 'Roll Over Beethoven.'" To escape this nonsense, the Beatles learned to find songs that were not so well-known and made them their own. They discovered and played a lot of b-sides to American records (the Shirelles, etc) that became sta-ples in their act. It was all-important to be different from the other bands. If, during a show, another band was being lively and enthusias-tic, they'd try to hold it down. Usually, however, they were alive and energetic in their sets.

Still, they didn't make any money in Liverpool and, with countless other bands cropping up there, the prospects looked bleak for our heroes. After temporary manager Allan Williams got them a gig in Hamburg, Germany, they found they weren't making any money there either. There's a valid reason they all look skinny in the old photos! But they were slowly, surely building a following. Maybe there was hope after all, for the upcoming year 1961.

By the end of 1960, the lineup for the Beatles was Paul McCartney (piano and guitar), Pete Best (drums), Stu Sutcliffe (bass), George Harrison (guitar), John Lennon (guitar).

McCartney's Höfners
by Claudine Purdue

It was never James Paul McCartney's intention to become the bass player for the Beatles. When, in April 1961, the 19 year old McCartney walked into Steinway music shop in the center of Hamburg, he pur-chased the Höfner 500/1 Violin bass he spotted in the window. It was light weight and inexpensive at approximately £30.

This first one held a 30" short scale (making the transition some-what easier for the guitar player), vertical Höfner logo, "Rugby ball" tuners, white/pearloid pick guard and unbound neck. The fully hollow body consisted of rosewood fingerboard maple sides and back, with an 11" spruce top, laminated with nitrocellulose. The pickups on the 1961 model were close together, towards the neck. Double coil, double pole pickups, covered with the Diamond plate. Sound knobs were two "tea cup" models, and basic up and down switches which controlled, treble on/off, bass on/off and rhythm/solo. The bass had a distinctive sound, making it resemble the tone of a tiny upright bass, especially with the flat wound strings of the era. It also had a special strap, with"dog-clip" ends, one end being tied beneath the neck and the other attached to the body with a clip.

This model was used with a Selmer Truvoice Stadium TV19T amplifier owned originally by George Harrison, from 1960-1961, then with a bass cabinet obtained from guitarist Adrian Barber of another Liverpool group The Big Three. Later a Quad II amplifier. McCartney continued to use this set up until 1963, (the exception of playing at the Star Club, in which they used the house amplifiers) then purchasing the first of many of the Vox "T" line.

In 1963, the Diamond shaped pickups of the original 1961 Violin Höfner began to literally fall out, having been held in place for some time with electrical tape. The Höfner company gave McCartney an updated 1962 model. The pickups now moved further apart to increase sound quality, as well as, having been changed to "staple" pickups. The logo having also been changed to script format. This would be the bass that the world would see on the Beatles first appearance of the Ed Sullivan show. Both Höfners were used from 1963 up through Rubber Soul, after which the Rickenbacker came to be the main recording bass. At some point during 1964 Höfner presented him with a gold plated, bound neck third 500/1 bass, which he politely refused.

In 1964 he sent his original 1961 "Cavern" model to be refurbished for use a backup bass to Sound City of London, having added a different style control knobs, a deeper color sunburst, and Selmer tweed hard case. McCartney swapped out the "new" style knobs for the original "tea cup" style later on. This bass would also reappear on "Thank Your Lucky Stars" in 1964, and much later in the *Revolution* video seen in 1968 with David Frost. The last appearance of McCartney's original violin Höfner was in the filming of the *Let It Be* movie. During the shooting it was stolen. The famous rooftop concert, in which the BASSMAN sticker is shown, is the 1963 model, the prominent sticker having been taken from John's Fender amp box. This is the Höfner that he continues to use currently, brought back into use in 1980 at the request of Elvis Costello, who enjoyed the classic sound.

Two

The New Bass Player
(1961)

1961 in Review

This is where the story truly starts, because 1961 is the year Paul McCartney stopped being the guitarist/pianist and became the bass player in the Beatles. Because of the switch, 1961 is a year of importance in Beatle lore. But to the Beatles, it was mostly another year of striving, starving and making extremely slow progress on their way to a success that must have looked to be light years away.

They had secured fairly decent residencies in Hamburg, Germany, playing for hours on end to drunken, brawling customers. As seedy and dirty as the scene appears to have been, it was perfect for the Beatles. For it was there that the Beatles honed their craft. They learned to "make show" as their German bosses would yell. John and George have both said that it was in Hamburg that they were at their best as performers. By year's end, they were a hot band who were honing their stage craft . . . and still going nowhere.

The Departure of Stu Sutcliffe

At the beginning of 1961, they were a five-piece band. John, Paul, George, Pete and Stu could not be called lazy. They had by now begun the lives of workaholics that the Beatles would retain until the end. You might say they were already a veteran band. They had spent a lot of time playing long hours in Liverpool and Hamburg during these early years. When their residence there ended in July of 1961, John, Paul, George and Pete made their way back across the channel to England. As they left, they said goodbye to bassist Stu Sutcliffe who remained behind with his fiancé, Astrid Kircherr.

It's never been made entirely clear as to why he left. There are certainly those close to him who claim it was his level of talent.

> "He stood a certain way, he had shades, he looked the part-but he wasn't that good a player. Any of our mates could look at the group and spot it; any of the guys who were in groups like us—King Size Taylor & the Dominoes, the Big Three—they would just spot it, and they'd say: 'Lousy bass player, man.'"
> ~ Paul McCartney
> (*Paul McCartney – Bass Master - Playing the Great Beatles Basslines*, 2006)

In the video to *The Beatles Anthology*, George Harrison shared McCartney's view of Stu's talent. Recordings of the Beatles with Sutcliffe certainly don't indicate that he played with much talent, mostly just thumping root notes, 1st beat of measure.

We should bear in mind, however, that none of the Beatles showed much talent in those days. Klaus Voorman, who was a huge fan of the group in their Hamburg days, said in a documentary. "Stu was a really good rock and roll bass player, a very basic bass player, completely different. He was, at the time, my favorite bass player . . . and he had that cool look." He went on to say that he liked the Beatles best when Stu was in the band. Rhythm-mate Pete Best has said that Sutcliffe was a better bass player than he has been given credit for—that he knew his limitations and worked hard with them.

Band politics may have been a contributing factor to his exit. McCartney, by his own account, had been giving Sutcliffe a hard time as had his close friend, John Lennon. But, he also saw a future for himself in the Hamburg art community; he had been awarded a scholarship and enrolled at the Hamburg College of Art.

When he left the Beatles, Sutcliffe loaned McCartney his bass (with the stipulation that he keep it strung for a right-handed player) and walked out of the history books. But I can't let him go without expressing *some* emotion about the young man who named the Beatles.

Sutcliffe was a short-time historical figure, a person who lives only in the books. Sadly, he's one who died before we could get to know him and so it's hard to imagine him as a real person. In fact, It only occurred to me when I read the book version of *The Beatles Anthology* that he was a real person and not a historical figure. There, speaking in the present tense, is Sutcliffe talking about how there were no bands to touch the Beatles in Liverpool. It was taken from a letter to his mother, but the fact that there was a quote from a living, breathing Stu Sutcliffe brought him to life for me.

He's been said to have been funny enough to be on par with Lennon. By all accounts, he was a bit of a visionary. In *Stuart Sutcliffe's Bass Playing*, Liscio calls him "an original thinker, highly intelligent, responsible and mature beyond his young years." He quotes Voorman as saying "[Stu] could see ten times more than other people" and that he was "miles ahead of everybody." He was a clear-thinking young man.

As time went by, Stu began suffering headaches that, according to Astrid Kircherr, had left him temporarily blind at times He died in Germany of an aneurism on April 10, 1962 in an ambulance with Astrid by his side. The Beatles arrived in Hamburg shortly thereafter for another engagement when they heard the news.

At the time of Stu's death, the Beatles were on an upswing. His old rhythm-section mate Pete Best was still in the band, and they had been signed to a management contract with Brian Epstein who was trying to secure a record contract for them (that would come a month later). But for Sutcliffe, who had spent countless hours playing with the band, it must have been emotionally dispiriting to not be a part of that inner circle anymore.

John Lennon, Paul McCartney and Pete Best have talked about this phenomena, and the same thing is felt by entertainers of all stripes, from musicians to sports stars. One moment you're doing something that is incredibly important, exciting and fast-moving with instant gratification from your fans. Next moment you're back to being a regular guy again. There are darned few, if any, who have handled it well and so we can only guess that Sutcliffe was not easy about the transition. The Beatles were a fast-moving train on the rise to stardom. And so they said goodbye to Stu Sutcliffe.

We Need a New Bass Player. Who Will it Be?

Sutcliffe's exit from the band provided a real problem to resolve for the remaining four. There were many questions to ponder. Should they remain a five-piece band, sharing the money five ways? The band has played together for hundreds of hours and are a tight unit. Did they want to bring in somebody new who would have to learn all of the songs (always the bugaboo of musician replacement)? Did they need three guitarists (John, Paul and George)? The bass was generally known as the instrument for the person with the least talent back in 1961. If they did decide to move one of the guitarists over, whom should it be? John did not want to make the move and neither did George.

In the end, they decided to move the best lead guitarist of the lot over and Paul McCartney became the first bass playing front man.[1]

> "it was like, Uh-oh, we haven't got a bass player. And everyone sort of turned 'round and looked at me. I was a bit lumbered with it, really it was like, 'Well . . . it'd better be you, then.' I don't think you would have caught John doing it; he would have said: 'No, you're kidding. I've got a nice new Rickenbacker!' I was playing piano and didn't even have a guitar at the time, so I couldn't really say that I wanted to be a guitarist."
> ~ Paul McCartney
> (*Paul McCartney - Bass Master - Playing the Great Beatles Basslines*, 2006)

It's amazing how small things can become so monumental in the study of history. Paul McCartney didn't have a guitar, did have a talent for the bass guitar, and history now reads that it was either during

April or May of 1961 that he became the Beatles' bass player and destined to become one of the most famous bass players in rock history.

> "In listening to Paul McCartney play, you hear how much feeling he puts into his playing yet he strictly stays within the harmonic context of the song. None-the-less, he does some incredible things underneath. In some ways what he does and how he plays might even be more difficult than doing a solo or taking it in that direction. I think that, to him, it's what's best for the song itself that counts. He does not need to solo because that would be taking away from the song and the message. After all, he is a songwriter at heart who happens to be a very talented musician."
>
> ~ Mark Fosella
>
> *(email, 2012)*

I think Mark has captured the essence of Paul McCartney's bass playing better than many who have gone before. He said in one paragraph, what I hope to elaborate upon in this book.

The First Official Recording Sessions

Despite many guitar players' opinions to the contrary, the bass guitar is not an easy instrument to learn. It takes much more than the ability to play notes to become effective at the instrument. It is, generally, a "behind-the-scenes" instrument that yields great power in the music, at times subtly, at other times right out front. As the main anchor between the drummer and the other instruments, the bass is both a rhythm and melodic instrument. What the bass player does in a song is not often heard or understood by a lot of listeners, but if you were to remove it from the song it would be immediately noticeable. A talented bass player knows how long to hold a note to be the most effective. (Listen to the breaks on "Come Together.")

Paul McCartney became a bass master over the years, as we will see. But, do you find yourself wondering how long it took for him to convert from being a guitarist and pianist to an adept bass player? Five years? Two? Less than what it takes most of us mortals.

Thanks to the inclusion of a few songs on Beatles' *Anthology 1*, we can answer that question right here. Keep in mind that he became the bass player in April or May 1961.

Somewhere on or around June 22nd 1961, back in Hamburg, the Beatles were called upon to go into a makeshift recording studio and backup lead singer Tony Sheridan on some tracks. The sessions were produced by German writer/arranger/producer Bert Kaempfert, who had orchestrated a hit record called "Wonderland by Night" and was, in later years, to write the music for "Strangers in the Night" and "Spanish Eyes."

My Bonnie (LP)

Sheridan's album was to be titled *My Bonnie*. There was time and room, apparently, to fill tracks for the album because the Beatles (credited on the record as "The Beat Brothers") recorded some tracks of their own. These are the songs included on the Anthology. Let's talk about two of them:

"Cry for a Shadow"
This is an instrumental song written and performed by the Beatles either in tribute to or in mockery of The Shadows, one of the most popular bands in England at the time. Aside from the fact that it is a fun, and catchy number, there are a number of factors that make the song interesting from a historical point of view.

❖ Paul's bass on this, one of the first songs he ever recorded on the instrument, is *already* first rate. You can tell he has the feel for the instrument. He features at the end of every chorus with a slick little run up the neck.

❖ Pete's drumming is state-of-the-art for 1961, utilizing a surf beat. But, as will be reported again later in this book, when it is compared to the heaviness that McCartney brought with his bass, it comes off as too light-sticked. Either McCartney should have lightened his touch or Best should have "heavied up."

The songs from those sessions were recorded in a school setting, far from a recording studio, and you're hearing the Beatles pretty much how they sounded live in those days. Paul's amp can barely handle the pressure, and that actually adds some charm to the sound of the bass. During most of his Beatle years and then again on *Wings Over America*, part of Paul's unique sound was driving his amp just to the edge of distortion. What a difference this makes with sound in general—adding an edgy touch to it—and Paul is getting it on this recording.

"Ain't She Sweet"

While the drums and guitars (and indeed the vocals) are playing staccato on the verses, McCartney is the only one who is sustaining his notes (legato). He is playing in counterpoint to the rest of the band, taking a leadership role in the music. His bass stands out from the crowd and not for the last time either. He is playing loose and clearly having fun. A lot of bass players, especially in those days, played in a *walking* style. This means that they would play notes as they moved from chord to chord. Starting with the first verse (under Lennon's vocal), McCartney stretches the time from the first to the second chord by walking his way up. This *stretching* is done only beneath the vocal parts. It uplifts the vocal from below.

For the rest of the song, he moves between walking notes and rhythm notes. Throughout his long career on the bass, as we'll see, quite often he has done the exact opposite of what you might expect a bass player to do. There's no exception when the band moves to the chorus of the song "Just cast an eye . . ." you'd expect him to continue the style he had used with the verse. Instead, he begins hammering the notes (playing and repeating the same note quickly, similar to what he did for the introduction to "Please Please Me"). Even if you don't notice what he's doing, it livens up the song by making the point that the bass guitar can have an incredible effect without being obvious. Listen to all three songs from the album ("My Bonnie," "Ain't She Sweet" and "Cry for a Shadow") and you'll see that his clear goal is to keep the music lively. Despite his aptitude for self-control, and control of his surroundings, he loved to let a song take flight—when he wasn't the one singing.

How Long Had McCartney Been Playing Bass?

The question was, how long did it take for McCartney to develop into the role of the bass player? It was in April or May, 1961 that he switched to the bass. It was June 22nd (or so) that the Beatles recorded "Ain't She Sweet," etc., Paul McCartney had learned and begun perfecting his use of the bass guitar as an influence on the music being played by the band. He had been playing the bass for just one or two months.

Hamburg was where the Beatles learned how to seize an audience and make them watch and listen. Dressed in leather, dirty, sleepless, either drunk or on pep pills or both, they played hour after hour to roaring, brawling drunken Germans. But they were getting better all the time.

> "I was fascinated to see how the Beatles were improving. Chivvied on by the club boss: *'Mak shau! Mak shau!'* (Make show, make show) every time a break went on too long, they pushed themselves to the limit to play for eight hours at a stretch. Under pressure, they'd become more professional, and they were achieving a fabulous effect. Even though they hadn't yet progressed to using their own songs, they were producing a sound that was special and unique."
>
> ~ Cynthia Lennon
>
> (*A Twist of Lennon*, 1980)

Playing eight hour gigs will do one of two things to a band: either they would find out they are not cut out for the line of work—or—

they would become very talented as a unit. The never-sleeping (a prerequisite for a professional musician) Beatles opted for the latter.

The Cavern Clubs and Hopes for the World Beyond

Although the Quarrymen had played there, it was in 1961 that the Beatles began their long series of engagements playing at the Cavern Club in Liverpool. The Cavern had been a jazz club, and the Beatles changed that (much to the chagrin of its earlier patrons). You got to the club by descending a stairway and standing in a small area, sweat dripping off of the brick walls. It's a wonder the musicians weren't electrocuted playing there, but this was Liverpool at its most exciting. The crowds loved the Beatles and they ended up lugging their equipment to and playing at the Cavern Club an incredible 250 times in the next few years.

Playing the Cavern, they had become one of the very top acts in Liverpool. They had even made a record, but in effect they were still nowhere. London was where you had to be if you wanted to make it in music. It was the springboard for money, fame and the actual real reason most of these guys got into the music business: women. As they put on their leather outfits and faced their cheering screaming fans for yet another rocking evening at the sweaty Cavern, part of their brain must have been pondering the fact that this club might be the height of their success. I don't know if the Beatles were religious, but even a nonbeliever could see that it would take a bona fide angel to get them out of this dead end.

The Angel Appears

Stories differ about exactly how their personal angel of mercy came to them, and even his own account is questionable. True, he owned a prestigious record store in Liverpool called NEMS (North End Music

Stores) in Whitechapel, a section of Liverpool. It's also true that he, too, felt that he was on a road to nowhere. It may or may not be true that on October 28, 1961, a young man named Raymond Jones entered his record store and asked him if he had a record called "My Bonnie" by a group called the Beatles. After a few other requests, the store owner was intrigued, made a series of inquiries, and discovered where he could find this strangely named group.

Whatever the case, November 9th 1961 is a day that we can hold as sacrosanct. It's the day that Brian Epstein first walked into the Cavern Club and saw the Beatles. He saw a crowd of kids cheering for their leather-clad, untidy heroes. They didn't look right to him, but they sure sounded good. And he fell in love with them, especially that one named John.

He came back many times to hear them play. He was a man with well-developed theatrical instincts and began to imagine what he could do with the group. He finally decided that he wanted to manage them. He sought advice from his lawyer who told him to forget about the whole idea. He sought advice from his family who gave the same sage advice. And so, on December 6th he met with the Beatles who agreed to hire him as their manager (the actual contract was signed on January 24th of 1962).

And he began pouring all of his energy into getting them known in London.

It wasn't long before Epstein's machinations attracted the attention of the head of Decca Records, Dick Rowe. A representative was sent to watch the Beatles at the Cavern and through a contract was not signed, an audition was set up at Decca Records' studio. In London! The date: January 1st, 1962. Heck, we better get to the next chapter quick to see where this story goes next.

Notes

1. "Who is the best" is always a point of conjecture, but McCartney certainly showed his credentials as a lead guitarist throughout the Beatles' recording career. He is the one who played the hot lead solo on "Taxman." It was he who played the slide guitar lead on "Drive My Car." He plays the dirty opening lead riffs on "Sgt. Pepper's Lonely Hearts Club Band" and then the lead on "Good Morning Good Morning" as well as the heavy metal guitar on "Helter Skelter." Official lead guitarist George Harrison must have had difficulty with being relegated to 2nd banana in that role through the years until he played the beautifully crafted and played solo on "Something."

Short-Scale vs. Long-Scale Bass

Scale, in this case, refers to the size of the neck of the instrument. Most basses you see are considered "large scale" basses. A point that is not so well known about Paul McCartney's early bass playing (1962-1965) is that what might be the most famous bass of all time, his ever popular Höfner 500/1 violin bass, has a very short neck. At the time of its issue, it was an inexpensive bass with a small neck. If one is used to *regular* basses, picking up a Höfner will offer a surprise. It is extremely light.

When playing it, there is a tendency to play fast little lines and, unless you have Paul McCartney's bass in your hands—which I can guarantee none of us ever will have—it will also be out of tune as you play up the neck.

Yet, even with that little bass guitar, Paul McCartney brought rock bass playing many a step forward. He used a Höfner for every concert and recording right up until *Rubber Soul.* There is some controversy as to which bass was used on various songs on that particular album. It would be *safe* to claim that both "Drive My Car" and "Think for Yourself" were done on his 1964 Rickenbacker model 4001S bass.

For non bass-players, there is a world of difference between the two instruments.

"Because the Höfner's so light, you play it a bit like a guitar—all that sort of high trilling stuff I used to do, I think, was because of the Höfner. When I play a heavier bass like a Fender, it sits me down a bit and I play just bass."

~ Paul McCartney

(*Paul McCartney – Bass Master - Playing the Great Beatles Basslines*, 2006)

Interestingly enough, he was only able to play up the neck efficiently when he switched to the Rickenbacker. The Höfner's neck was not aligned until recently (by Mandolin Bros. in New York). Until then, its intonation (best defined as its ability to remain in tune with itself) would decline after the third fret according to its owner. The switch to the Rickenbacker "sat him down" but it also allowed him to move up the neck with a far steadier and more powerful style. This can well be witnessed by his playing on "Rain," "Paperback Writer" and the *Anthology 2* version of "And Your Bird Can Sing." He *could not* have obtained the same sound or effect on his Höfner.

The interesting aspect of this whole subject of McCartney's bass playing is that he was (and is) not merely a bass player. It is quite obvious that he hears and feels the entire range of the song as it is being developed. He has definite ideas on what the guitars should sound like (frequently plays them), what the keyboard should sound like (frequently plays them) and what the drums should sound like (and frequently plays those as well). Even with his "high trilling stuff," he remained a bass player. His technique, while trilling, was still rhythmic and not like a lead guitar (as so many claim). If you want an argument from me, all you have to do is say he played lead bass. The only exception I can think of to this rule is during the end piece of "I Want You (She's So Heavy)" where he purposely went on great flights of bass playing fancy, and is another case of something that could not have been done on his small scale Höfner. But it is also another case of Paul having great fun on a John song.

THREE

Waiting on the World (1962)

1962 in Review

Although the year started on an incredible high, 1962 was a year that almost ended the Beatles. Had not a peculiar set of impossible coincidences taken place, Brian Epstein would never have secured a recording contract for the group. Had that not happened, it is most probably that they would have eventually splintered as a group, never to be heard from by the rest of the world, and—far less importantly—never causing this book to be written.

The year started off with a failed audition at Decca Records on January 1. The head of the studio, Dick Rowe never lived it down until he died in 1986. Lest we feel too badly for his thumbs-down to the Beatles, and we don't, he did sign the next promising act that came along: the Rolling Stones.

A look at the Beatles' schedule for the year shows that they spent most of their time playing around Liverpool and other dates in northern England.

The band was apparently experiencing some inner turmoil. There were signs that drummer Pete Best was not in favor with the group. Despite that, in mid-year, Brian Epstein made it happen: the Beatles were signed to a recording contract with EMI, one of the biggest record companies in the world. This culminated with Best's exit and the welcoming of Ringo Starr into the group. It was now John, Paul,

George and Ringo. The four had come together at last, and the world would have to step aside as they made their ride for success.

Paul began establishing himself as a top-notch bass player around Liverpool. There were other bass players out there who could play, but few were also front men.[1]

The Beguiling Tale of the Elusive Recording Contract

The Beatles were in a fragile situation as the year began. They were successful in the clubs around Liverpool and in Germany, but they knew that the one and only way to break out of the small time was to land the ever-elusive recording contract. Without that they would not even merit a footnote to history.

To make their journey more fragile, the Beatles were northerners. They were provincial, northerners, perpetually snubbed by those in the all powerful London music scene. In those days, before the Beatles changed everything, "provincials" had to change their accents and style and forget about their lower class ways.

The Decca Audition / Epstein Management Contract

So it was with this tense realization in mind that the Beatles drove down to London on January 1st through terrible weather to play in a real recording studio for the first time. We can only guess at the conversations that transpired as they made their way to the big city and their shot at the big time.

Decca Records had shown interest in them and here was their moment in the (wintry) sun. They recorded 15 songs, all picked by Brian Epstein. The Beatles were nervous and edgy, which becomes clear when you listen to the recordings (many available on the Beatles *Anthology* CD).

There was no producer for the session but the engineer, hung over from an all night New Years Eve party, seemed positive. This seemed like great news, and the Beatles went home excited and happy, ready for the fame that was right around the corner.

As they awaited news and with a new regard for Mr. Epstein, on January 24, 1962, the Beatles signed with him to a five year management contract and waited for word from Decca that their future was in good hands.[2]

In early February, the crushing news came that they had failed the Decca audition. "Guitar groups are on the way out," they were told. They blamed themselves for letting manager Epstein supply their list of songs to play and vowed never to let him interfere with the musical side of things again. It looked as if the Beatles' story might be at an end before it could seriously begin.

Epstein told them to hang tight while he went down to London to give one last go. Armed with the tape from the failed Decca session, Epstein visited just about every recording company in London and was turned down on each occasion.

Here is the part of the story where one false turn could have changed musical history. Had Epstein given it up for lost and gone home, we may never have heard of this group called the Beatles. Maybe it would have been another band entirely that conquered the pop music world . . . or maybe even that would never have happened.

As it was, Brian Epstein reached a point where he decided to give himself one more day to find a recording company that would be interested in his charges. What followed was an incredible series of events tied together by merest coincidence and chance.

After leaving his hotel on this historic day, Epstein decided to pay a call on a friend, Bob Boast, who owned a record shop in London. Boast did not know how he could help but suggested that a 78 rpm demonstration disc be cut from Epstein's Decca tape. This would make it easier for Epstein to present the Beatles music to those he might meet. In fact, Boast told Epstein, they happened to have a small studio right in the building. It could be done there.

There, Epstein met disc cutter Jim Foy. As the music was transferred from tape to record, Foy decided he liked what he heard and referred Brian to the publishing office of Ardmore & Beechwood.[3] They might be able to be of assistance, and they happened to be in the same building. Epstein went up and paid a visit to general manager Sid Coleman.

During the meeting, Epstein made it clear that his main priority was a recording contract and not a publishing contract. Hmmmm. Well, Coleman happened to be a business acquaintance of a man who was the head of Parlophone Records, a small subsidiary of the recording conglomerate EMI. The man's name was George Martin. Coleman could, if Mr. Epstein wished, give him a call right then. After all, it couldn't hurt.

George Martin was in the office when the call came through and decided it couldn't hurt to meet the manager of this band called the Beatles. He had been on the lookout for a pop group to rival the success of the Shadows who were making hit records. A meeting was set up. Brian Epstein and George Martin, soon to be purveyors of the biggest act in pop music history, met for the first time the next day (May 9, 1962).

Epstein played his 78 RPM record for Martin. George Martin later said that he didn't feel the music was all that good, but that there was something there that piqued his interest. He wanted to meet them in person, and this happened at last on June 6, 1962. John, Paul, George and Pete came to London to show their stuff.

Knowing that the Beatles had a tendency to be tense with each other before big dates, Epstein had told the Beatles EMI had signed them to a recording contract. Truthfully, this was to be a test session only.[4] How he would have explained that one away should the Beatles had failed this audition is anybody's guess.

In the studio, as he listened and watched, Martin didn't think much of their music, especially their originals. But he had a soft side for rebels and irreverence, both of which the Beatles had in abundance. He also felt that they were extremely charismatic and knew that that special energy that they had would work in their favor.

The thin chain of success went from shop owner Bob Boast to disc cutter Jim Foy to Ardmore & Beechwood general manager Sid Coleman to Parlophone head George Martin and even then required "that something" that piqued his interest. Folks, they don't write movies that good.

The End of the Line for Pete Best

During the session, the group recorded "Love Me Do," a song written by McCartney, according to Lennon, in the 50s. But as they played, drummer Best committed a fatal act: he sped up the song, not once but twice.[5] It should be noted that being a drummer in a studio setting is one of the hardest jobs ever, far different than playing live. Record producers don't have much patience for drummers who lose control of tempo in the studio.

At the end of the session, producer George Martin took manager Brian Epstein aside and told him "this drumming isn't good enough for what I want. It isn't regular enough. It doesn't give the right kind of sound. If we do make a record, I'd much prefer to have my own drummer."

At that moment a bell, a death knell, rang in the London fog for Beatles' drummer Randolph Peter Best. It was time for a change. So, at the request of John, Paul and George, on August 16th, 1962, before their first serious recording session, Brian Epstein fired Pete.[6]

I wanted a second opinion on the above, and so asked my brother, a long time studio drummer:

"Regarding studio drumming 'back in the day' there were no click tracks (an audible sort of metronome to keep the band on the same page tempo-wise). Could this have saved Pete's job? I doubt it, the whole band is required to play in time, not just the drummer and Pete was a fairly accomplished drummer, he

could have played steady time. After a couple of passes everybody tends to settle down a bit. I think style was more the
issue." [7]

~ Mike Alstand

(email, 2013)

Pete, instead of riding the fast train to stardom, was out and sub-
jected to a long life of "what might have been?" After his departure
from the band, he had an intriguing appearance on the American TV
show, *What's My Line* and then—like Stu Sutcliffe—walked out of the
history books and into the world of the ordinary. It's only in the past
years that he's come around to talking about it much, and his insights
are a welcome addition to the Beatles' story. He had truly been in the
trenches with the group, helping to build the story from the ground up.
He had spent countless hours in the van with the others, eating, sleeping, playing, sweating, surviving the turmoil. After his firing from the
band, and as he watched his former mates take each step towards the
fame he had hoped to be a part of, it would be an easy guess to hazard
that he was devastated beyond our comprehension.

The Beatles needed a new drummer. Who would it be? This time
they couldn't look from within. They needed an outsider, but someone
who was familiar with their act and song arrangements. It turned out
there was just such a man. Ringo Starr, drummer for Liverpool group
Rory Storm and the Hurricanes, had sat in for Pete Best a number of
times when he was UTP (Unable To Perform) in Germany. They got
along well with him, and he was an excellent drummer. The problem
was that the Hurricanes were in the midst of a series of dates up in
northern England. Was Ringo available? Let's just say that he *became*
available very quickly. He gave a three day notice to Rory Storm and
took off to conquer the world with his new mates, the Beatles.

Making the replacement changed a whole lot of things. It changed
our view of the Beatles (John, Paul, George and Pete?). Obviously, it
changed the way the group looked. Instead of the moody, hair combed
back, Pete Best, we had the Beatle-styled Ringo Starr. It changed the
music in ways we can not imagine.[8]

The Beatles got their recording contract, the small Parlophone label got a burgeoning talent, and the portals of fame seemed to be at last in sight.

They've Got the Contract. Now What?

The first thing George Martin had to do once he decided to sign them in July, 1962 was to determine which of them was to be the front man and star. What? Front man? Well, in Martin's defense, all of the big groups of the day all had one star singer, a focal point. It just was not done to have an entire group act as *star*. He, at first, decided to make Paul the front man and leader of the group. Then had second thoughts about changing them.

> "I couldn't imagine a group being successful as a 'group.' Then, after some thought, I realized that if I did so (make one of them the leader) I would be changing the nature of the group. Why do that?"
>
> ~ George Martin
>
> (*All You Need Is Ears*, 1994)

It hadn't been done, but George Martin was willing to take the chance. For that, alone, we owe the man a large measure of thanks.

For their first real session, Martin had told the Beatles to learn and be ready to record Mitch Murray's song "How Do You Do It?" (You might remember the version eventually recorded by Gerry and the Pacemakers). The Beatles went up home to Liverpool to make their own arrangement of it but must have agreed not to put too much of their charm into the recording. They had original songs they wanted to record.

"Love Me Do" (Single)
"P.S. I Love You" (B-side)
(Released October 5, 1962)

On September 3rd, the Beatles played the Cavern Club at lunchtime where George got into some nasty business with some of the patrons, receiving a black eye for his efforts. The group played in Lancashire that evening and then flew down to London to record their first single, recordings to commence on September 4th.

The Beatles recorded their arrangement of "How Do You Do It?" and tried to convince George Martin to let them record their own songs.

He was agreeable to the opportunity and gave them the okay to record "Love Me Do" which they did. After their day of work, they headed back up to Liverpool to play at the Cavern Club the next day.

After touring around for a week, they played the Cavern again on the 10th and drove through the night down to London to be ready to record again. There, they recorded "P.S. I Love You" and re-recorded "Love Me Do." Thus began the Beatles' style of cramming trips down to London for recording neatly between gigs hundreds of miles to the north. They spent endless hours together riding around in their little red van.

As for the recordings of "Love Me Do" and "P.S. I Love You," Paul McCartney was admittedly nervous as he sang. John had been singing the lead vocal on "Love Me Do" but now he was going to be busy playing the harmonica during that part. So, Paul was handed the lead, and you can hear his voice breaking from the tension. After all, this was a monumental moment for the Beatles. They were being given a chance to record one of their own songs, a true novelty then in the world of recording.

As for his bass playing, Paul played as he did so often in the early days: simple but effective. It's the best way to play when you're new to the studio, forever balancing enthusiasm with the perfection needed to make a tight recording.

George Martin decided to release "Love Me Do" and "P.S. I Love You" for the Beatles first ever single. It made the charts but was not a sensation, peaking at number 17. There is some evidence that, in order to boost sales figures, manager Brian Epstein purchased thousands of the records.

Recording artists are not generally given a lot of chances to achieve success. Fortunately, the Beatles were given another shot at the big time. This time, they did not disappoint.

"Please Please Me" (Single)
"Ask Me Why" (B-side)
(Released January 11, 1963)

Here's a snippet of what the Beatles went through to record "Please Please Me." On November 24th, they performed at Prestatyn in Flintshire. The next day, they drove 40 miles to perform at the Cavern Club in Liverpool. Then, in the late fall weather, they loaded into their van and drove for 200-plus miles to London to record their new song along with the flip side, "Ask Me Why" and (the never finished) "Tip of My Tongue." The next day, they recorded some of their songs at the BBC and then made the long drive up to Cavern for yet another performance there. The point is "Please Please Me," one of their most exciting ever records, was done in a haze of gigs, driving and recording. Not bad!

"Please Please Me" was the next step in their drive to success: a number one record.

The song was written mainly by John. He had always been fascinated with the double use of the word please in Bing Crosby's 1932 hit "Please," a song his mother Julia sang to him. The song had the lyric "Oh, Please. Lend your little ear to my pleas" and now it was time for the British record buying public to become fascinated with the word play.

Lennon may have written the song, but it is the first time that the Beatles/Martin recording relationship became a real two-way street. On September 11th the Beatles had tried out a slow, Orbison-like version of "Please Please Me." [9]

Martin asked the band to tidy it up and bring it back. They did and, as John recalled in an interview in 1963, "we're glad we did. In the following weeks, we went over and over it again and again. We changed the tempo a little bit, we altered the words slightly and we went over the idea of featuring the harmonica, just like we did on 'Love Me Do.' By the time the session came round, we were so happy with the result, we couldn't get it recorded fast enough."

Paul McCartney said "George Martin's contribution [to 'Please Please Me'] was quite a big one, actually. It was the first time that he actually ever showed that he could see beyond what we were offering him. 'Please Please Me' was originally conceived as a Roy Orbison type thing, you know. George Martin said, 'Well, we'll put the tempo up.' He lifted the tempo and we saw that it was much better."

As with so many of their songs, especially the early ones, there wasn't one particular Beatle responsible for the sound. Each one's part was exciting and well played. They all come together to produce an unforgettable sound.

This is the first time we hear the Beatles as the "four-headed monster" as Paul has referred to them. It is as if each Beatle submitted his personality and style into one large effective unit: a Beatle song machine that, in the end, gave a sound that was far larger than the sound of four men playing together. "Please Please Me" has a clear focus, with no one veering from the path of making the song as exciting as it possibly can be.

The song ends with an airy exchange of vocals between John, Paul and George sung over an interesting chord structure: E / G / C / B / E. The chords only add to the tension that has been building throughout the song.

Allow me to introduce musicologist Alan W. Pollack. During the time I was writing the genesis for this book, Mr. Pollack was writing very scholastic and interesting essays about the Beatles' songs. Ten years of his effort paid off with his *Notes on . . . Series* that covers every song in the Beatles recorded canon. Thankfully, he has consented to many of his notes being included in this book.

> "The bluesy hint [at the end of 'Please Please Me'] of the minor mode plus the implicit cross-relations of the G and C naturals against predominant sharps of the E Major key makes an extremely bracing effect. For laughs, try this last phrase with the more 'correct' diatonic chords of G# Major and c# minor and see how hopelessly square it sounds by contrast."
>
> ~ Alan W. Pollack
>
> (*Notes on . . . Series*, 1989-2000)

Paul's Bass

After that incredibly catchy two-note guitar intro, the harmonica comes to the forefront. But the bass "hammers" (constant steady beat) eight notes up high on the neck while the harmonica and guitar play the hook melody line. Once the vocals begin, the bass recedes (appropriately) to the back of the song. John and Paul's voices are delivered with energy, enthusiasm, and are a force to be reckoned with, and an aggressive bass part would only get in the way.

Throughout the song, McCartney keeps the bass steadily rocking, sometimes following the drum pattern, usually playing eighth note rock and roll runs. Ringo shines throughout this song and Paul is right with him all the way. The Beatles rock and roll rhythm section is clearly going to be a force to be reckoned with.

George Martin says he was thrilled with what he was hearing from the control room, and who can blame him? What a thing it would be to go back in time and listen with him to this song being recorded.

"The whole session was a joy. At the end of it, I pressed the intercom button in the control room and said, 'Gentlemen, you've just made your first number-one record.'"

~ George Martin

(*All You Need Is Ears*, 1994)

And they had.

Other Thoughts on the "Please Please Me" (Single)

This was a make or break moment for the Beatles, especially John and Paul. Their first single, "Love Me Do" / "P.S. I Love You," did not sell well, reaching number 17 on the charts. If Lennon and McCartney, who were adamant about writing their own music, had not come through with "Please Please Me," things might have ended up differently. They might not have been allowed to take up studio time and expense with their originals again. It's a credit to George Martin that he saw their potential as songwriters at this early stage and gave them a second chance with this song. Not many producers would have done so. Aside from some of the great American rock 'n rollers of the 1950s this idea of being one's own songwriter just wasn't done. It's one of the many barriers the Beatles crashed through.

Finally, if you listen to the song "Please Please Me" directly after "Love Me Do" and "P.S. I Love You," you can't help but wonder where the Beatles learned everything they needed to learn to make their new record. They'd certainly grown!

As purveyors of music that would stun the senses, they had improved markedly in several areas.

❖ Playing technique: Ringo especially seems to have been released from bondage. His playing was integral to the sound of the record (and would remain so throughout their time together).

❖ Song structure: "Please Please Me" is a complex song very much in the classic Lennon style. He liked to write songs that created tension and had a release. In this case, the tension begins with the exchange "Come on (Come on)" and builds up to the climactic "Please please me, whoa, yeah . . ." He was to revisit that tension/release style many times in his career.

❖ Interchanging and contrapuntal dynamics: From the very beginning, the four musicians are playing parts that interchange with—and are not the same as—the other parts.

❖ Theme introduction: The opening harmonica provides the melodic theme of the song, which is echoed by the melody of the vocals.

❖ The arrangement of it is light years ahead of anything they had done previously.

They had come a long way in a very short time. Where and whatever that source was, it was the fuel for a Beatles' song-making machine that would last to the end of their days.

1962 Recap

1962 was a heady year for the Beatles. But a musical act can never sit on its laurels. Show business is all about "What have you done for me lately?" Although they had a number one record, they could easily have disappeared during the next year and think of how different a place the world would be. No Beatles, no British invasion. The American artists of the day would have been happier, but the thought almost makes a fellow want to cry out in the darkness.

By the end of 1962, the lineup for the Beatles was the one we grew to know and love: Paul McCartney (bass), Ringo Starr (drums), John Lennon (guitar), George Harrison (guitar).

Notes

1. A front man (or woman) is the person who interacts with the audience, chatting between songs, etc. John and Paul shared this duty throughout the Beatles' career as live players. It was around 1962 that John and Paul developed an often used stage bit. Paul would introduce their last song and ask the audience to clap their hands and stomp their feet. John's response was to clap, stomp and speak spasmodically. It would be considered politically incorrect today, but that might make it even funnier.

2. This was a management contract. It should be noted that there are many who scorn Epstein for taking 25% of their gross income. This is indeed a high percentage, when you consider that the Beatles then shared income from the rest of their income after various expenses. Source information about the contract signing taken from Wikipedia's entry on Brian Epstein. Pete, Paul and George were all under 21 at the time the contract was signed (their parents did not sign), and so it appears that it was not a binding contract. Also, Brian Epstein did not sign the contract, apparently leaving himself an out in case things turned sour as they often did (and still do) with young musicians.

3. Music publishers play a crucial role in the lives of songwriters. By taking a share of the ownership of a song, the publisher will help to promote the song and—perhaps most importantly—insure that the songwriters are paid royalties for the sales and performance of the songs. Or, in the case of many music publishing companies through the years—not make sure the writers are paid. As an extra note, the Ardmore and Beechwood still exists on Charing Cross Road in London.

4. The entire story of Brian Epstein's improbable journey to get the Beatles a recording contract is taken from many places. It is told in a charming way by Mark Lewisohn in *The Beatles Recording Sessions* as well as by Sir George Martin himself in his book *All You Need is Ears*.

5. This historic recording of "Love Me Do" is available to us on the Beatles *Anthology 1*. Best has difficulty in maintaining the slower tempo of the song during the bridge "Someone to love . . ." It is noticeable in the first bridge at 1:00. His drumming then becomes unmistakably faster under the harmonica solo at 1:40. When the song comes back to the verse, the band has a difficult time for a moment readjusting to the proper tempo. Rule #1: If there is a tempo problem it's the drummer.

6. The real reason for Best's firing goes deeper than his tempo issues. The real reason will probably always be unknown. To this day, Pete Best says he has no idea why he was fired.

7. Mike's comments went further, and they're interesting enough to make a rather long footnote: "Also, in earlier days, the drummer would have to get the entire song down, start to finish, with no internal editing of the track: no 'cut and paste' editing, that is. It's hard to splice into a tape, what with all of the various sounds coming from a drum set; some sounds with sustain such as a crash or ride cymbal, some

more staccato sounds like a snare drum, and not end up with a choppy, Frankenstein, sound to the track. In the Beatles early days, they had this limitation plus the additional factor of difficulty added by taping most of, if not all, of the entire bands performance at one time; they all had to get it right at the same time!

A type of recording I did recently required me to listen to the songwriters concept of a song on an acoustic guitar, listen to his explanation of what might be added to the track in the future; harmonies, types of instruments to be added, solos etc., and then record along with only the bass player. I had to project where the songs dynamics should change and use different sounds, say, switch to a ride cymbal for a chorus or add crash cymbals during the peak of what would be a guitar solo. At the same time, I had to play it somewhat "safe" enough to allow the writer and editor flexibility to change the shape of the song as it evolved and not leave them locked into parts that were dictated by specific choices I had made. I love this flexibility in the studio. Some previous sessions, using tape, and doing repeated passes at a track would have the crew in the booth with their heads down on their folded arms, despair prevailing in the studio and fear of failure intensifying. Imagine getting to the finale of a now much contested track and then tripping up right at the final moment. Yeah, technology!

8. Pete Best was a solid drummer. After years "in the trenches," he could only have been. It may be that, like Sutcliffe, he kept a basic beat going that really added to the intense rock and roll atmosphere of their live dates from those days. It's possible that between Best and Starr, the former was the better live, club drummer. Best used snare rolls frequently. He also used the rock and roll drum standard of hitting the snare on the beats of 2, 2+ and 4. Paul's bass playing style was far heavier than Pete's drumming style and so the rhythm section tended to feel out of balance. As for Ringo, there doesn't seem to be a drummer alive—jazz, rock or whatever—who doesn't think Ringo was a great rock and roll studio drummer. One thing that is clear is that Best had a much lighter-sticked attack than Ringo. In the end, it's impossible to fault the Beatles. Ringo became one of the best rock and roll drummers ever. Creative and on-beat, he lifts the spirit of all of the Beatles' tracks. He is a huge reason as to why the early Beatles songs sound like so much fun. His drumming balanced McCartney bass playing; the Beatles rhythm section became one of the best in the industry, John said, "Ringo's a damn good drummer. He was always a good drummer."

9. Astute owners of the Beatles' *Anthology 1* will note a discrepancy here. The Anthology states that the version on the CD is from September 11th. However, this recording is not slow or bluesy. The main difference between it and the released version is that George's guitar plays the line that the harmonica eventually took over. Mark Lewisohn's book *The Beatles Recording Session* places the date of the "slow, bluesy" version at September 11th. It's my view that the slower version was played for producer Ron Richards on September 4th during a rehearsal. Richards recalls George playing that opening line over and over throughout the song and suggesting that he

only "play it in the gaps." So, either the writers of the Anthology are incorrect in their placement of the date or Mark Lewisohn is. Does it matter? Of course it does!

The Beatles as a Team Through 1966

At the end of a baseball playoff game recently (October, 2010), I was listening to commentary about a team that had come together and surprised everybody with their level of success.

The commentator, former pitcher Mike Krukow, was familiar with the players and said something along the lines of "The players on this team have all come to know and trust each other. Even when they're down, they just know that someone is going to come through; that someone is going to make something happen. This is the kind of team you dream about playing on throughout your career."

That last comment immediately made me think of the Beatles because the more I've studied their story, the more I've come to be in awe of their total commitment to their success and, touchingly, to each other. Once they settled on the right four people, they became a team of such incredible personal magnitude that they would wield a power that perhaps no one has ever done before or since. Even without their success, these are the kind of people you dream of playing with.

Playing off of each other's strengths (and weaknesses) the group climbed the ladder together. There were others who were all instrumental in their own way in helping the Beatles along. Manager Brian Epstein and record producer George Martin come to mind immediately, but it was John, Paul, George and Ringo who did the driving. If one Beatle was struggling, which happened frequently, the others would cover for him. In a statement that is incredibly revealing about this aspect of their closeness, John Lennon once said that each one of them had saved the lives of all the others at one time or another.

During all of their years together, they were all fiercely protective of each other and loyal beyond comprehension. It wasn't until they broke up that knowledge of their disputes and tension became known. But for now, as they headed into 1963 and the incredible fame they were to achieve, it would be that iron-bound togetherness that would keep them going.

FOUR

Today, England. Tomorrow . . . (1963)

1963 in Review

1963 is by far the most intriguing year in the Beatles' story. They started the year with a few solid hit records under their belt and began their tireless climb towards the top. As the year passed by, they were everywhere all the time (well, in their home country anyway). They'd be in London one day, driving up to the north of England on the next, and then maybe back down to London once again. They never stopped. They worked virtually every day, performing non-stop, driving in their little van. It was, as Ringo said later, the year of the van that they could not stop.

They began to achieve unheard of fame in their home country as the months went by. On January 11th, the single "Please Please Me" (recorded in 1962) was released and became a number one hit on most charts. Shortly thereafter, they recorded the Please Please Me LP. And then the hits started coming. "From Me to You" came in April; "She Loves You" came in August; *With the Beatles* (LP) came in November along with the accompanying single "I Want to Hold Your Hand." Unlike so many groups who made a big splash with a record, the Beatles were able to keep making high energy records that would go to number one on the charts without fail. During 1963 they began making major TV appearances and were soon on their way to the next major stop on their ride to success: being the Kings of London. On October 13th, they performed at what was always considered the place to play if you were a big star: the London Palladium.

Screaming fans inside and out, this had never been seen at the Palladium before. The London Press (known until the 1980s as Fleet Street) noticed the Beatles at last. The term Beatlemania was used for the first time to describe the scene.

Throughout the year, the Beatles records, doing so well around the world, were never released in America by Capitol Records, the American subsidiary of EMI (the Beatles' recording company in the UK). Some of the records were released by smaller companies but could not catch on with the American public. It was frustrating for the Beatles because America was the final hurdle on their dizzying drive to success. It was where the money was. It was where all of the Beatles' musical heroes came from. While they became more famous than any performers in the history of their home country, notoriety in America was not to be in 1963. But things were looking up on that front: at the very end of the year, Capitol Records decided to release (and promote) the Beatles latest single, "I Want to Hold Your Hand" in America.

The Beatles
Early Songwriting Style

We should pause for a moment and reflect on what was to become, during the year 1963, the Beatles' style of songwriting. While they were fans of the black blues and rock and roll artists, they made a conscious decision to steer their songs away from the blues format. They learned early on that while older people might love the blues, the kids didn't. And they knew that their drive to success was being fueled by the kids who were buying their records and coming to their shows. What they wanted was something more upbeat, positive and exciting and something that would catch your attention the moment it came out of the radio speakers.

They wanted to create songs that kids would sing along to, the kind that stay in their heads until they went and bought the record. During

1963, they learned the tricks of the recording trade very quickly and became masters of recording high energy, fresh sounding songs that would virtually leap out of the radio and capture the listener. It didn't take long, however, for the musicologists to see behind the "pop for kids" to discover that the music was actually quite intelligent in its creation.

With the exception of "I Saw Her Standing There," the Beatles did not release a blues based record until 1964 (both sides of the "Can't Buy Me Love" single).

Please Please Me (LP)

Released
March 22, 1963

Cover Notes
George Martin's original cover idea was to photograph the Beatles in front of the beetle display at the London Zoo, but this was fortunately nixed by zoo officials. Instead, the Beatles were driven, all in a rush, to EMI's London Headquarters where Angus McBean took the photo.

The photo became steeped in confusing Beatle album cover lore. A photo from the same session was used for *The Beatles / 1962-1966* cover. Then, the Beatles were re-photographed for the LP cover for *Get Back* (which was unreleased). A photo from that session ended up on the cover of *The Beatles / 1967-1970*.

Peak Position
Number 1

Number of Weeks on the Chart
70 (a year and 3 months. Not bad for their first LP!)

Please Please Me (LP)

Number of Days in the Studio
3

First Song Recorded for the Album
"There's a Place" on February 11, 1963

This started a trend that continued right through to the end of the Beatles' recording career. The first song to be recorded was almost always a strong Lennon song.

The single "Please Please Me" (see page 32) was released right at the start of the year. It was a nationwide hit and record producer George Martin wanted to follow that success with a new album. They recorded most of that album in one day.

Let's take a look at what the Beatles were up to on and around the day they recorded their first LP.

On February 9th, they performed in Sunderland, Durham which is almost up in Scotland. The next day they loaded up the ol' van and drove almost 300 miles through the English winter to London. On February 11th, 1963, the Beatles recorded almost the entire first album, to be entitled *Please Please Me* (so named and timed to capitalize on their hit single).

They started at 10 AM by recording "There's a Place" and finished up with take two of "Twist and Shout" at 10:45 PM.

It was a long day, especially after their winter escapades on the road. Two of them were down with colds but to capitalize on their time in the studio, they skipped lunch opting to practice during the break. It was all a recipe for disaster. Instead, they produced an unforgettable debut album that rode the top of the charts in England and stayed there for months (eventually being displaced by their second LP, *With the Beatles*). It contains some of the best Beatle songs, although many of them are forgotten (as "forgotten" as a Beatles song could be, that is). John's rendition of "Anna (Go to Him)" (written by black rhythm and blues artist Arthur Alexander) is full of power and soul.

There aren't many songs more fun to listen to than "Boys" or, for that matter, "Please Please Me" itself.

Producer George Martin had a strict philosophy on how the running order of an album should be laid out:

- ❖ The catchiest song from the batch should open side one. It is the song that will determine whether the listener will continue on.
- ❖ The last song on side one should be something that makes the listener want to get up and flip that album over.
- ❖ Start side two with a song that keeps the energy going.
- ❖ End the album with the most powerful song of them all.

Let's take a closer look at some of the other songs from the LP.

"I Saw Her Standing There"

With its raucous count-in (actually taken from a different take), raw McCartney vocals and passionate Beatle sound "I Saw Her Standing There" was the perfect song with which to open the new album. It grabs your attention and may well be the catchiest of all the songs on the album. Written early on in the Lennon-McCartney partnership, the song is simple in structure and effective on record. The Beatles later became devoted fans of the tambourine. In these early days, handclaps were used to provide rhythm and excitement to their songs. I heard this song at a dance club not too long ago and was pleasantly surprised to find that it stood up well to the heavy dance songs that were out at the time.

"'I Saw Her Standing There' is one of the boys' first fast, hard rockers. It was probably the most blazingly original song they had yet written at the time of its recording. Appropriately and auspiciously, they chose to crown it with the lead-off spot on their first album."

~ Alan W. Pollack

(Notes on . . . Series, 1989-2000)

"That's Paul doing his usual good job of producing what George Martin used to call a "potboiler." I helped with a couple of the lyrics."

~ John Lennon

(The Playboy Interviews With John Lennon and Yoko Ono, 1981)

Paul's Bass

A talented bass player will create a part for the song that moves it along, and Paul is not in the mood for taking prisoners here. He plays a line he copied from a Chuck Berry song; it's a strong eight-note-centric part that keeps moving the song forward.

For this fast dance song, John, Paul and Ringo joined forces to provide an energetic rhythm section that was certain to get people up and dancing—you can hardly help it.

"'I Saw Her Standing There' . . . I feel this is THE song which moved the bass player to the front of the band, not only driving the song in its entirety . . . **play** the bass line alone, and everyone knows what song it is . . . **but** also demonstrating that one could sing lead while playing a driving bass line."

~ Christopher P. "Duffy" Hughes

(email, 2009)

More than any other instrument it drives the song, playing nicely off of Ringo's hi-hat work. There's also my perennial favorite, a tremolo guitar, played by John.

"Boys"

Thus began the tradition of giving Ringo one song to sing on each Beatles album. "Boys" was a minor hit by the American girl group, the Shirelles, and may well be the archetypical bop-shoo-wop song of all time. Fast, full of frenzy and bop-shoo-wops, the song is instantly fun to listen to. Ringo was singing about boys, but who cared?

> "Any one of us could hold the audience. Ringo would do
> 'Boys' which was a fan favorite with the crowd. And it was
> great—though if you think about it, here's us doing a song, and
> it was really a girls song. 'I talk about boys now!' Or it was a gay
> song. But we never even listened. It's just a great song. I think
> that's one of the things about youth—you just don't give a shit.
> I love the innocence of those days."
>
> ~ Paul McCartney
>
> (*Rolling Stone*, 2005)

With "Boys," Ringo and Paul give us a demonstration on how all you need is a strong rhythm section to make a song sound fresh. Paul is showing off his hammering bass style right from the start of this song. He plays an exciting part, and you can hear his voice all over the background, howling and screaming. Ringo's drums and belting lead vocal make up for the other half of the fun on this song. "Boys" could have been a real minor recording of theirs, a bit of a dud. When you consider it was the ninth song recorded on that marathon of a day, it's thanks to the Beatles endless energy, and especially Ringo and Paul that this recording still makes you want to dance.

"Misery"

"Misery" showcases John and Paul for the first time on record singing most of a song in unison (not counting the first verse in "P.S. I Love You"). The John/Paul voice mix was unique to them. Paul's voice had a rounder tone than John's. The softness of his voice housed Lennon's sharper vocal and the powerful mix was used to great advantage in many songs to come, including "I Want to Hold Your Hand," "Thank

You Girl," "I Should Have Known Better," "Eight Days a Week," "Day Tripper," and the chorus to "Baby You're a Rich Man." It's possible that the choruses of "Ticket to Ride" are John and Paul. They sang them in unison live, but the studio recording sounds like John double-tracked them. Frequently, it would be easy to mistake this lead vocal as being John's alone (as in "Eight Days A Week"). This is largely due to McCartney's ability to impersonate Lennon's voice (just check out "Let Me Roll It" from Wings *Band On The Run* LP).

"Misery" was recorded in six takes. George Martin's piano "walkdown" mirrored a line that Lennon played as they sang and played the song live in the studio.

"Twist and Shout"

This was the last song the Beatles recorded during the day-long stint in the studio. The group had not eaten lunch, had been singing and recording for almost 13 hours and it's amazing to think that Lennon pulled himself together enough to deliver one of the great rock vocals of all time. The version you hear today was their first attempt at it (referred to as "Take one"). Had he not been able to sing it on that first take, we may never have heard their version of the song because when they tried a second take, Lennon's voice was gone.

You'd think the Beatles would be exhausted when they finally went to record "Twist and Shout", but you'd never know it by listening to the record. Perhaps all of those long nights playing in Hamburg kept them going. Whatever it was, here they play with a driving force and clarity of vision that is astounding. Paul's bass playing has become a standard run for I-IV-V songs,[1] but when you realize he's playing live and singing like a bird, it's pretty impressive. It's a driving bass line for one of the great songs in history.

Other Thoughts on the Please Please Me LP

From the standpoint of power, songwriting and delivery, John Lennon was out front on this album. As for musical prowess, listeners could tell that the group had a seriously talented bass player, the best musician in the band to date; George and John were still clumsy and a little stiff on the guitars. They certainly were adequate as players, but neither of them *took charge* of the sound like they would in later years. This left openings for Paul to shine through with his tasteful and driving bass playing. When the song called for simplicity ("Anna (Go to Him)," "Chains," "Love Me Do," "Baby It's You," etc.), his playing was spot on. When it called for a hook-filled driving line, "I Saw Her Standing There," "Please Please Me," "Twist and Shout" and "Boys" Paul McCartney showcased on his instrument.

John and George had colds on this wintry February day and are sadly unable to reveal their excellence in close harmony singing. Paul's voice shines throughout, but John and George's voices will have to wait for their second album to shine, and shine they will.

Note: The next day, weary after their marathon session, the Beatles piled back in the van and drove 200 miles through the snow to play in Sheffield, Yorkshire.

Musicologist Walter Everett provides what might be the best post-script of all to the *Please Please Me* LP. It's one of those thoughts that never occurred to me, but once I grasped it, it seemed so obvious and powerful.

"In records to come, [George] Martin would have a much more obvious role than he does in 'Please Please Me.' However, it is for this album that he makes his greatest contribution to them as their producer. For he let the Beatles have their way. Instead of handing them certain ready-made hits, he allowed them to develop more deeply by recording their own material . . . the LP's performance is earnest, the overall energy of the performers is quite infectious, and Lennon's confidence and expressive power are instantaneously recognizable. While 'Please Please Me' contains no original masterpieces, the listener is transfixed by the fun the Beatles can create in a single day."

~ Walter Everett

(*The Beatles As Musicians*, 2001)

Come to think of it, fun must have been what the British record-buying public had been craving because the LP shot to number one on the British LP charts and stayed there for 30 weeks! Let me repeat that: 30 weeks at number 1. And what LP finally knocked it off of the charts? *With the Beatles!*

Is America Ready Yet? America Might Have Been But, Well, Capitol Records Was Not.

George Martin, seeing what a hit he had on his hands, tried hard to get Capitol Records, who was actually owned by EMI (the company for which the Beatles recorded), to release the song in America. The President of Capitol Records, Alan Livingston replied "We don't think the Beatles will do anything in this market." Wow. With the hindsight of history, it seems farfetched that they would fail to see the monster they had on their hands, even at this early date. Part of me wants to defend them with the reminder that having a successful British act in America would be unprecedented, but a bigger part asks why they did not even try.

Please Please Me (track listing)

Side One	Side Two
1. "I Saw Her Standing There"	1. "Love Me Do"
2. "Misery"	2. "P.S. I Love You"
3. "Anna"	3. "Baby It's You"
4. "Chains (Go to Him)"	4. "Do You Want to Know a Secret"
5. "Boys"	5. "A Taste of Honey"
6. "Ask Me Why"	6. "There's a Place"
7. "Please Please Me"	7. "Twist and Shout"

Note: In 2012, *Please Please Me* was voted 39th on *Rolling Stone* magazine's list "500 Greatest Albums of All Time." The magazine also made note of the fact that the Beatles basically invented the "self-contained band," writing their own hits and playing their own instruments. What a first album!

"From Me to You" (Single)
"Thank You Girl" (B-side)
(Released April 11, 1963)

The legendary Beatles' van that never stopped continued its roller coaster ride, showing up to play their dates night after night. On March 4th, they played in St. Helens up near Liverpool. When they were done, they raced through the night for the 200 miles to get to London to record their next single, "From Me to You" / "Thank You Girl" and an attempt at an "oldie" of theirs: "The One After 909."

"The One After 909" was a song that John and Paul had written years before (there is a home recording of them playing it in 1960 with Stu Sutcliffe on bass). Now it was to be the Beatles' first attempt at following up their *Please Please Me* LP with a single.

This early version, to be found on the Beatles *Anthology 1*, showcases Paul attempting gamely to play a solid hammer rhythm without benefit of a pick, which he generally used while playing. In a phenomenon that is probably unique amongst bass players, Paul tried picking with too much pressure and fell victim to a stiff picking wrist. Once this happens, it's extremely difficult to loosen it up quickly.

The song breaks down under the fierce thunder of the waylaid bass, but Paul, being no quitter, tries gamely to keep it going. In this case, John wonders, "What are you doing?" Paul tries again and again. The problem appears to have been irresolvable because his playing sounds the same through to the last take.

The new single was not to be and "The One After 909," sadly, was not to be heard again until they dusted it off for the *Let It Be* LP. Instead, the Beatles recorded "From Me to You" and "Thank You Girl" and watched as they became the two sides of their next smash hit single.

"From Me to You" was released in April, 1963 and became their second consecutive number one single. It was a big hit in England, and George Martin tried again to get Capitol Records in America to release it. Capitol once again decided against it.

"I'll Be On My Way"
(BBC taped recording)

The Beatles appeared on BBC radio shows many times throughout the year. Generally, they played songs from their old stage show days, usually songs by American artists.

But on April 4 they made their only recording ever of Paul's ramblin' guy ballad "I'll Be On My Way." Their arrangement started off in a very similar fashion to the later Dave Clark Five song, "Because," with it's A, A+5. A6, A+5 chords. The song is an early one of Paul, replete with Lennon and McCartney's usual nice touch at harmonizing. It also features an interesting chord progression on the bridge.

There are a few fascinating aspects to this recording. It's a complete Lennon/McCartney original Beatles song, available on the 1994 CD release *The Beatles at the BBC*. Aside from being a nice early Beatles' tune, it's a rare treat to hear a song for the first time. Furthermore, it's also the only original song on the CD that was never recorded in the studio. Billy J. Kramer with The Dakotas recorded the song, the first Lennon/McCartney song recorded by another artist.

"She Loves You" (single)
"I'll Get You" (B-side)
(Released August 23, 1963)

The Beatles had now had a number one hit with the "Please Please Me" single. The similarly named LP was also number one on the album charts. To corner the market, their EP (extended play record, popular in England at the time). "Twist and Shout" also went to number one on the singles charts, the first time that an EP had ever done so. Their next single, "From Me to You," hit number one. It was looking as if the Beatles had staying power. George Martin told them he wanted more. By June, they were ready to come back and record what was to become a pop masterpiece.

Just to make sure they were good and tired, they played to over 3,000 people in Yorkshire and then drove 225 miles to play at Great Yarmouth, Norfolk (on the north side of the hump of eastern England) and then drove 135 miles down to London to record their amazing new song, "She Loves You."

> "It was written together and I don't know how. I remember it was Paul's idea: Instead of singing 'I love you' again, we'd have a third party."
>
> ~ John Lennon
>
> (*The Playboy Interviews With John Lennon and Yoko Ono*, 1981)

> "I originally got an idea of doing one of those answering songs, where a couple of us sing about 'She Loves You' and the other one sort of says the 'yes, yes' bit. You know, 'yeah, yeah' answering whoever who is saying it. But we decided that was a crummy idea anyway. But we had the idea of writing a song called 'She Loves You' then. And we just sat up in the hotel bedroom for a few hours and wrote it."
>
> ~ Paul McCartney
>
> (*beatlesinterviews.org*, 1963)

Aside from documentation of the recording, there has been very little discussion about how the Beatles came about making the monster single of their early years. This was the sound of Beatlemania, but was it just a matter of luck and happenstance that they turned the song into the biggest selling record for years to come? The Beatles aren't talking, but there is one thing that they have made clear: they listened to a *lot* of records when they were on their way up. Whether or not they knew the musical definitions of what they were hearing, they certainly ended up using some very sophisticated aspects in their music and "She Loves You" is no exception.

Take a ride with me and some authors more schooled in music than I; we need to talk about "She Loves You" at some length because the Beatles hit upon something extremely deep with this song. I wonder how they could get to a point so soon in their career where they could create such a combination of masterful songwriting with tension-filled arranging and performance; tension being the keyword.

> "The song contains a musical vocabulary and arrangement that is shot through with quirky details and nuances that were soon to develop into trademarks of the group; their special 'sound' is already apparent."
>
> ~ Alan W. Pollack
>
> (*Notes on . . . Series*, 1989-2000)

> "Of all the early singles, no other combines their mastery of pop-styling with the rapture it incited from their audience— Beatlemania—as maniacally as 'She Loves You.' Everything here can be traced to earlier material, but nothing that came before hints at this kind of power."
>
> ~ Musicologist Tim Riley
>
> (*Tell Me Why: a Beatles Commentary, 1988*)

Praised and glorified by the lay fan as well as the serious musical scholar, "She Loves You" shows that the Beatles had learned the underpinnings of making a pop single like no songwriters or performers that had come before.

By the way, there's a reason the song doesn't sound as clear—even on CD—as other Beatles recordings. In an effort to save space, EMI had a fairly standard policy of wiping the tapes of lesser artists and re-using them. Once the Beatles' legend became ensured (after this record) they stopped the practice with tapes of Beatles recordings. This means that the song can not be remixed. It will probably never sound better than it did when it came out on record in 1963!

The Intro

The little tom roll is the perfect touch. Lasting less than a second, it is immediately recognizable and ushers the song into the chorus which was an unusual move for those days and probably by suggestion of George Martin.

After the tom roll comes the voices of power. It is a generous mix of the three voices and the recording process that makes the "yeah yeah yeah" so effective. On the final "yeah," George sings his famous sixth note (The song is in G. George sings an E, the sixth note in the G major scale.) As John is singing a D, close by, it adds a nice touch of dissonance at this vital moment. If you're not hooked yet, you might as well change the station to the news.

The Song Proper

And then there is the first of the guitar flourishes that populate the song. Each time a verse starts, George plays a (clearly overdubbed) guitar flourish on his Gretch "Country Gentleman" (Chet Atkins model). "Growling," says Alan Pollack. But when you hear the flourish, you know the song is going to continue. The first of these happy ones happens just after the first refrain (at 0:12). The verse is ready to start.

"You think you lost your love," John and Paul start off the verse singing in unison until they reach the word *love*. John's note drops down while Paul's goes up; a small but effective detail. "Well I saw her yesterday-ay-ay." For this line, George joins Paul on his harmony part (when done live, Paul would sing the first line on mic, then stand to the side so George could slide in and sing his part on the same mic). They repeat the formula for the second part of the verse "it's you she's thinking of . . ."

"There's a heavy syncopation that just about pulls us out of our seats at the beginning of the third line of the verse. It comes right after 'She said she loves you' (it happens at 0:52) and it occurs on the off-beat between the second and third beat of the measure; try this—tap straight 4 with one hand and sneak in a hard whack between 2 and 3 with your other—you'll see what I mean about falling out of your seat."

~ Alan W. Pollack

(*Notes on . . . Series*, 1989-2000)

It's not an original idea, but it works well here. Paul's bass follows the syncopation, going up to a B over the G chord. At the same time, George begins a succession of chords that walk down, leading to a louder (and clearly overdubbed) hook line at 0:56. It lends a jazzy feel to the proceedings and could easily be translated to horn lines.

To ring in the second verse, George plays the second of the guitar flourishes (0:37) letting you know that the song will continue.

When we get to the next refrain "she loves you yeah yeah yeah," Ringo takes-the-wheel and drives the song forward by falling off of the cymbals and playing on the toms, including some nice triplets between the "she loves you yeah yeah yeah" vocal lines. After the chorus (1:15), we have the guitar flourish from George. This is the third guitar flourish, still the happy one, indicating yet again that the song is not yet ready to finish.

The Notes of Doom . . .
Here Comes the Ending

The song follows this format through another verse and a refrain...and then come the Notes of Doom from George's guitar. This walk down of guitar notes occurs quickly. . . . The Beatles had become so adept at making music that lifted the listener up to a different place, many of us find it difficult—in the heat of the moment—to remember, "was that the second or third refrain?" Checkout time comes with the flourishes and The Notes of Doom at 1:52. It's almost time to say goodbye. But there's another trick in store on the very last note of the song. George's famous sixth note, sung with John's fifth and Paul's root note on top.

The sixth note was used frequently by the Beatles for the last guitar chord, but this time they added it to the vocal.

> "Their pride in the sound of that final chord, with their three voices singing B, D, E, close together, is manifest in the way they sustain it a brief instant after the instrumental sound has died away. The sensuous experience of singing three notes like that with two of your friends is worth having at least once in a lifetime; something about what acousticians call the rapid beats that result from small intervals that are not perfect consonant."
> ~ Alan W. Pollack
> (*Notes on . . . Series,* 1989-2000)

But to George Martin, the sixth note just sounded cheesy, like something that Glenn Miller would have used 20 years before. The Beatles talked him into leaving it in. Note: if you don't know what's meant by the added sixth note, just listen to the last "yeah" of the song, the one that keeps going after the music stops. It has a dissonant sound to it. There's something not squeaky clean about that chord. It's Harrison's sixth that does that.

Paul's Bass

McCartney gives a clinic on "She Loves You" on how "less can be more." While his bass line lays the foundation for the chords through-out the song, he plays the same rhythmic pattern throughout (1 2+ 3, the pattern is more easily recognized in Mungo Jerry's 1970 hit "In the Summertime"). The only time he sways from this rhythm is when he follows Ringo's syncopation (the "pull you out of your seats" one) and so the effect of that change is amplified. McCartney has learned that if you play the same thing over and over and then suddenly change it, even if the change is subtle, it arouses the listener's ear.

Other Notes

You think about all of this substance and genius for song creation and make the assumption that a lot of careful thought went into it only to discover that the song was written after a show on Wednesday, June 26th when John and Paul wrote it in a hotel room. The following Monday, the Beatles recorded it, and it became the biggest selling single in British history (up until 1977, that is, when McCartney's "Mull of Kintyre" outsold it). The song transformed everything, and "yeah yeah yeah" became a catch-phrase amongst young and old alike.

Something magical happened to John Lennon and Paul McCartney as songwriters and the Beatles as a group right around this time in their history. Compare the songs they had recorded before with "She Loves You" and it becomes clear that John and Paul had opened up a gold mine, found their holy grail and taken a giant leap upward. Now that they had discovered the elixir, they would not give it up for a long time.

Its lyrics were different from the songs they'd written before. It was not the typical *I* and *you* song. John Lennon later said that they were beginning to write another *you* and *I* song but that Paul had the idea of bringing a third person—known only as *She*—into the mix. This song was about some other girl and you, and considering the way it was performed, it seems as if you're hearing the greatest news you could hear. "she loves you And you know that can't be bad." I always thought that the lyrics were *nice*. What a swell bunch of people coming to tell us that she loves us. But maybe there's something more to those lyrics. Alan Pollack says "I think the focus here on extreme, raw feelings in the choice of words and imagery is a fresh twist; she almost lost her mind, and pride can hurt you too."

Is America Ready Yet For "She Loves You"? Still No?!

As noted above, "She Loves You" became the biggest selling record in the history of England. George Martin was sure this time that America was ready for the Beatles. Again, EMI's American label, Capitol Records, turned them down. Brian Epstein, searching for a record label in America, found Swan Records, a small record company in America. The song didn't chart.

"Fools!" said the Canadians, and not for the first time. Noted Beatles' historian Bruce Spizer points out that Capitol of Canada released "She Loves You" in September of 1963 (and an LP entitled *Beatlemania! With the Beatles* on November 25th). "She Loves You" rose through the charts during the month of December and reached #1 on January 13, 1964, well before they hit #1 in the U.S.

The Final Word

Norman Smith was their engineer from 1962-65. Let's give him the last word on the subject.

> **"I was setting up the microphone when I saw the lyrics on the music stand. I thought I'll just have a quick look. 'She Loves you Yeah Yeah Yeah, She Loves You Yeah Yeah Yeah.' I thought Oh my God, what a lyric. This is going to be one that I do not like. But when they started to sing it—bang, wow, terrific, I was up at the mixer jogging around."**
> ~ Norman Smith
> (*The Complete Beatles Recording Sessions*, 2005)

The day after they recorded "She Loves You," they went to Maida Vale Studios in London to record a radio show. For the show, they recorded "That's All Right (Mama)," "There's a Place," "Carol," "Soldier of Love (Lay Down Your Arms)," "Lend Me Your Comb," "Clarabella," "Three Cool Cats," "Sweet Little Sixteen" and "Ask Me Why," many of which can be found on *The Beatles at the BBC*. Nine songs in one day! And all well done. Raise your hands if you ever thought you could record a bunch of songs in one day only to find out that it takes forever. No hands? Let's move on.

With the Beatles (LP)

Released
November 22, 1963

Cover Notes
The cover was considered extremely arty at the time, and many groups subsequently borrowed from the idea. It was the first serious cover for a successful pop-group, borrowing from the jazz LP cover idiom. The cover is ironic, considering the joyful music inside of it.

It was shot by Robert Freeman (who also provided the covers for the Beatles' next four LPs) inside the Palace Court Hotel in Bournemouth, with the black turtle-necked Beatles placed (Paul behind George behind John with Ringo sitting) by a window in a darkened room.

Peak Position
Number 1

With the Beatles replaced *Please Please Me* as number 1 and stayed there for 21 weeks. This means the Beatles were at the number one slot for 51 continuous weeks. So when your British friends tell you that the country "wasn't balmy" over the Beatles when they came out there, you can argue otherwise.

Number of Weeks on the Chart
51 (one short of a year)

Number of Days in the Studio
7

First Song Recorded for the Album
"You Really Got a Hold on Me" on July 18, 1963

A song from one of Lennon's heroes, Smokey Robinson.

It was now July, 1963. "She Loves You" was still riding the charts, looking like it would stay there forever. Producer George Martin and group manager Brian Epstein understood the axiom that time waits for no artist, no matter how big of a hit they have. It was time to record a follow up album to the ultra successful *Please Please Me* LP. The Beatles had begun to hear the question that would haunt them for the next year or so: "When will the bubble burst?"[2]

> "They've been trying to knock us down since we began, specially the British press, always saying 'What are you going to do when the bubble bursts?' That was the in-crowd joke with us. We'd go on when we decided, not when some fickle public decided, because we were not a manufactured group. We knew what we were doing."
>
> ~ John Lennon
>
> (*Interview*, 1964)

To prove they knew what they were doing, they went on and created *With the Beatles*. We know now that they enjoyed a string of unbroken fame that lasts to this day, but back in 1963, there were no assurances of that. It was time to make their next move. So, on July 18th, the Beatles drove on down to EMI's London studios on Abbey Road to begin work on their phenomenal second album, soon to be entitled *With the Beatles*. The Beatles were touring constantly but, with two recording dates in July and six more in October, they squeezed in just enough time to record fourteen tracks for the new album. Seven of those songs were attempts by the Beatles to mirror back to the world the music of the black artists that had so inspired them.

Songs from With the Beatles Written by or Inspired by Black Artists

❖ "You Really Got a Hold on Me" by Smokey Robinson
❖ "Please Mister Postman" by the Marvelettes
❖ "Money (That's What I Want)" by Barret Strong
❖ "Devil in Her Heart" by the Donays
❖ "Roll Over Beethoven" by Chuck Berry
❖ "All I've Got to Do" [*]
❖ "Not a Second Time" [*]

They clearly held these artists strongly in mind from the first recording session for the new album where they proceeded to work on—in order: "You Really Got a Hold on Me," "Money (That's What I Want)," "Devil in Her Heart" and "Till There Was You," the last one being from the Broadway musical *The Music Man.*

They had a touring schedule that would have broken the most ardent and fervent collection of human beings. Brian Epstein had booked the Beatles all over the country for 1963, and often times for the low wages they were being paid before fame set in. He could have easily bought those dates out but, being ever the "on the square" businessman, Epstein wanted the Beatles to keep those dates. And, being the ever ready to please Beatles, they drove all over hell to play them.

John, Paul and George's vocals shone brightly on this LP. Their close harmony was superb, and their lead vocals were nothing short of fantastic. Their prime focus in those days was always the vocals, and this album was no exception to the rule.

---

[*] The final two were originals that both John and Paul said were inspired by Smokey Robinson and the Miracles.

Paul's Bass Playing on *With the Beatles*

As for McCartney's playing, up until *With the Beatles*, most contemporary bass playing was jazz (played on an upright bass) or rock and roll (played either on an upright or Fender electric). But it was an extremely primitive technique used by rock and roll bass players that generally mimicked the style of horn lines.

With The Beatles was the album where ROCK bass playing first crawled from the ocean and breathed air.

But even with the advent of the CD and remastered tracks that we have now, the bass is still low in the mix. That's because the cheap turntables of the day weren't able to handle the bass if it was mixed too loud on a record. It wasn't until 1965 that the Beatles bass could actually be heard. But when you can hear the bass, it is solid and wild, especially for the times. By the time they came to record this LP, Ringo and Paul had developed an awesome matching of power that few other bands could boast. They both avoided showing off too much, but more importantly they sought and always seemed to find just the right way to present a song.

Pressing along with John Lennon's guitar on "Hold Me Tight," the rhythm rolls like a tank. Hanging back on "All I've Got to Do" (discussed further), they don't play perfectly—meaning that it is just important what they would leave out as what they would put in. Every Beatle album had a particular flavor that contrasted it with all of the others. No two of them are alike in any way, but you can find similarities between *With the Beatles* and *The Beatles* (the white album) in that each instrument on most songs was well defined both in sound and in style. This was also true of *Rubber Soul*.

As a band, they could play about any kind of style, and they could do it both ways. They could create a tight, cohesive sound that was overflowing with energy and would draw you into their tremendous spirit—or—they could play as four musicians working expertly with each other as on both *The Beatles* and here on *With the Beatles*.

Let's talk about some of the songs.

"It Won't Be Long"

For those who were excitedly awaiting this, the Beatles next album, I doubt if any were disappointed once they put it on their turntables. What an album opener! The album starts right off with the tried and true call (John "It won't be long") and response (Paul and George "yeah") . . . Undeniable!

After the song's emphatic opening, at 0:10, a series of events follow in quick succession to bring us to the verse. John sings "till I belong to you" while Paul and George sing "ahhh" below this. Beneath that, John strums a few power chords on his guitar, down in the mix. At 0:12, George plays that hook guitar line that can only be in E.

Then George repeats the line, but this time there are hi jinx going on. The verse is coming, and it's time to shift gears down a little bit. Downshift? Well, they do that by having Paul double the guitar line, and Ringo add a nifty little fill of his own. The idea is to signal the lower level of intensity by playing at a higher level. Interesting.

The dynamic of the instrumentation on the verse is confusing at first listen. As it begins, the energy seems to drop a notch, but from whom is it dropping? Not the drums, because Ringo goes from a semi-closed hi hat to a ride cymbal. The solution seems to be only that the background vocals have dropped out.

At the end of the verse, George's guitar plays the hook line on guitar and repeats as earlier, but this time the rest of the Beatles get involved (0:27). Paul's bass begins to follow the guitar line down but makes a quick turn at the end of the line to bring us back to the chorus. Ringo follows the guitar line with his toms and John plays a cool roll on his guitar.

And on the song goes until that final dive into a melodic ballad ending ("till I . . . belong . . . to-o you"). Beautiful. They never did this song live, and you wonder why until you realize that they were playing shorter sets by now and only their hit records as their fame soared. And, in case you wonder why "It Won't Be Long" was not the hit record from this album, the Beatles had other plans ("I Want to Hold Your Hand").

Paul had a slightly distorted sound on the song, especially on the hook lines. Martin/Smith (producer and first engineer) are to be given a lot of credit for not only leaving that in but also for bringing it to the forefront of the mix where it can be heard clearly.

It is dynamics that make so many of the Beatles songs what they were. They were, even at this early stage of their career, masters of when to go all out and when to lay back. Because you've gone through a mini roller-coaster ride of dynamics when listening to much of their music, you tend to reach each conclusion feeling some exhilaration. "It Won't Be Long" is no exception to this rule. It might be that the vocals and guitars provide the roller car you're riding in, but Ringo and Paul provide that car's wheels.

The *With the Beatles* LP starts off with this song and doesn't trail off there.

"All I've Got to Do"

The opening chord to "All I've Got to Do" carries deliberate dissonance. The chord's note structure is E, G#, C, F# and A. Walter Everett calls it a "mixture-colored V minor ninth with root omitted, sounding over anticipatory." guitarworld.com calls it "E+5sus4add9." I like to simplify and call it a"C dim over E with the upper root omitted."

I suppose that's why they call it music *theory*; there is no definite way to describe some things. Whatever it is, a tab would look like this:

```
E    -  5
B    -  7
G    -  5
D    -  6
A    -  7
E    -  -
```

The chord is simple to play, but carries a nice effect. The interesting aspect to this chord is that it is similar to chords used in blues progressions on the V turnaround to indicate the key of A—and that A would be the next chord. Instead, the song is actually in E and the first chord is the VI m (C#m). The C#m is indirectly related to A (could be an Amaj7 without the root). The C#m gives it a tentative and sadder feel. The chords beneath the bridge "call you on the phone and you'll come running home" gives it a more concrete, sure feel as if John has switched from feeling unsure to being confident in the situation. Interestingly that section starts with another minor, F#m. The bridge rounds out with Am, then finally to the E root.

The next point of interest is Lennon's used of "I-yi-yi . . ." (Walter Everett refers to them as re-articulated melismas. Whatever.) This was an early Beatle Lennon feature and he used them with style and confidence on such of his originals as "Ask Me Why," "Anna Go to Him)" and "Not a Second Time." Conversely, Paul McCartney used them only one time that I'm aware of, and that was on the Decca audition of "Like Dreamers Do." It just didn't work for him.

Next up is McCartney's descant harmony on the line "All I've got to do-oo-oo . . ." Clearly, care was taken into how he would follow Lennon down the scale. Listen closely and you'll note that he doesn't follow Lennon, note for note. Following is a table with John (lead vocal) and Paul's (high harmony) trip down the scale. The two notes in bold notes show where Paul held his note one time longer than John.

Paul	g#	f#	e	f#	f#	**e**	e	c#	b	c#	b	g#
John	e	d#	c#	d#	d#	c#	b	g#	f#	g#	f#	e
lyric	All	I've	got	**ta**	do	oo	oo	oo	oo	oo	oo	oo

The first six notes have Paul singing a third above John. On the seventh note, without Paul changing, John has dropped a fifth below him and stays there until the very last note of the run. There's a reason for that, and it becomes painfully obvious if you try to sing Paul's part but changing the 7th in the run note to a d#. It just doesn't work.

"All I've Got to Do" is the second song from the album, and to the best of my knowledge it's the first time in R&R or rock where the bass player plays double-stop chords as a vital part of the song (a chord is where an instrumentalist plays two or more notes simultaneously). As the guitars are creating space with understatement, Paul's instinct to fill the sound with chords is effective. The minor tension he creates with his chords is of utmost importance to this track during the verses. He is riding the drum's syncopated rhythm in a herky-jerky way that will get your foot tapping.

Some technical notes about the drumming: again, dynamics are well to the fore this time with Ringo at the lead. As the song heads towards the choruses ("is call you on the phone") he starts opening his hi hat a bit and by the time the chorus is reached ("and the same goes for me . . .") the song reaches up to new heights. Beneath this line, Ringo is pounding his bass drum on the quarter notes in a way that adds tension. The chorus is full of life and strong with the vocals leading the way. But the rhythm section is playing in a decidedly mature way for such young men. You would think there would be a tendency to rush the tempo a bit. It's an easy thing to do when things get exciting, but Ringo and Paul keep things steady. And then, even more suddenly than it started, the chorus ends. Ringo kicks a perfectly timed hi-hat stroke (telling the other musicians where the beat is), and they're back down to a low-key verse. The second time the song heads towards the chorus, Ringo is bringing the song to a higher level so that when the chorus is reached, the musicians are already pouring it out—dynamic, exciting stuff. On this song, none of the playing—bass chords aside—is new or extraordinary, just very well done. Note: The recordings for "All I've Got to Do" and "Not a Second Time" were both begun and completed on the same day, September 11, 1962.

"All My Loving"

While John is mashing triplets on his Rickenbacker guitar, the first half of each verse of "All My Loving" has Paul's bass walking from chord to chord in good ol' swinging jazz style. The typical R&R bass lines would work with this song, especially considering what's happening on rhythm guitar, but the walk works even better.

But then on the chorus, where you generally expect the band to pick it up, the Beatles fall way back. The triplet guitar stops, the bass stops walking, and the background vocals are hushed, used almost as an organ effect. The bass, here, stands to the side as well until the guitar solo starts. In effect, it becomes a whole new song during the choruses. "All My Loving" is a catchy song alright, one of Paul's catchiest ever. Following George Martin's rules for album layout, this would easily have been the opening track on their previous album. Here it is relegated to 3rd song, side one.

"This song may have been my initial awareness of a musical 'hook.' For the first time in my listening memory, Paul's masterful bass creates a swinging *counter* to the lead and rhythm guitar, yet maintaining a fine quality bounce through the whole of the song. In the version on the Anthology, there exists a *joy* in the bass playing, entirely playful. The bounce remains in the released version, but something was removed or lost during the continual refinement; something a non-musical person such as myself would be hard-pressed to explain. He dances with his bass up and down the neck at double the rhythm—perhaps it is that which creates the happy, joyful bounce. The harmony after the solo . . . wow. . . . Could this be the perfect pop tune?"

~ Gary Alstand

(*email, 2013*)

"When I read (the above comment) I thought , that is exactly what the song makes me feel as well. There is a certain 'hope' or 'joy' to the rhythm, that's hard to describe. A bit like being happy on a first date . . . happy enough to want a second date and learning in turn that the person you're with feels the same way. 'You just gotta call on me' really brings that out. It's like lyrical reassurance."

~ Claudine Purdue

(*email, 2013*)

"'All My Loving' was written by Paul, I regret to say because it's a damn good piece of work. But I play a pretty mean guitar in back.."

~ John Lennon

(*The Playboy Interviews With John Lennon and Yoko Ono*, 1981)

"Till There Was You"

"Till There Was You" is included here because the level of musicianship is, suddenly seemingly, at a much higher level than they had exhibited previously on record. Paul McCartney's bass playing sounds as if he's been playing Bossa Nova style for years. He anchors the song nicely, and Ringo provides a strong background. But give a listen to the acoustic playing of John Lennon. Well, he was always a good masher on the guitar; sometimes imaginative, usually perfect for rock and roll. But now he's playing at a level of taste and competence that is surprising. George Harrison had shown flashes of brilliance in the past, but he truly shines here on his nylon string guitar. That's his playing you hear up front at the start of the song as well as during the incredibly tasteful solo.

"A couple of details betray the Beatles' own fingerprints; e.g., the flat-VI chord (D-flat Major) in the coda and the final F-Major chord with the added Major seventh are definitely **not** part of the original. Despite this, the musical essence of this song, with its chromatic winding that pervades both vocal melody and bassline (and which indirectly affects the choice and progression of chords) is something quite off the Beatles' track."

~ Alan W. Pollack

(*Notes on . . . Series*, 1989-2000)

"Not a Second Time"

As I'm a disciple of George Martin, I realize some of these words will be blasphemous. Listening to "Not a Second Time" one wonders what happened to the loud(er) bass playing we've been hearing on *With the*

Beatles until now. For "Not a Second Time," it has been nearly dropped from the mix. The reason becomes clear when you pick the electric bass out from George Martin's over-dubbed heavy-handed piano bass.

As any bass player will tell you, playing with a piano player who uses their left-hand a lot can be frightful. If they're both carrying a rhythm, as they are in "Not a Second Time," the two instrumentalists must either play precisely the same notes and rhythms or one of them has to drop out.

The surprising part about this addition of piano bass is that McCartney plays a nice bouncy bass line on the electric which would have moved the song well. Why would the piano part be added over it? A good first guess would be that George Martin added the part in the Beatles' absence due to issues with the bass in the mix. But studio documentation shows that Martin added the part during the day of the recording. The difficulties with the piano vs. Paul's bass and John's acoustic guitar become apparent immediately if you're listening for them. In the second bar between John's first two vocal lines, there is a serious stumble of rhythms.

Then, to add to the calamity, there is a missed piano note, as well, at 0:37 (just before "you're back again"), the piano skips to a B over the Am. Martin, realizing his error, drops quickly back to the Am. He was probably anticipating the Bm under ("no no no, not a second time"). The fact that he doesn't repeat the note next time around (1:40) indicates that it was a mistake. We all do that kind of thing, but in this case, it's surprising that it was left in especially when you consider that the piano part was laid down after the rhythm section was recorded.

Did You Hear That?!

As the Beatles head into the piano solo on "Not a Second Time," Ringo provides a drum flourish, under which you can clearly hear Paul McCartney shout "Woo!"

As with so many songs on *With the Beatles*, a less-than-careful listening shows that Ringo was the prime mover of the music in those days. He plays a snare rhythm in the verses of the song that was a trademark of his. Instead of the surf style snare of 2 2+ 4, Ringo drops the first of these beats.

Of more interest is the drum fill noted in the "Did You Hear That?!" above (0:44). It has been double-tracked to add emphasis to it, and the stereophonic ploy works like a charm. It was "doable" at this point because it was the only instrument being played and so took up both sides of the 2 track mix. Sadly, the effect is not used again when the drums bring back the vocal (at the end of the piano solo). As good an effect as it is, it makes one sadly wonder what *With the Beatles* might have sounded like with enough tracks to record the drums in stereo.

"Don't Bother Me"

Poor ol' George complained to the end of his days about how the Beatles always gave him short shrift while recording his songs. Looking at the session info, it's true that John and Paul were always the first to get their songs done when recording an album. But it's also true that they did not slack when it came to recording George's songs, and "Don't Bother Me" (the first song he ever wrote not counting his co-writing credit for the guitar solo in "Cry For A Shadow," 1961) features some outstanding ensemble support for his tune.

The recording was made in the middle of a lot of projects being attended to and far-off gigs to play. But despite the minimal amount of time available overall, the musicians were determined that George's offering would be given the full Beatle treatment.

It took 11 takes to perfect the song with Paul on bass, John on tremolo guitar, Ringo on drums and George on guitar and double tracked vocal. To give the song the rich, rhythmic feel it still retains, the Beatles added claves (Paul), tambourine (John) and an Arabian bongo (Ringo).

The sound of Lennon's tremolo rhythm guitar features on the intro. It settles us into a rhythm and from there until the end they deliver top notch ensemble playing, each player adding vital ingredients to the final mix. Paul's bass part follows John's rhythm on the intro, but under the verses he plays a syncopated and funky bass line that is subtle in the recording but moving to the song. For the second chorus ("I've got no time . . ." found at 0:34), Paul increases the pressure by breaking out his patented (for 1963) two note chords. As he did not feature chords on the first chorus, this subtle change marks an increase in the intensity of the rhythm section. He continues the practice each time they reach the chorus for the remainder of the song. It may be either that Paul forgot the first time or that he tried it the second time, liked how it worked, and decided to keep it going.

There are a lot of crisp breaks in "Don't Bother Me," one that stands out can be found at 1:58. The band breaks but this time Paul holds on to his note. It's a little thing, a touch of color that is barely noticeable, but it showed some bass guitar wisdom. A good bass player will know instinctively how long a note should be held. This one is well done.

Holding the note on breaks became a bit of a staple in the bag of McCartney bass stylings, especially in live shows, and one that was employed to fantastic effect on "Come Together" in 1969.

Notes on the *With the Beatles*

One thing that worked heavily in McCartney's favor all through the recordings on *With the Beatles* was that John and George's guitars were tastefully played, rarely overplaying, or strumming for the sake of strumming. The spaces they left in the music allowed McCartney to be inventive and have fun with the music. All this would sadly change on the next album.

"Little Child" and "Roll Over Beethoven" are both pure rock 'n roll and McCartney plays a pure (and perfect) rock 'n roll bass line on both. "Till There Was You" has accomplished playing by all of the Beatles. The arrangement is excellent and shows considerable understanding of chord structure. I've always considered the song "Hold Me Tight" to be a sleeper in the Beatles catalog. Although hated by both

John and Paul, it's one of my favorite Beatles songs due in large part to Paul's stylized singing and Lennon's raw sounding rhythm guitar.

With the Beatles was recorded on two-track, which meant that they had to be careful with overdubs and the craft work of the studio. Despite, or perhaps because of, this extreme limitation, it is one of the best albums the Beatles ever did. Like the one that followed, it is largely a collection of John Lennon songs. It's largely his voice throughout, and his songs and vocals are forever memorable.

Which album was the most fun? If your best memories are of when they were all working together like a machine, not editing each other too much; if your taste in Beatledom is for the fun, rocking Beatles, but with some sophistication, then *With the Beatles* might be the one for you. It's a powerful testament to how exciting a band can sound when they've played together long enough to work like a machine, but not so long that one of the personalities emerges as the nay-saying leader. Those days would come, but not for a few years.

With the Beatles (track listing)

Side One	Side Two
1. "It Won't Be Long"	1. "Roll Over Beethoven"
2. "All I've Got to do"	2. "Hold Me Tight"
3. "All My Loving"	3. "You Really Got a Hold on Me"
4. "Don't Bother Me"	4. "I Wanna Be Your Man"
5. "Little Child"	5. "Devil in Her Heart"
6. "Till There Was You"	6. "Not a Second Time"
7. "Please Mister Postman"	7. "Money (That's What I Want)"

A New Höfner for Paul

In late September, McCartney picked up another Höfner 500/1 bass with a difference to his old one. The pickups were further apart which would allow him a wider array of tones from high to low.

Late in 1963, he also got new Vox amplification: an AC-100 (100 watt amp) and a speaker cabinet with two 15" speakers. It seems like he really improved his amplification, but the amazing thing is that he would never be heard with 100 watts in the vast places they were getting ready to play in.

"I Want to Hold Your Hand" (Single)
"This Boy" (B-side)
(Released November 29, 1963)

Things were breaking big for the Beatles. They played the London Palladium (the big time in England) on October 13th and on the 17th they went down to London to record the song that would break them at last in America: "I Want to Hold Your Hand." If you were to be writing a novel about the group, this would be the climax.

First Four Track Recording

Unknown to us until much later, "I Want to Hold Your Hand" was also the first recording the Beatles made on a four-track recorder. This allowed the group to record their parts in sections. George Martin now thought of the studio as a workshop. They could put the bass and drums on track 1, the guitars and other instruments on track 2 and 3, and the vocals on track 4. At the end, they would mix all four tracks down to stereo, and they had a record. For the Beatles, the best part of the innovation (which had already been used extensively in America) was that they did not have to record their songs live in the studio. They could work in sections, and if they made mistakes the whole band didn't have to stop and begin the song again.

Song Notes

"I Want to Hold Your Hand" is full of dynamics, stumbles and hooks. At the outset it's the rhythm guitar with its celebrated stumble on the open chords, seemingly but not quite falling out of 4/4. This is followed by a delightful little build-up, to end the intro, which is almost over-professionally done.

On the bridge ("and when I touch you I feel happy"), just as in "All My Loving," the guitars and drums fall way back, and Paul's bass leaps to the fore, playing chords. The whole song changes feel for a short time, but not for long. The dynamics that result when the guitars re-enter at "I can't hide" are, at the very least, catchy.

Here, at a stage where the Beatles were conquering the world, John and George both stood back and let the dynamics flow. The boys had learned, quite early in their professional recording careers, to bring the hooks to the fore.

"just about every one of the Beatles' early trademark tricks of the trade is to be found within it: the abrupt syncopations, non-intuitive two-part vocal harmony, falsetto screaming, an occasionally novel chord progression, even some elided phrasing. And of course, don't forget the overdubbed handclaps!

Perhaps it is just this paradoxical contrast between familiar and more daring elements that is at the heart of the song's phenomenal success."

~ Alan W. Pollack

(*Notes on . . . Series*, 1989-2000)

"I Want to Hold Your Hand" is a yet another pop music masterpiece. Short and concise, it takes you through changes both subtle and obvious.

This song and its B-side "This Boy" (one of the classiest flip sides of all time) were recorded on October 17, 1963. It was released on November 29th, 1963 in the UK where it was number 1 for six weeks. Note: "I Want to Hold Your Hand" was released in England a week after the *Meet the Beatles* LP (which contained "I Want to Hold Your Hand") was released in America. So while the British record buying public was out buying yet another brilliant Beatles' single, most of

America was hearing them—at last—for the first time. Sadly, also, it was suddenly time to say goodbye to about 90% of the American recording artists who had been enjoying thriving careers.

Is America Ready?
As a Matter of Fact, Yes.

"I Want to Hold Your Hand" became number 1 in America. Brian Epstein appears to be the man responsible for making this—a huge step in his master vision of success—a reality. After the failure of past attempts with smaller labels in America, the task was clearly going to have to be handled by a large record label in America that had the resources to finance a publicity campaign. Since the Beatles British record company (EMI) owned Capitol Records in America, it made sense that Capitol would be the ones to do it.

But why now when they had refused twice before? Perhaps Brian Epstein was aided by Beatles' record sales numbers throughout the world. It is hard to overemphasize that EMI was making a lot of money from the sales of Beatles' records. Capitol was not.

So, with "I Want to Hold Your Hand," Capitol Records was ready at last. At the end of 1963, the company put forty to fifty thousand dollars into a campaign to break the Beatles in America. Capitol planned to release the record in January of 1964, but a Washington DC disk jockey by the name of Carroll James was playing it, public demand was growing, and release was pulled up to December 26th, 1963.

"America mattered," said George Martin. "It mattered because, quite simply, it was the biggest record market in the world. If our excitement seems over-dramatic in retrospect, it is crucial to remember that no British artist had got near breaking into that market."

1963 Comes to an End

So the year came to an end; the busiest year they would ever experience as a group. They'd driven all over the country many times and played many hundreds of dates, sliding the odd recording date between. By year's end, the group was famous beyond their dreams in England. Records were selling at history-setting amounts. They were all over the radio and television.

But the fun had already worn off for them. They had to wear disguises out in public. Their shows had become ridiculous: they needed to be smuggled into and out of them, they needed police protection and you couldn't hear the group for the screams. As they traveled around the country, they were worried about their families who were besieged by the press and fans alike.

But by year's end, 1964 looked like a year of expansion for them. They had booked to perform in France and Australia. They had also signed to do a movie. At the end of the year, Capitol records had released "I Want to Hold Your Hand" in America. Finally, Brian Epstein had traveled to New York to talk to Ed Sullivan, and the two arranged an appearance by the group for early in the new year. Was the world about to find out what England had already known? What would become of all of these possibilities? They could only guess.

Notes

1. This refers to the position in the major scale a chord is in. "Twist and Shout" is in the key of D and the main, repeating chords are D, G and A. D is the first note in the D major scale, G is the fourth and A is the fifth, hence I IV V)

2. The question "When do you think the bubble will burst," meaning "When will your amazing run of fame end?" was asked so many times that it became almost a standing joke of the press in Britain and America, and was an extremely irritating question for the group. When you have something that hot going, the last thing you want to hear about is the constant reminder that your luck might not last long. Paul McCartney was the only Beatle who seemed to try to answer the question seriously. In 1963, he would talk in serious tones about how the band might go for another year or so and then he and John might become songwriters for other artists or maybe get into movies.

She Loves You? Apparently Not

Here's an insight into the power of suggestion. For years we've been listening to the song and gleefully accepting the lyrics as they've been suggested to us: "She loves you yeah yeah yeah" etc. But what are they actually saying?

While giving this song a close listen to prepare for this book, I noticed that what they were actually saying was a bit different than what I had been hearing all of these years.

I heard the opening lines as "She loves you yeah yeah yeah . . . she'd love to yeah yeah yeah." Obviously I liked that because it's so suggestive. Seemed like something the Beatles would try to get away with.

Wanting an extra pair of ears, I elicited the assistance of my Australian friend Richard Goodwin. We delved into this matter and came up with about as many answers as there can possibly be.

Richard writes "What I hear, from the introduction to the final chorus, is 'She loved you'; it occasionally sounds like 'She loves too' and occasionally the harmonies and lead sing 'loves' and 'loved' at the same time. Early on, John sings 'She love you,' I believe."

The conclusion we've drawn is that it is indeed all about the power of suggestion. We've all listened to this song hundreds of times over the years since it was released and we've heard the words 'she loves you' every time. And yet it turns out that the phrase hardly appears in the song. "Whatever they're saying," says Richard, "it's not 'She loves you'—even though we all knew it was?"

FIVE

Runaway Fame
(1964)

1964 in Review

The Beatles had survived the incredibly busy 1963. They were famous beyond all dreams in England. To manager Brian Epstein, it was "today England, tomorrow the world." The Beatles started 1964 in less than grand style, putting on a series of performances in Paris. Recordings from these engagements show the Beatles, mainly Paul, trying to engage the near silent crowd with a word or two in French. "For our next song, chanson. . . ."

They had to wait for the world. Was it possible the world wasn't ready for the Beatles? Was the capitulation of their homeland to be the zenith of their careers? It wasn't long before they had an answer to that. After their set of Paris shows on January 16th, they received the news they'd been waiting for. "I Want to Hold Your Hand" had jumped straight to number one on the American charts.

There had been only two one-off records by English artists that had found success in America. To make it there would be unprecedented, unbelievable yet—for our heroes—undeniable. Still, a number one record did not mean continued success there. As far as they knew, it might be yet another "one-off" hit for a British act there. Indeed they were already booked to perform on *The Ed Sullivan Show* in a month, and it was hoped they might increase their popularity there ("might" . . . ha ha ha).

Brian Epstein's final two steps of the master plan were ready to fall into place, much sooner than anybody thought. First, he wanted the group to have a hit record in the states. And, he wanted long-term success there. "The Beatles," he kept claiming to anyone who would listen, "will be bigger than Elvis."

1964 was the year that changed the world, and—as far as years go— it didn't take long to get going. At the start of the year they were (big) stars in the UK and well known in some other countries, and as early as February 9th, they had done what no other British act (or army) had done in history: they conquered the new world.

The dam burst at last in America, and that is not really being overly playful with words. Unless you were in America and alive at the time, it's difficult to describe what a monstrous hit the Beatles suddenly became there. It is impossible to find the right superlatives that don't sound downright silly. One day there was no Beatles; the next day they were on Ed Sullivan and then there was . . . BEATLES. Everywhere.

But *everywhere* didn't stop with America. The interesting aspect to their jump to success is that at the same time they were breaking in America, they were breaking around the entire world. Everywhere, at the same time. In just about every continent, subcontinent, country and hamlet the Beatles became famous or at least known (to be fair I haven't read about their breakthroughs in Antarctica in early 1964, but I'm sure they became known).

Sociologists far and wide attempted to explain what truly was a phenomenon. Dry and clinical discussions about girls wetting their seats in a tribal ecstasy would have been funny if they weren't too boring to get past the first few paragraphs. Interviews of the Beatles in 1964 reveal that the question, "Why are you so popular?" was the never-ending question of the year. They never had an answer other than "We don't know." They were as mystified as the rest of us. After all, what causes success to flow? Word of mouth? If so, how did they become well known even in the remotest of places? My view is that it is a question that will never be answered.

In 1964, they could do no wrong. There success was far more than just the songs we have today.

Whatever styles they wore, the world wore.

The Beatles had long hair . . . The boys of the world wanted their hair long.

The musical instruments they used . . . Companies like Höfner (Paul's bass), Rickenbacker (John and George's guitars) and Ludwig (Ringo's drums) suddenly had major manufacturing problems. How can you stock the music stores of the world with enough product to satisfy the demand of thousands of budding musicians?

There were some serious downsides to this onslaught of fame. Many musical careers were either ended or put on hold by the invasion of British musical acts. The old rock and rollers ceased to exist in the minds of the record buying public. It's hard to fathom how hard it was for them to be so popular one moment and then totally forgotten the next.

Secondly, whatever excitement they had held out for being world-wide stars only further secured them as prisoners of their own fame. A cursory glance at photos of the group as 1964 progressed shows them getting more and more tired as the year went by.

1964 meant they finally could say "so long" to the van they had put so many miles on. But it was also "hello" to endless long airplane rides, the Ed Sullivan show, screaming teenagers, tours of Australia, the Netherlands, Denmark, Hong Kong (that was the tour where Ringo had tonsilitis and was replaced by Jimmy Nichol), Sweden, screaming teenagers, another tour of England, a seemingly endless tour of North America (each show with lousy amplification), press conferences that started out as fun and ended up being less than dreary, death threats and famous predictions of their deaths, screaming teenagers, meeting mayors and their families, a Christmas show, a (surprisingly good) movie, two new albums, three new singles, Bob Dylan, pot, George's Rickenbacker 12 string guitar, John's switch to acoustic guitar, Paul's expansion of writing for other artists and . . . how they did all of this in one year, especially after surviving 1963, is quite sincerely beyond belief.

Here are some facts about record sales in America in 1964

❖ "I Want to Hold Your Hand" sold nearly 5 million records in the US by 1968, making it the best-selling single of the 1960. (*Capitol Records press release*, 1968)

❖ In 1964, the Beatles had the never matched total of 15 American million selling records (9 singles and 6 LPs), representing US sales of over 25 million in 1964 alone. (*Wikipedia*)

❖ "Can't Buy Me Love" sold 940,225 copies in the US the day it was released (March 16, 1964), shattering all previous sales records. The single went on to sell over 3 million by the end of the year. (*Spizer*, 2000)

❖ The motion picture soundtrack *A Hard Day's Night* sold 1 million copies in the first four days of its US release making it one of the fastest selling LPs of the 1960s. (*Billboard*. 1964)

❖ By August 1964, the Beatles had sold approximately 80 million records globally. (*Wikipedia*)

Their first single of the year was "Can't Buy Me Love" and the last was "I Feel Fine" two very different songs. Somehow, through all of their travels, travails and an imprisoned lifestyle, they were able to keep moving beyond what they had done before.

Paul McCartney's Bass Playing in 1964

Listening to the Beatles' records from 1964, it's clear that Paul McCartney had continued to progress with the mastery of his main instrument. Unfortunately, especially on *A Hard Days Night* (LP), it's harder to hear what he's playing than in albums past. The production level of the bass seems to have leveled off or actually decreased, especially when you consider the manner in which it had been brought to the fore so often in 1963 (see "It Won't Be Long" on page 65). A number of theories can be put forth:

❖ In 1963, John and George played their guitars somewhat sparingly and very tastefully. In 1964, Lennon began using an acoustic guitar most of the time. Also, George started using his new Rickenbacker electric 12-string. Both instruments were mixed well to the fore all through *A Hard Day's Night*, providing a blanket "wall of guitar" sound.

❖ As the year progressed, Bob Dylan's expanding influence on Lennon/McCartney's writing called for more acoustic/less rock songs, especially on their *Beatles for Sale* LP. There was just not much opportunity for McCartney to shine.

❖ The monstrous schedule they maintained through the year meant that the recordings were somehow made even more fast and furiously than the ones they had made the previous year. There must not have been much time to sit and think about what the bass could do for a song.

❖ Paul McCartney's interests were expanding (as they have to this day). He was playing more piano and guitar than before. He also wanted to be a songwriter of greater renown. While Lennon typically gave his songs to other artists—if he felt they were not up to par for the group (i.e., "Bad to Me")—McCartney was busy writing songs specifically to be done by other artists (such as "World Without Love" and "Woman," both recorded by Peter and Gordon).

"Can't Buy Me Love"
 "Komm, Gib Mir Deine Hand"
 "Sie Liebt Dich"
 (January 29, 1964)

Before they made their first trip to America, and while they were performing in Paris, they made their first recordings of 1964.

There was interesting business to attend to. It was felt by EMI's German branch that Beatle songs would only be successful there if they were sung in German. The Beatles were against the idea. Producer George Martin was for it. So it was that they found themselves recording

"Komm, Gib Mir Deine Hand" (I Want to Hold Your Hand) and *"She Liebt Dich"* (She Loves You). The original master recordings of "She Loves You" had been erased by EMI and so they had to re-record the song.

They had time left over in the studio, and so they set in to record a new song Paul had written, and this time they were singing in English. It was "Can't Buy Me Love."

The first takes, as heard on the Beatles *Anthology 1*, have an altogether different feel than the released version. In its first try, the song is slower and bluesier, with Paul's voice sounding more like it did on "She's a Woman" and "I'm Down." John and George have vocal *answering parts*, such as "Woaaahhhh love me to."

Paul's bass on this early version, however, is very similar to the released one, mostly anchoring the rhythm with a I-V bass line.

Aside from the occasional vocal flub, it's a very good version. But it's hard to deny the enthusiasm and energy of the final version. It was a worldwide smash hit and was the perfect song for the romping field scene in the movie *A Hard Day's Night*. All this and, according to Mark Lewisohn, the whole song—including the major change in style—took less than an hour to record. That's the Beatles' machine at work!

Here's an interesting note on "Can't Buy Me Love." After recording the basic tracks in Paris, they brought the tape back to England for tidying up. Geoff Emerick, who would later become their 1st engineer was acting as 2nd engineer during this time, and (historically) this was the first time he sat in the seat of the 1st engineer.

"It had the same level of excitement as previous Beatles singles and was quickly slated to be an A-side, but first there was a technical problem to be overcome, discovered when the tape was brought back and played at our studios. Perhaps because it had been spooled incorrectly, the tape had a ripple in it, resulting in the intermittent loss of treble on Ringo's hi-hat cymbal. There was a tremendous time pressure to get the track mixed and delivered to the pressing plant, and due to touring commitments the Beatles themselves were unavailable, so George and Norman took it upon themselves to make a little adjustment.

As I eagerly headed into the engineer's seat for the first time, Norman headed down into the studio to overdub a hastily set-up hi-hat onto a few bars of the song while I recorded him, simultaneously doing a two-track to two-track dub. Thanks to Norman's considerable skills as a drummer, the repair was made quickly and seamlessly"

~ Geoff Emerick

(*Here, There and Everywhere*, 2006)

Going to America

The Beatles were breaking in America in a (put your own superlative here) way. It was as if a conquering army had landed and was now marching across the land, shoving any form of resistance aside. The main stronghold was in New York City, where by January 13th, "I Want to Hold Your Hand" was selling 10,000 copies per hour. How is that possible? At the same time, various companies that had claim to Beatle songs were putting their records onto the market. Every record they made in 1963 was bulling its way onto the American charts at the same time. It was looking as if there would be more songs than there was room on the charts to contain them all.

Capitol Records was not idle. Within days they had slapped together an album that contained tracks from the UK *With the Beatles* LP, and included "I Want to Hold Your Hand" as well as "This Boy." The new Capitol album, *Meet the Beatles*, was released on January 20th. Quick job? It's amazing what a company can do when a lot of money is at stake.

In retrospect, it all seems like part of a master plan that the records would be selling in astronomical numbers just as the group was coming to America. But it was a coincidence. Epstein had booked the prime time Ed Sullivan Show months before, with no knowledge that they would even be known. At the time, they were not selling records in

America and getting the group on the show was his latest, and most deft, ploy to get notoriety for the group

And here they came, landing in America on February 7th. Even with their record sales, they had no idea what was waiting for them here. It didn't take them long to find out.

Most events that are burned into the memory of Americans (Pearl Harbor, the deaths of FDR and JFK, 911) all have to do with sudden and surprising loss of life. Those of us that were lucky enough to be sitting in front of a TV on the evening of February 9th, 1964 have a similar reaction when asked "where were you . . . ?" But it's a much more positive and all-encompassing memory. For that was the night that the Beatles performed for the first time on *The Ed Sullivan Show*. According to AC Nielsen, the show was watched by 73 million people, by far the most ever to watch a TV broadcast at the time. Here's a pop quiz. What was the first song performed by the Beatles on that show? You already knew? It was "All My Loving."

As was their style in those days, the Beatles didn't stay long. Boom, they came and then they were gone, like four Shanes riding off into the sunset. It was perfect. They flew home on February 21st with not much time to get ready to make their upcoming movie and record all the songs for it. The next day, back home in England and still jet-lagged, the Beatles taped a television show, staying there until 10:30 p.m.

"Can't Buy Me Love" (*Single*)
"You Can't Do That" (*B-side*)
(*Released March 20, 1964*)

As noted above, "Can't Buy Me Love"—soon to be jetting its way to worldwide fame and acclaim—was recorded in France during their stay there in January.

Then, three days after returning from their dizzying trip to America, they began recording songs for the upcoming movie. When the Beatles showed up at the studio on February 25th, producer George Martin wouldn't have known what they had ready to record. He knew they needed to record a B-side for "Can't Buy Me Love," quickly, but he probably wondered if the writers had found time to come up with anything worth recording. Imagine how he felt when they demoed "You Can't Do That." Producers dream of stuff like this. The Beatles were pulling hit songs out of their travel bags and using them for B-sides. Let's talk about this fantastic single.

"Can't Buy Me Love" sounds like a hit from the opening bar. As per George Martin's direction, they started the song off with the chorus ("Can't buy me love, oh"). For the lay listener, the opening of the song might seem hectic and exciting. The reason is that the key of the song isn't reached until the verse ("I'll buy you a diamond ring my friend"). The song is not grounded until then. An interesting thing about the verses is that there are only four instruments creating a barrage of sound.

The verses are based on a blues chord progression, but the sound is far from blues. Put through the Beatles' machine, it is Paul McCartney's most inspired and enthusiastic song to date.

> "The appearance of **any** amount of straight-blues in a Beatles' original is noteworthy in and of itself. A recurring theme in our studies has been Lennon and McCartney's predilection for bluesy cover material, going back all the way to the Quarrymen era, made ironic by the virtual dearth of such material in their canonical songbook; you'll find that the number of twelve-bar Beatles' originals can be counted on less than the fingers of two hands."
>
> ~ Alan W. Pollack
>
> (*Notes on . . . Series,* 1989-2000)

Alan also goes on to note that the B-side, "You Can't Do That" is also based on a 12-bar blues progression.

"You Can't Do That" is bluesy and sounds like a precursor to the hard rock they would be recording four years later. It starts off with a catchy line played on George's new Rickenbacker 12 string guitar. That's Paul on the cowbell as well as the rock bass. Ringo is there with his ever present cool drum breaks (and barely discernable bongos). Paul and George's incessant and engaging background vocals are reminiscent of 1963's "Money (That's What I Want)." But this is John Lennon's baby. He delivers the hard edge vocals and even plays the guitar solo. If I'm not mistaken, it's John's first guitar solo on record. What he also delivers is one of the great rock and roll screams at 1:29.

What a powerful single! Both songs sound as electric and exciting today as they did when they came out; both are full of wild enthusiasm and energy. And it's hard to believe that this is the same Paul McCartney and John Lennon who would—for the upcoming movie—also write the beautiful ballads "And I Love Her" and "If I Fell."

A Hard Day's Night (LP)

Released
June 26, 1964

Cover Notes
Robert Freeman snapped the photos. The style was copied in the movie itself with George facing a cameraman and making various faces.

Peak Position
Number 1

Number of Weeks on the Chart
51 (one short of a year)

Number of Days in the Studio
8

First Song Recorded for the Album
"You Can't Do That" on February 25, 1964

One of Lennon's best from the early days. It ended up as the B-side to "Can't Buy Me Love" and the performance removed from the movie until the DVD release.

Even though the Beatles were riding a speeding train of fame that seemed like it would never stop, Lennon and McCartney were up for the challenge. They had to write and record seven new songs to be included in the upcoming movie (to begin filming on March 2).

A Hard Day's Night is the final piece in their trilogy of albums that constitute what might be called the early years. These were the albums that reflected and caused Beatlemania. They were full of youthful electrified and enthusiastic excitement that would not be reached at this sustained level again. At only one other point in their career would they enter the studio with so many songs ready to record and that would be after their time in Rishikesh, India in 1968.

> "God bless their little cotton socks, those boys WORKED! Here I am talking about an afternoon off, and we're sitting there writing! We just loved it so much. It wasn't work."
> ~ Paul McCartney
> (*The Beatles Recording Sessions,* 1990)

As they worked their blessed cotton socks off writing all new songs for the upcoming (as yet unnamed) movie, John and Paul were on a quest. They must have had it in mind that the film would be an opportunity to bring the power and excitement of their music to an even larger audience in the world. They wrote with passion and skill and the Beatles went into the studio every day and recorded those songs. Put through their song making machine, shaken, stirred and rising asunder, each song from the album easily could have been a hit single for any other group.

The recordings were made at the same time the movie was filmed. Frequently they would be filming during the day and recording in the evening, and they had to appear as if they were enthusiastically having fun doing it all. The Beatles clearly had an energy source that went deeper than that of mortal humans.

The movie and LP were, surprise surprise, incredible successes throughout the world. In America, over one million copies of the LP were bought in the first four days of its release alone. It was getting beyond ridiculous, in fact, it was starting to look as if the entire national economy was now based on the moving, storing (not for long), shelving, and selling various Beatles' products. Let's talk about some of the songs.

"A Hard Day's Night"
The movie's producer said that a title was needed. Later that evening, John Lennon became inspired and told the driver of his car to take him home. The next morning he had the title and the track ready. That's

John's story, and if it's true, then he wrote the song on the night of April 16th with the movie almost done. He got the title line from Ringo who, at the end of a long day told someone, "It's been a hard day." But then, noting that it was now night time, added "day's night."

The album, the song and the movie all start off with *The Chord*. It is, by certain fact, the most argued about chord of all time. What is that chord? The world wants to know. One thing is for sure, you would recognize that chord if it was played quietly in the back of Beethoven's fifth symphony, or while a rocket lifted off in your backyard. Alan W. Pollack is always good for great quotes:

> "Wake me up from the dead of sleep many years hence and play it (the chord) for me by itself out of context, and not only do I trust I'll be able to identify it immediately, but also summon with close to total recall just how it shot through my consciousness the very first time I heard it as a mere not-so-pimply adolescent."
> ~ Alan W. Pollack
> (*Notes on . . . Series*, 1989-2000)

What is that chord? What are the notes they played? George Martin has always passed it off as something they just came up with. John just happened to strum a chord and they said "That's it!" However, as was the case with a lot of their recordings, there is something far more sinister involved. They always claimed wide-eyed innocence, and happenstance, as to how they got their sound. Yet there were people in that studio who really knew what they were doing, and this chord—I think—proves it.

Let's bring a mathematician into the fray to (hopefully) bind this issue up once and for all. But read on only if you dare, because the holy grail is about to be revealed to you.

> "Four years ago, Jason Brown was inspired by reading news coverage about the song's 40th anniversary—so much so that he decided to try and see if he could apply a mathematical

calculation known as Fourier transform to solve the Beatles' riddle. The process allowed him to break the sound into distinct frequencies using computer software to find out exactly which notes were on the record.

What he found was interesting: the frequencies he found didn't match the instruments on the song. George played a 12-string Rickenbacker, John Lennon played his 6 string, Paul had his bass—none of them quite fit what he found. He then realized what was missing—the 5th Beatle. George Martin was also on the record, playing a piano in the opening chord, which accounted for the problematic frequencies

So how was the chord played you ask? George Harrison was playing the following notes on his 12 string guitar: a2, a3, d3, d4, g3, g4, c4, and another c4; Paul McCartney played a d3 on his bass; producer George Martin was playing d3, f3, d5, g5, and e6 on the piano, while Lennon played a loud c5 on his six-string guitar."

(noiseaddicts.com, 2008)

So, at long last, there is the answer: an F chord mixed with a G chord.

But what happens after The Chord has altered our consciousness? If you're the average person, like me, you must think "A Hard Day's Night" must be full of subliminal machinations. It's hard not to fall into a Beatle-induced trance during the song. With it's driving tempo, it's difficult to listen to in an objective way: Harrison-played electric 12-string guitar, wild bongo playing, reverberated lead vocals, heavy guitars, and solid rhythm section (with Ringo's ride cymbal enthusiastically and exhaustively played). In fact, it may be Harrison's guitar and Ringo's cymbal that is the driving force of the song. It is played and recorded in a way that encompasses the rest of the sound.

One of the lovable aspects of "A Hard Day's Night" is that it is one of the few times that John and Paul share separate lead vocals in a song. Other examples are "Any Time at All," "I've Got a Feeling" and "Free as a Bird."

Although their last album was full of excitement, the album-opening "A Hard Day's Night" heralds the new Beatles' wall of sound that pretty much describes the album.

"I'll Cry Instead"

Throughout the Beatles' recording career, Paul had a distinct tendency to play in a more lively fashion on songs written by John or George. This is a good example of Paul's lively playing on a John song.

It was recorded in an interesting manner. Lyrically, it's sad and introspective, but the Beatles put their magic touch on it. It rolls along nicely, Paul playing a I/V country-western influenced style, all upbeat. But wait. Whose idea was this? At 1:05 and 1:35 the band breaks (under "show you what your lovin' man can do") and, lo and behold, a bass break! Try to name a song in the world of pop that had a bass break by 1964. When these points are reached, Paul pumps harder on the strings with his pick than otherwise throughout the song. It makes sense: if he's going to be the prime factor in the instrumental section, he's going to "crank it up" a notch.

"Things We Said Today"

Very good ensemble playing. The first thing to listen for is the counter rhythms being employed during the verse:

❖ Ringo is playing a fast 4/4 high-hat and a snare beat played on the 2nd and 4th beats

❖ George is striking alternating chords (Am and Em7) on beats 2 and 3+

❖ John is being more liberal with his acoustic guitar strum, but basically following the 2 and 3+ rhythm with George

❖ Paul decides that his bass should, in effect, follow the 2 and 4 rhythm with Ringo's snare; a basic line that does the job.

Above all of this is Paul's reflective, softer-edged vocal with which he harmonizes over the bridge of each verse. The chords beneath that little section represent the Beatles in a nutshell. They sound good and sound fairly basic, but they do not constitute a simple progression by any means. They are, in fact, effectively strange. The first chord is a jump to Am's relative major C ("some day when I'm") followed by a C7 ("lonely"), then F ("wishing you weren't so") and Bb ("far away") and then back to the melancholy old Am.

The chord structure and playing style of the actual bridge ("me I'm just a lucky guy") seem to indicate that Paul had skillfully melded two wholly different songs together. The first pass through: A(major now), D, B E7, A, D, B Bb Am. The B/Bb/Am walk-down acts as a sort of slide transition from the upbeat bridge to the softer verse.

It would have been called a "slow dance" song at the time. But it's played at a fast tempo, 139 Beats-Per-Minute (BPM), the same tempo as "Please Please Me"! So, what defines a slow song or fast song? It's not necessarily the drumbeat: Ringo's eighth-note hi-hat beat during the slow sections is somewhat similar to a rock-and-roll beat. In the end, it must be the energy of the performers. In this song, Paul delivers both forms of energy to his vocal. During the slow part, his voice covers the sound almost like a blanket; it's very soothing. During the rock part, his voice carries the tension of a rocker.

This is one of the early examples, to be shown many times over their career, of the Beatles' ability to shift in and out of tempos, time signatures, and moods with stealth and ease. For another one of their all-time best examples of this, refer to the 4/4, 3/4 change in "We Can Work It Out."

"And I Love Her"

This was the first song recorded specifically for the album, done on February 25th. While it is not a song that you hear as much these days, it stands as a testament to Lennon (claimed to have written the middle eight) and McCartney's fully formed song-writing skills way back in 1964. Its melody has a high "haunt count." The chord progression is intriguing in that it showed some knowledge of musical theory on the part of the writer. Each verse starts out in C# minor and winds its way to its relative major, E.

The recording is very reminiscent of the styles used on the *With the Beatles* LP, especially "'Till There Was You." George plays uncommonly creative parts on his nylon string guitar over John's tasteful acoustic guitar strumming. And there they are, back again, Paul's double-stop chords right from the start. Ringo's claves add a Latin touch to the proceedings.

Listening to the version on *The Beatles Anthology* shows that the song was much heavier in the earlier takes. Ringo is playing rock drums while George plays electric guitar. It took them three days of trying to get it right. The fact that it was one of the few times that a Paul song was used to start recording an album (it was almost always a John song) and that they took three days on it shows his emerging leadership within the group's structure.

"Tell Me Why"

It becomes difficult, when discussing the album *A Hard Day's Night* to refrain from becoming redundant. Just about every song is either exciting and fresh or beautiful and melodic. It's not difficult to guess which category "Tell Me Why" falls under. As with "Can't Buy Me Love," the song doesn't find its key until vocals start. This adds tension to the introduction. Once the drum laden intro is finished, Paul gets to let loose and he walks the song from chord to chord. The entire song is exciting, but to me it is the bass part that makes it happen.

> **"**Who else would have come up with that bass line? Nobody! Not that it's so complicated or hard to play, but it is a near perfect expression of how the bass can fit and give the song 'ass' as Paul has said. It makes me think of good carpentry, when the pieces just fit square, smooth and strong. Ringo locks in so well and punctuates perfectly. If you can't respect mac's bass parts, you should go play sax or something. This band changed my life, and I am glad of it.**"**
>
> ~ Dave Ryan
>
> *(email, 2008)*

A Hard Day's Night (track listing)

Side One

1. "A Hard Day's Night"
2. "I Should Have Known Better"
3. "If I Fell"
4. "I'm Happy Just to Dance with You"
5. "And I Love Her"
6. "Tell Me Why"
7. "Can't Buy Me Love"

Side Two

1. "Any Time at All"
2. "I'll Cry Instead"
3. "Things We Said Today"
4. "When I Get Home"
5. "You Can't Do That"
6. "I'll Be Back"

Moment for the Ages

For the week of April 4, Billboard's top 100 reported that the Beatles had the top five songs on the US charts. They were "Can't Buy Me Love," "Twist and Shout," "She Loves You," "I Want to Hold Your Hand," and "Please Please Me." It's interesting to note that "She Loves You" was released by Swan Records and "Please Please Me" was released by Vee-Jay. These were the companies that took over those songs after Capitol had considered them losers in 1963.

Long Tall Sally (EP)
(Released June 19, 1964)

EPs (Extended Play records) were popular in England in the 1960s. Considering Lennon and McCartney's desire to stay out of the blues related market, EMI's selection of songs for this EP is interesting. Three of them use a standard 12 bar blues chord progression and one of them, "I Call Your Name," has a very bluesy feel to it. Two of the songs were written by black rock and roller pianists in the 50s, one was written by a rockabilly star and one was written by a Beatle.

"Long Tall Sally"

Paul, of course, sang this high-energy rocker performed originally by Little Richard. This song, "Long Tall Sally," was the closing number in the Beatles set list for years and was the last song they ever performed in their last tour. There are countless live recordings of the Beatles doing the song and in every case, like Mr. Penniman himself, Paul McCartney gives his all to the song. Aside from Paul's "leave it all on the stage" delivery, another highlight is Ringo's machine gun drumming in the last bridge ("gonna have some fun tonight").

Little Richard played piano and wrote and sang some of the greatest songs ever in rock and roll, including "Good Golly Miss Molly," "Slippin' and a Slidin'" and "Tutti Frutti." His all-out, screaming style of singing was a huge influence on McCartney.

"Slow Down"

John sang (shouted) the 12 bar blues/rocker "Slow Down," written by 50s rocker Larry Williams. The Beatles' arrangement is similar to Williams' original version but with much more forced energy and some all time great screams. Lennon's treatment sounded angry, while Williams' was sung with more humor.

Like Little Richard, Williams played piano and wrote great rock and roll songs, including "Bony Moronie," "Short Fat Fannie," "High School Dance" and three songs that Lennon covered with the Beatles: "Slow Down," "Dizzy Miss Lizzy" and "Bad Boy."

In fact, Williams and Richard were close friends, carousers and lived the underworld life (trying to be subtle here). Listening to Williams' versions of his old songs, you can tell that—like Little Richard was to McCartney—he was a strong influence on John Lennon. And, like McCartney with "Long Tall Sally," John tried maybe too hard to capture the energy of the original.

In both cases, however, the energy of the Beatles' cover versions are undeniably energetic.

"Matchbox"

Carl Perkins' "Matchbox" was Ringo's vocal contribution to the early 1964 recordings and was also included on the Beatles' new EP. Ringo sings the song with great energy and amidst a lot of reverb. More notably is Harrison's masterful guitar impersonation of Carl Perkins.

A sad note about Perkins: he was on his way to a TV appearance in New York, the one that was hopefully going to catapult him to nationwide stardom, when he was involved in an accident that nearly killed him. He never got his big shot again, but if nothing else his fame for writing "Blue Suede Shoes" made him a legend. The song on this EP, "Matchbox" was a minor hit for him. His fame also derives from the Memphis guitar sound that he helped create, and Harrison does a pretty nice imitation of him on the Beatles' version of "Matchbox."

[Look for all three of the above artists on YouTube if you would like to get an idea of how the people the Beatles idolized sound.]

"I Call Your Name"

Lennon wrote the verses to "I Call Your Name" before there were Beatles, and added the bridge "Don't you know I can't take it" later. He gave the song to Billy J. Kramer and the Dakotas but quickly soured of Kramer's treatment of the song. Lennon decided the Beatles should do it the right way with some legitimate power in the vocals (which he did single-tracked).

Interesting note: the cowbell comes in one bar after the lead vocal starts. It's possible the player (probably John or Ringo) forgot when to start and they decided to leave it in.

"I Call Your Name" is yet another example of the Beatles shifting styles midstream and making it sound easy. The song seems to be in three parts: 1) the gentle 1st part of the song, 2) the ska-laden (guitar in the crack) guitar solo and 3) the upbeat part that takes the song from the solo to the ending.

"During the solo section, the back-beat is modified even while the tempo is kept constant. When the original beat returns after this break, it too sounds like a change yet again! This is possibly the first time we've seen this trick in a Beatles' song, though in the future it would become one of John's own trademarks."

~ Alan W. Pollack

(*Notes on . . . Series*, 1989-2000)

Long Tall Sally (track listing)	
Side One	Side Two
1. "Long Tall Sally"	1. "Slow Down"
2. "I Call Your Name"	2. "Matchbox"

Furthering the account on their activities that long ago summer: On June 1st and 2nd, the Beatles recorded the entire second side of *A Hard Day's Night*: "I'll Cry Instead," "Slow Down," "I'll Be Back," "Any Time at All," "Things We Said Today" and "When I Get Home." At the same time, they finished the forthcoming *Long Tall Sally* EP (described above). On June 3rd, Ringo being sick, they rehearsed replacement drummer Jimmy Nichol for their upcoming tour. June 4th were on stage in Denmark to begin a world tour (Denmark, The Netherlands, Hong Kong, Australia, New Zealand and back to Australia).

They were back home playing in London on July 7th, made television shows and toured England, jumped over to Sweden, back to England for more touring. On August 16th they played in Blackpool, the tourist resort on the west coast of England. On August 19th, they were on stage at the Cow Palace in San Francisco, kicking off a 25 show tour of America and Canada. They flew from city to city without regard for distance (Thanks Brian!).

Beatles for Sale (LP)

Released
December 4, 1964

Cover Notes
The world-weary looking Beatles were photographed for the cover by Robert Freeman in Hyde Park, London. Like With the Beatles, this cover was somber. But this time, a lot of the music inside the record sleeve actually reflected the feeling of the cover.

"It was easy. We did a session lasting a couple of hours and had some reasonable pictures to use. . . . The photographer would always be able to say to us, 'Just show up,' because we all wore the same kind of gear all the time. Black stuff; white shirts and big black scarves." ~Paul McCartney

Peak Position
Number 1

Number of Weeks on the Chart
46

Number of Days in the Studio
8

First Song Recorded for the Album
"I'm a Loser" on August 14, 1964

"I'm a Loser," Lennon heaving aside the adorable mop-top image.

Somehow it all changed. It was time to leave the head-shaking wooohs of early Beatlemania behind. Supposition tells us that the Beatles got tired of being the lovable moptops during this year. There was no way they could keep up the grind they were on and remain fresh and exciting.

It's quite possible that the entrance of Bob Dylan and pot-smoking into their world saved them. Without a step down from the tension, who knows how long they would have lasted as a group. Lennon was particularly influenced by the bard of folk. He discovered that not only can you write compelling and meaningful lyrics, but you can still have a sellable commodity, as well. And, oh, did his lyrics change for their next album.

As for pot, it's easy to guess that being high allowed them to laugh at the surreal atmosphere they were living in. Another aspect to consider is that John and Paul had, despite surviving a grueling schedule, written every song on their last album. There must have been no way they could do all that again.

> "No band today would come off a long US tour at the end of September, go into the studio and start a new album, still writing songs, and then go on a UK tour, finish the album in five weeks, still touring, and have the album out in time for Christmas. But that's what The Beatles did at the end of 1964. A lot of it was down to naivety, thinking that this was the way things were done. If the record company needs another album, you go and make one."
>
> ~ Norman Smith
>
> (*John Lennon Called Me Normal, 2008*)

These were now the slowed down, mellower, introspective Beatles. Have a look at the album cover. Was it just that day, or were they looking like old men now?

As for their songs, they might write about being losers, spoiling parties and their baby being dressed in mourning colors. A far cry from being happy just to dance with you or their desire to let you know that the girl loves you.

Released on December 4th, *Beatles for Sale* (in my opinion) vies with *Yellow Submarine* as the two least interesting Beatles albums. But being the least engaging of their albums doesn't mean they didn't have some fab stuff on them.

"No Reply"

This song opens the album and, in that role, makes the immediate statement that this is not going to be the same old Beatles. There is not a lot of un-tendered enthusiasm in the song. It's very acoustic guitar oriented. John Lennon's lyrics had always been capable of being somewhat downcast ("I Call Your Name," "You Can't Do That," etc.) but the music would mask the sentiment. No more!

However, "No Reply" has some impressive studio work, filled with little things that maybe don't strike the ear on first listen. The piano, which had always previously been prevalent, was now down in the mix. Ringo's snare pattern (playing on 1, 2+ 4, 2, 3+) is reminiscent of the latin beats of the day. The song also features what had become, and would always remain, a Lennon staple: a build-up and satisfactory climax. The verses (double-tracked Lennon) are sung somewhat softly. The choruses, with Paul's patented added rock harmony sound, elevate the song. The bridge ("If I were you I'd realize . . .") brings the satisfying climax. John and Paul had long ago perfected using their voices together to elevate a song. Now they were doing it on a different, more subtle platform. Hearing them sing the words "no reply!" together brings to mind their mix of voices on "Don't Let Me Down" (*Let It Be*).

Paul's bass is lost in the mix. It sounds a bit like a string bass, thumping along with Ringo's bass drum. But then, no electrifying and dynamic bass part was called for in this performance.

"I'm a Loser"

If the message wasn't made clear as you played the first song on the new Beatles' album, it must have sunk in when the second one started. These weren't happy songs.

But still, the Beatles' professionalism in the studio shone forth.

Probably arranged by George Martin (who never quite took credit for being such an integral part of the Beatles vocal layering), the intro has John singing his plaintive cry, sung in a straightforward style. It's the harmony part that adds a melodic touch to the intro. Paul is, as usual, singing up high, but you can't hear his voice until the "zuh" of loser. John sings a lower harmony that adds a touch of bounce to the proceedings.

The verses have two acoustic guitars accompanied by a decidedly country-western sounding, note-bending, Fender Stratocaster playing George Harrison.

As usual with John's best songs, Paul McCartney is there to provide liveliness. Here on the chorus, his bass—now fully audible—takes off on a walking gallop (if one can gallop while walking). He also provides a strong harmony part. Ringo picks up the pace as well, his hi-hat coming to the fore. And what's this? John's trusty harmonica is back with us for a nice ride on the first solo. Listening to the guitar solo on headphones reveals something not readily apparent before. There is another electric guitar there, along with the acoustics, being played very subtly and low in the mix. In the stereo version, it makes the lead guitar sound as if it were echoing across the channels.

The Beatles seemed to be playing a bit more dismally than we might have hoped for, but the songs were not without lots of delightful little subtleties.

"Rock and Roll Music"

I mention this song because it makes it's own statement: "We'll still play rock and roll, but when we do, it's gonna be with acoustic guitars." John's voice is strong, second only to a song that was—for some never explained reason—left off of the album. And that song was:

"Leave My Kitten Alone"

This song remained locked in the vaults and unheard of by most of us until the *Anthology* CD came out. Listening to it, I think "Why did we have to wait all of these years to hear this?" Quickly followed by, "How cool is this? A new Beatles song!! And not only a new Beatles song, but a new Beatles song that smokes!!!"

> "That was a Johnny Preston song that we'd rehearsed in
> Liverpool along with all our Cavern stuff and it was just in our

repertoire. It wasn't a big one that we used to do, we'd pull it out of the hat occasionally, and we also recorded it."
~ Paul McCartney

(The Beatles Recording Sessions, 1990)

In a twist of irony, "Leave My Kitten Alone" was recorded on the same day as "Mr. Moonlight." Why would "Kitten" be left off the album while "Mr. Moonlight" was left on?

"There's the basic guys-fighting-guys premise here that would seem to be conspicuously outside the Beatles perimeter. While we're all quite familiar with John's dealing with the irritation of an interloping other guy by taking it out on the girl, shades of 'You Can't Do That,' I dare you to find another example in which he addresses the interloper directly, with threats, no less!"
~ Alan W. Pollack

(Notes on . . . Series, 1989-2000)

Similarly, the version they copied—replete with "meow" being sung at the end of each line—was, safe to say, pummeled by the way John sang "Kitten."

"The Beatles recorded many covers but often never released them, after all they had a pretty good catalogue of their own stuff! Here is a cover that I'm really mad for . . ."
~ A Big Ball of Stuff

(email, 2013)

"One of The Beatles' finest "lost" songs . . . had the song been re-leased on Beatles for Sale, it would surely have been one of the highlights. Why it was rejected is unclear, although it has been sug-gested that it was dropped in favour of 'Everybody's Trying to Be My Baby,' in order to give George Harrison a lead vocal."

(beatlesbible.com, 2009)

"Kansas City/Hey-Hey-Hey-Hey!"

"Despite having mostly dropped it by 1963, The Beatles revived the medley when their first American tour arrived in Kansas City on 17 September 1964. It was rapturously received by the crowd, leading the group to consider recording it in the studio."

(beatlesbible.com, 2009)

This they did a month later, when a shortage of original material for their fourth album led to The Beatles reviving a number of old songs.

"Kansas City/Hey-Hey-Hey-Hey!" became one of The Beatles' most successful cover versions. Perfected in just one take, it was one of the first songs to be recorded during a mammoth session on 18 October 1964.

It's the recording in one take that is so impressive. It's reminiscent of Lennon's one take on "Twist and Shout" from the previous year. According to McCartney, Lennon prompted him to sing his heart out. He sure did.

"Eight Days a Week"

Fortunately, "Eight Days a Week" was given the big-sounding Beatles' treatment.

"Big, huge, fat Höfner bass part underneath. To me, this defines a rolling, moving feel. Swing style line under powerful guitar parts, with each guitar doing its own thing to create drive, musical flavor, and interest. Where the hell did these guys come from? It's neat to hear how this song evolved from the early takes into such a dynamic piece. Like a sculptor, they knew just what to add, what to take away.

But oh, how the bass part is wicked cool. Paul is by far the best player of the four, and this proves it.

This band was indeed greater than the sum of the parts, like having that "ringing chord" in a barbershop quartet when everyone nails their note, and the blend creates something extra in the sound. The Fabs produced that essence in so many of their songs. In these songs, the bass takes the song to another level, made a good song great."

~ Dave Ryan

(email, 2011)

"Eight Days a Week" was apparently one of George Harrison's favorite Beatles' songs. During the *Let It Be* process, when John and Paul were searching for one of their *oldies* to record, George recommended this one.

Beatles for Sale (track listing)	
Side One	**Side Two**
1. "No Reply"	1. "Eight Days a Week"
2. "I'm a Loser"	2. "Words of Love"
3. "Baby's in Black"	3. "Honey Don't"
4. "Rock and Roll Music"	4. "Every Little Thing"
5. "I'll Follow the Sun"	5. "I Don't Want to Spoil the Party"
6. "Mr. Moonlight"	6. "What You're Doing"
7. "Kansas City/Hey-Hey-Hey-Hey"	7. "Everybody's Trying to Be My Baby"

When the *Beatles for Sale* album was finished at last, Lennon told an interviewer that they had had real difficulty making the album, but they were satisfied with what they achieved with it.

Final Notes on 1964

And so we say goodbye to the year where we, the citizens of the world, were ensnared in the Beatles' trap. They gave up their nervous systems, and we gave up our hearts, souls and money. Sounds like a fair swap. Can there ever again be a year like this? It's possible, but let's just hold out hope that if someone can sweep the entire world under their feet again, that they are as reasonable and positive as the Beatles were. And let's hope that—like the Beatles—they come marching with guitars and not guns.

As for those Beatles, there would never again be another year where they were everywhere at once. They would have endless tours of the civilized world—and America—and they would have some rough times. But they must have closed the year out with a meeting with Brian Epstein in which they laid down the law.

Stalled Careers

Some years ago, while looking through Joel Whitburn's book *The Billboard Book of Top 40 Hits*, I noticed how many long time hit-makers whose careers took a nose-dive just after the Beatles first hit the American charts in January of 1964. Wouldn't it be interesting, then, to dust that book off and make a list of those whose careers plummeted after January of 1964? These turn out to be some of the biggest names in the business, from Nat King Cole to Elvis Presley . . . all relegated to secondary status. It's hard to imagine what it must have been like to be working hard on a career and suddenly find that you were no longer wanted.

To make it on the following list, the artist had to have at least 10 top 40 hits leading up to January of 1964 and then have a noticeable drop-off afterward.

Paul Anka
> 23 Hits from 1957 *to* 1963
> Last hit: "Remember Diana" (May 1963)

Tony Bennett
> 11 hits from 1956 *to* 1963
> Last hit: "The Good Life" (June 1963)

Brook Benton
> 20 hits from 1959 *to* 1963
> Last hit: "Two Tickets To Paradise" (October 1963)

Ray Charles[*]
> 19 hits from 1957 *to* 1963
>
> Last hit: "That Lucky Old Sun" (October 1963)

Chubby Checker[*]
> 18 hits from 1959 *to* 1964
>
> Last hit: "Hooka Tooka" (January 1964)

Nat King Cole
> 24 hits from 1955 *to* 1963
>
> Last hit: "That Sunday, That Summer" (September 1963)

Perry Como
> 23 hits from 1955 *to* 1963
>
> Last hit: "I Love You Don't Forget It" (July 1963)

Bobby Darin
> 19 hits from 1958 *to* 1963
>
> Last hit: "18 Yellow Roses" (May 1963)

Dion (Di Muci)
> 13 hits from 1960 *to* 1963
>
> Last hit: "Drop Drop" (November 1963)

Fats Domino[**]
> 13 hits from 1955 *to* 1963
>
> Last hit: "Red Sails In the Sunset" (October 1963)

Connie Francis[*]
> 33 hits from 1958 *to* 1963
>
> Last hit: "Your Other Love" (November 1963)

Johnny Mathis
> 18 hits from 1957 *to* 1963
>
> Last hit: "Every Step of the Way" (June 1963)

Ricky Nelson[*]
> 31 hits from 1957 *to* 1963
>
> Last hit: "For You" (January 1963)

Lloyd Price
> 10 hits from 1957 *to* 1963
>
> Last hit: "Misty" (October 1963)

Bobby Rydell
> 18 hits from 1959 *to* 1963
>
> Last hit: "Forget Him" (December 1963)

Neil Sadaka
> 13 hits from 1958 *to* 1963
>
> Last hit: "Bad Girl" (December 1963)

The Shirelles***
> 12 hits from 1960 *to* 1963
>
> Last hit: "Don't Say Goodnight" (July 1963)

Bobby Vee
> 11 hits from 1960 *to* 1963
>
> Last hit: "Be True To Yourself" (July 1963)

Jackie Wilson
> 20 hits from 1958 *to* 1963
>
> Last hit: "Shake! Shake! Shake!" (August 1963)

Source: *The Billboard Book of Top 40 Hits* by Joel Whitburn, 1987

* Ray Charles, Chubby Checker, Connie Francis and Ricky Nelson each had one or two minor hits in 1964.

** Fats Domino is still alive and kicking although he doesn't tour outside of New Orleans any more. Domino must be considered *the* victim of Beatlemania in America. With 36 top 40 entries before 1964, he was credited with more charted rock hits than any other classic rock artist except for Elvis Presley. And then that was it. He continued to record steadily up until the 1970s, always hoping for the elusive return to popularity. Although he was immensely popular leading up until the time of the Beatles, his last top 40 hit—ever—was in October of 1963. Hello Beatles, goodbye Fats.

*** The Shirelles, whose almost naive-sounding vocals were a big part of their success, are the only "group" on the above list. They were partially a victim of the British wave, but a bigger part of their downturn in 1963 may have been due to their discovery that their record label, Scepter, did not have the money they had been "holding for them." They are but one of many groups—white and black—who got a serious shaft from their record companies. The irony of this is that the Beatles were fans of the Shirelles; in fact they were fans of many of the entertainers whose careers they stalled.

Interesting Thoughts About the List

You'll notice that, with the exception of The Shirelles and Dion, all of the above artists were individual artists (not in a band) and had careers that started in the 1950s. Many of them were MOR (middle-of-the-road) style singers. If you were one of those singers, by February of 1964, your career was *stalls-ville*, and your agent wasn't returning calls. Very sad times for those who were *so* successful up until then.

Considering the above list, it is inexplicable that Brenda Lee, Roy Orbison, Bobby Vinton and Andy Williams enjoyed continued success right through that graveyard year of 1964.

Elvis Presley was too powerful to keep off of the top 40 charts, but the slide still happened for him. His list of top 10 hits leading up through 1963 is endless and stops suddenly after "Bossa Nova Baby" reached number 8 in November of 1963. He did not have a top 10 hit again until 1965 ("Crying in the Chapel") and then had to wait some years to do it again.

Frank Sinatra did not make the list because his last pre-Beatles hit was in 1962, too long before the Beatle wave to say that the Beatles slowed his career down. He enjoyed a top 30 hit with "Softly As I Leave You" in October of 1964 and then laid low until he hit number one with "Strangers In The Night" in 1966.

It's also interesting to note that many of the above artists, like Sinatra, enjoyed renewed success in late 1965 and in 1966. The American listening public began to want to be crooned to again.

SIX

The Emerging Maestro
(1965)

1965 in Review

None of us knew it at the time, but it was becoming taxing to be a Beatle. To us, they were a happy-go-lucky band of four guys who romped around the world telling jokes with Liverpool accents. The Beatles seemed to be everywhere. Somehow, the very name, THE BEATLES, had become something more than a group of letters. There was—and still is—power in that name. Underneath that particular combination of letters, there were images of world tours, screaming girls at concerts (including their most famous concert ever at Shea Stadium), long hair, exciting music being played on cheap record players, press conferences with funny repartee, beautiful faces, Höfner basses, Rickenbacker guitars, Ludwig drums with that logo across the front, the boys escaping and romping on a field to the tune of "Can't Buy Me Love," parents shaking their heads, and what about the exciting moment when you're hearing a new Beatles' song for the first time on the radio?

Maybe you can go back through your memory and pull out these moments, add more of your own, and put them back together under the umbrella of the name "THE BEATLES."

In 1965, there were more of those memories to add. They made another movie, they toured the world again, and their songs were all over the radio again.

In 1965, they—along with their musical counterparts in England and America—redefined pop music. Again. It was a new style, conceived by two parents who tried in vain to keep each other at arm's length: rock and roll and folk music. The British Invasion groups and Bob Dylan ruled the day.

In writing about every year they were together during their touring days, you can make the claim that it is remarkable that the Beatles were able to do what they did. See, all we have today are the albums. There was so much more to their story that is long ago forgotten, but it's the albums that we listen to now. And somehow even the albums from this year of boredom and weariness that was the Beatles' remain incredibly likable.

As we'll see, *Rubber Soul*, considered by many as their best album, was hastily thrown together amidst touring. Regarding those hectic touring days, the Beatles have all referred to their lives as being in the "eye of the hurricane." Everything around them was mayhem and craziness, while they sat giggling at the world from their glass terrarium.

The thing that was probably much more evident in England than in America, Australia and other outlying countries was that in 1965, the Beatles really slowed down their appearances on radio and television shows. They were in the unique position of knowing that they didn't need to go sell their new stuff. If it had the words "THE BEATLES" on it, it sold, and that was more than enough. Wait, I should modify that last claim. *Rubber Soul* didn't even have thier name on it.

Just a small note of interest: The last song the Beatles recorded in 1964 was "Honey Don't." The first song recorded in 1965 was "Ticket to Ride" for the upcoming film.

Paul McCartney's Bass Playing in 1965 . . . "The Main Musical Force"

There was a point of time, about mid-year, when McCartney began to stake his claim as a master bass player. His playing on the *Help!* LP, while good and tasteful, was somewhat ordinary. But then came the

Rubber Soul sessions. It's clear that he had been listening to bass players and thinking about what he could do in the studio. He had learned subtle tricks that he now employed that showed the power of the instrument in a band setting. In this day and age of incredible bass players, it's a bit difficult to picture the pop world as it was back in 1965. The bass guitar was simply not an instrument that commanded attention (although Motown/Jamerson/Kaye fans knew this already). The fact that the most popular musical group in the world had a front-man who played the bass guitar brought a lot of popularity to the instrument. It was around this time that "being the bass player" no longer meant that you were the weakest guitar player. Guys like Paul McCartney, John Entwistle and Jack Bruce were changing that image in a big way.

Listening to "Drive My Car" and "Michelle" from the *Rubber Soul* LP will give you a good idea of what McCartney had become capable of. Those songs are both also signs of what was to come in 1966 when he truly became a master of the bass guitar.

Paul McCartney was, in 1965, the emerging maestro in other ways. He was learning the ropes of the studio and how to employ them.

> "There is no doubt at all that Paul was the main musical force. He was also that in terms of production as well. A lot of the time George Martin didn't really have to do the things he did because Paul McCartney was around and could have done them equally well. The only thing he couldn't do was to put symbols to chords: he couldn't write music. But he could most certainly tell an arranger how to do it, just by singing a part—however, he didn't know, of course, whether the strings or brass could play what he wanted. But most of the ideas came from Paul."
>
> ~ Norman Smith
>
> (*The Complete Beatles Recording Sessions*, 2005)

I don't know if you've read this quote before, but it is a telling one about how the power behind the scenes had not-so-subtly shifted from group leader Lennon to McCartney at least in the studio.

McCartney seems to have, for some time, been the type of person who was happy to allow another person to take the limelight, but to be the leader, in fact.

Recording Techniques in 1965

According to Mark Lewisohn, the Beatles/George Martin adopted a new recording style in 1965. Instead of endless amounts of takes as before, they would now have a commercially viable song ready in just one or two takes. What they did was to record the rhythm section first (bass and drums) and then start overdubbing on to that. A song like "We Can Work It Out," which is a pretty complex song, was done to perfection in just two takes. But it took four hours and a lot of work to finish the song.

Help! (LP)

Released
August 13, 1965

Cover Notes
Another cover shot by Robert Freeman. The letters, in semaphore, spell "NUJV."

"I had the idea of semaphore spelling out the letters HELP. But when we came to do the shot the arrangement of the arms with those letters didn't look good. So we decided to improvise and ended up with the best graphic positioning of the arms." ~ Robert Freeman

Peak Position
Number 1

Number of Weeks on the Chart
44

Number of Days in the Studio
12

First Song Recorded for the Album
"Ticket to Ride" on February 15, 1965

Yet another Lennon classic started off the proceedings. Note that on the same day the Beatles began working on songs by Paul ("Another Girl") and George ("I Need You").

Based on the plan to make one movie a year, it was time for a new movie, so it was also time to start recording the soundtrack for that movie.

It all began on February 15th, a Monday as the group recorded "Ticket to Ride." Note that the Beatles were still honoring the age-old system of recording during reasonable hours. They started the sessions early and almost never went past 10:30 p.m. All that was to change later.

A close listening to the *Help!* LP shows Paul stringing along mostly in a 1-5 (root fifth) fashion. His playing is always appropriate and in almost no case experimental. Here in early 1965, it seems to have simply been a case of McCartney not thinking yet about taking a lead position with his bass. Along with that, there just weren't many experimental bass players on the pop scene. To expand a song by expanding the bass part wasn't considered by a lot of people in the industry at the time. *Help!* is a very good album of 1965 British rock.

> "Listening to *Help!* was like having these wise elders—who weren't that much older than me—giving you all of this information about what love is. It was like having four great teachers show you how to write songs."
> ~ Stevie Nicks
> (*Tell Me Why*, 2002)

"Ticket to Ride"

John Lennon, in his 1980 Playboy interview, noted that Paul's only contribution to "Ticket to Ride" was "the way Ringo played the drums." Ahh! We have some nice controversy here.

> "John just didn't take the time to explain that we sat down together and worked on that song for a full three-hour songwriting session, and at the end of it all we had all the words, we had the harmonies, and we had all the little bits.
>
> We wrote the melody together; you can hear on the record, John's taking the melody and I'm singing harmony with it."
> ~ Paul McCartney
> (*Paul McCartney: Many Years From Now*, 1998)

As noted above, "Ticket to Ride" was the first song recorded for the LP. Considering that they finished recording the *Beatles for Sale* LP only four months before and immediately gone on a tour of England,

"Ticket to Ride" sounds amazingly fresh. In that short space of time, they had redefined themselves again. "Ticket to Ride" or, for that matter, all of the songs on the new LP sound nothing like the band that they were four months prior. They always had their ears open for new sounds and styles and somehow managed to stay a step ahead of everybody else.

The drums are what drive the song and give it the groove that makes the song more than just another pop song. It's also interesting to note that Ringo's drum pattern changes from the first verse to the last. One possibility is that Ringo altered the pattern subconsciously and simply followed the up-beat feel of the song at that moment.

John Lennon loved to write songs that started off simple enough, built towards a climax and then . . . climaxed! This last verse is the climax of the song. It's quite possible, then, that the change in the drum pattern is another case of the Beatles coming up with a way to make a song exciting to listen to.

Little things. Michael Palin (Monty Python) once commented that it was difficult to tell what made their sketches work sometimes. "It might be that a car was coming and so we wanted to get the shot done quickly, and that made it work." It's little things that shove a song over the edge and in the case of "Ticket to Ride," I've always felt that Lennon's voice sounded tired and soulful, restrained and cool. It being the first song for the new album, maybe he looked at the road ahead (make an album, film a movie) and was feeling a little down. Or, maybe he was stoned.

> "Two things instantly stamp the song as original: the glistening opening guitar riff that establishes the beat, and the jagged, whack-and-jump drum pattern that rams the beat forward. The song is a Lennon composition, but what it illustrates above all is the fertility of the collaboration. For it is McCartney who contributed both of these rhythmic ideas. Without them, John's song would be a shadow of itself."
> ~ Mark Herzegaard
>
> (*email*, 2012)

Mark makes a great point. Paul McCartney knew how to make a good song great. The collaboration, it goes without saying, was priceless. I never knew that Paul wrote the opening guitar riff.

"The song features a coda with a different tempo that extends the song's length past three minutes, the first Beatles song to do so."
~ Joel Benjamin
(*email*, 2012)

"Another Girl"

The movie, *Help!*, could be considered the direct ancestor of the videos that used to be seen on MTV. The background scenes of the songs generally have nothing to do with the songs themselves. For the poetic "I Need You" and the yearning "The Night Before," what more perfect location than out on the furthest reaches of Salisbury Plain surrounded by snipers and tanks? For "Another Girl," the setting was the beach with Paul playing his "other girl" like a left handed bass guitar. Not sure who the actress was, but we can rest assured that if that one was busy, a couple million others would have forced themselves to go through with the job.

As for the actual song, the Beatles employed some of their favorite 1965-66 studio tricks. John Lennon plays the upbeat (off the downbeat) rhythm guitar that he employed on "She's a Woman" and "Taxman." It clearly was the Lennon approach to livening up a song; he seemingly, purposefully, *crunched* it in different ways throughout the song—not playing it picture perfect which would have become monotonous. There is an acoustic guitar that is way back in the mix (a nice break from the way-to-the-front guitar on *A Hard Day's Night*) and guitar fills that sound suspiciously like Paul McCartney's sound and style. In fact, I'd bet on that one.

For the bass playing listener, the mix is well done! The guitars are mixed out of the way of the underlying bass guitar, much like they were through the recordings in the latter part of 1963. The Höfner bass, especially now that the songs have been remastered, sounds woody and pleasant. For the first time in a while, Paul's bass is actually heard! While the playing is in McCartney's rather typical early Beatles' style, you gain a new appreciation for it here. It moves the song, as Paul is wont to do, rather nicely!

"Another Girl" is yet another example of a Beatle song that sounds simplistic until you learn to play it. The chord progression beneath the verses was not typical for the day, going from the root (A minor) to the flat vii (G) back to Am and up to D.

"Another Girl" (the bridge)

If you, like me, had always suspected that something unique was going on in the bridge, you'll not be disappointed. For this ("Another girl who will love me to the end") the song changes key without fanfare to the relative major key of C. It gets tricky here, but stick with me.

I'm convinced that Paul created the chords for the bridge by just playing and seeing how things worked out. Under the words "she will always be my friend," we go from E to A major, which would be a Beatle-esque way of switching the key to D major (E and A being the ii and v of the key of D). Instead, the song repeats the E to A, but this time lands on the initial root, A minor, and returns directly to the verse without pause.

It would have been easy to hold the second trip to A (major or minor) for a bar and then begin the verse, but McCartney had apparently become "versed" (don't pardon the pun) in swift behind-the-scenes changes in his songs.

"If You've Got Troubles"

This is another song that tends to be written off as an undesirable piece of work, mostly because it was never released. Reviewers have panned it. Had it been released instead of its replacement, "Act Naturally," a different view of the song may well be held today.

But I disagree. It contains an excellent rock bass/guitar line, an early example of what was to come to the rock world a few years later. In

1965, the prevailing style in England was to come up with a catchy guitar hook (i.e., Satisfaction). While "If You've Got Troubles" has that line, it still appears to be ahead of the times, and the reason is that they are doubling the bass line beneath it, sort of like "Drive My Car," which was to come some months later. The guitar line with bass doubling from an octave below is a potent weapon and "If You've Got Troubles" benefits nicely from it. The main problem with the song is that the Beatles just never finished it. I think this could have been a Beatles classic.

"Tell Me What You See"

There's irony in "Tell Me What You See." If you were to go up to 20 people, sing the opening line to the first verse of this song and ask them to quickly name it, 19 of them would scrunch up their face and search their minds. 5 might call you back in the middle of the night with the answer. Ask the same 20 people what album it was on and even that one person who could name the song will be stumped. I had forgotten myself until doing a rewrite on this chapter. Though "Tell Me What You See" is a nice song, it's pretty forgettable. And that, in itself, is unforgettable. There's the irony.

"Yesterday"
"I've Just Seen a Face"
"I'm Down"

Monday, June 14th, 1965 was a major day in the history and life of Paul McCartney. For it is on that day that the Beatles recorded three McCartney songs of completely different styles: the folky "I've Just Seen a Face," the sand-blasting "I'm Down," and the song he will always be best known for, his beautiful ballad "Yesterday."

"I've Just Seen a Face" is like no other Beatles' track. While the instrumentation, especially the escalating acoustic guitar intro, is interesting, it is the vocals and lyrics that drive the song. Paul said that he liked the lyrics and felt that each line sung seems to call for the next line, and they do, sung in a breathless fashion. "Yesterday" is, by far, the song that has been recorded the most times in the history of music, with over 2,000 cover versions. It is also the first time a string quartet appeared on a pop record. All this and it was never even released as a single in England!

Paul was understandably nervous about this being a solo track (never having been done by a Beatle to that point), and George Martin knew the song needed something more than just the acoustic guitar.

> "I suggested a classical string quartet. That appealed to him but he insisted 'No vibrato, I don't want any vibrato' . . . There is one particular bit which is very much his—and I wish I had thought of it!—where the cello groans onto the seventh the second time around."
>
> ~ George Martin
>
> (*All You Need Is Ears*, 1994)

The rest of the string arrangement came from the pen of Sir George Martin.

The recording of "Yesterday" finished off the day. It had started off at 2:30 with the recording of the folk-rock "I've Just Seen a Face," Paul's toe-tapping, sing-alonger. From there, the Beatles went into Paul's latest throat-shredder, "I'm Down." He clearly wanted to write a song that could replace "Long Tall Sally" in the Beatles' act, and he found it with this. The instrumentation, according to *The Beatles Recording Sessions* included drums, bass, organ (John), lead guitar, bongos, rhythm guitar and backing vocals. It's a blast! A roaring barn burner, a riotous powerhouse of a song and one of the hardest rockers they ever made. More? Well, the Beatles' approach to the song is very unlike the usual McCartney song, where the playing tended to be more controlled. In this case, they're allowed to run hog-wild and free-spirited. And, if you ever get a chance to see their performance of the song at Shea Stadium on August 15, 1965, they somehow amp things up even further. During the performance, John went hog-wild on the organ, playing with his elbows. Paul, George and John all look like they're having the most fun they ever had playing live.

The next time you hear "Yesterday" (while swaying to McCartney's sentimental and melodic vocalization) it might be a bit mind-bending to bear in mind that he had recorded "I'm Down" only an hour or two before.

"Well done. Beautiful."

~ John Lennon

(The Playboy Interviews With John Lennon and Yoko Ono, 1981)

This was a historic day for McCartney, and yet it is one that he has never mentioned.

Help! (track listing)	
Side One	**Side Two**
1. "Help!"	1. "Act Naturally"
2. "The Night Before"	2. "It's Only Love"
3. "You've Got to Hide Your Love Away"	3. "You Like Me Too Much"
4. "I Need You"	4. "Tell Me What You See"
5. "Another Girl"	5. "I've Just Seen a Face"
6. "You're Going to Lose That Girl"	6. "Yesterday"
7. "Ticket to Ride"	7. "Dizzy Miss Lizzy"

"Help!" (Single)
"I'm Down" (B-side)
(Released July 23, 1965)

A casual, uninvolved listening to the song gives you the impression that it's a fairly basic folk song with a bunch of stuff added. It's impossible to say what makes the song work so well because there is no one thing that stands out (aside from the fact that it's a damn brilliant song). But would it work without all the Beatle-esque touches? There's the rub! If you can imagine John Lennon sitting and singing the song with just his Jumbo acoustic guitar, it passes the test.

Some random thoughts about the song "Help!"

❖ I suspect that the song has the most chords in it of any song recorded by the Beatles (in alphabetical order A, Bm, C#m, D, E, F#m, G. Some version of every letter in the musical alphabet).

❖ The arrangement: the song starts with a bang. And there, again, is the Lennon propensity for a song that builds to a climax. In this case, the climax is "Won't you PLEASE PLEASE help me!" The rest of the song seems fairly basic by comparison. The buildup starts with "Help me if you can I'm feeling down." The rhythm changes completely. The snare drum leads us in with a roll. The acoustic and electric guitars start playing an offbeat pattern (sort of reggae-ish). Tension starts to fill the room. Harrison's electric guitar follows the melody. Paul starts adding harmonies to John's lead. It's all building up, and there it is: the climax!. Listen to the way the band sounds right on the word "me." Harrison's guitar, it's job finished for the moment, fades away. The jangling acoustic guitar comes back to the fore. It's a very nice moment.

❖ Who's idea was it to have the background vocals introduce John's lyrics? Brilliant. It sounds like another perfect McCartney touch to a great Lennon song.

❖ John Lennon told David Scheff that he was inspired to use words such as "independence" by a reporter who told him that the words to his songs were rarely multisyllabic.

❖ Lennon combined the use of "big words" with a soul searching narrative that was hidden behind the facade of the great pop sound of the song. "I was singing Help! for a kicker," he told one interviewer.

"When Help! came out, I was actually crying out for help . . .
And I am singing about when I was so much younger and all
the rest, looking back at how easy it was."

~ John Lennon

(The Playboy Interviews With John Lennon and Yoko Ono, 1981)

Let's see what Mr. Pollack thinks about "Help!"

"The public relations hype said that we were all affected especially hard by John's more confessional songs because
they revealed a surprising vulnerability we'd never have expected was lurking beneath his tough, cool, and zany public
persona. The fact that such songs can be found from one
end of the songbook (e.g. 'Misery' to the other (e.g. 'I Want
You') should have mitigated anything in the way of 'surprise' but that's PR for you.)

But don't be fooled into thinking that we're dealing
with a kind of perverse impulse to recklessly cast John
'against type,' running the risk, big time, of blowing such a
carefully cultivated image. Rather it's precisely because of
the cross casting here that the overall production works as
well as it does! Consider the alternatives. Tough guy singing
tough songs is okay but predictable. Nebbish singing
nebbishy songs is, yech, pathetic. Nebbish singing tough
songs is not fully believable. But take the one who always
jokes and laughs like a clown and have him admit to his
private indulgence in copious tears that fall like rain from
the sky—and now you've really got something. Maybe
those PR folks really knew what they were doing :-)"

~ Alan W. Pollack

(Notes on . . . Series, 1989-2000)

Rubber Soul (LP)

Released
December 3, 1965

Cover Notes

Firsts and lasts. *Rubber Soul* was the first pop album to omit the name of the artist. This was the last album cover shot by Robert Freeman, with the again unsmiling Beatles posed in John Lennon's back yard.

According to Freeman, he showed the Beatles some potential cover photos by projecting them onto an album-sized piece of cardboard. The cardboard fell backwards with this photo showing. The Beatles were excited: "Can you do it like that?" That's why the cover photo looks stretched.

Peak Position
Number 1

Number of Weeks on the Chart
59

Number of Days in the Studio
17

First Song Recorded for the Album
"Run for Your Life" on October 12, 1965

Another Lennon song, not one that he was proud of. But note that the second song worked on that day was "Norwegian Wood (This Bird Has Flown)."

What happened between the recordings for *Help!* and the ones for *Rubber Soul?* How did they, all four of them, advance so far so quickly? The Beatles began to take a serious interest in expanding the use of sounds for their recordings on *Rubber Soul*. It was the first time where they appeared to have sat down and decided they want people to "listen" to their music, not just groove to it. While "Yesterday" is along the same lines, it was the exception on the *Help!* LP. In fact, "Yesterday" would fit right into *Rubber Soul*. Engineer Norman Smith began to use a lot of compression on some of the instruments (a tact that Geoff Emerick would use more of on their next album). Further, regarding their sound, the instrumentalists stayed out of each-others' way. In other words, there is no crowding of sound (as was so true on *A Hard Day's Night*). As you listen, you can hear all of the instruments.

Rubber Soul is the last true Beatles album, where all of the songs appear to have gone through the Beatles' music-making machine. Through that machine, the Beatles could take songs that were written literally overnight (such as the last two songs recorded, "Girl" and "You Won't See Me") and make them into stunningly beautiful and moving Beatles' songs. It is the album with the most complex and best vocal arrangements from the early period (leading up through *Revolver*).

It's clear that the Beatles had kept an ear tuned to the music of the world. As they influenced everyone else, so did they have those that influenced them. This may have been part of the reason for this swift escalation of their songwriting and recording talents.

> "It's just amazing when you consider this was 1965 . . . you could call *Rubber Soul* ahead of its time, but it was really the beginning of that time. It was a watershed moment."
>
> ~ Colin Meloy
>
> (*Tell Me Why*, 2002)

Dramas

There were dramas surrounding the recording of *Rubber Soul*.

Innocent little ol' *Rubber Soul* is an important chapter for the novel in which the Beatles lived. It began with the near departure of George

Martin from the Beatles' fold and ended with the actual departure of long-time engineer Norman Smith.

Drama #1: The Departure of George Martin

By August of 1965, Martin was fed up with the financial pettiness of EMI. They were making millions upon millions of pounds from his work while he was making a couple grand a year. Furthermore, the company refused to increase the meager amount of money the Beatles themselves were making from their recorded successes. It was time to go and so George Martin left EMI (along with a few producers, engineers, secretaries, etc.) and formed his own company, Associated Independent Recording (AIR).

Martin, the Beatles and Norman Smith had been an incredible team of creators of music. Each was integral to the whole, and when you consider the amount of success this combination had produced, to have your lead man leave the company could be a heavy blow. It wasn't clear to Martin at the time if the Beatles (or EMI for that matter) would want him to come back or if they would be dealt a new producer.

Drama #2: Not Enough New Songs, Not Enough Energy

Here in the autumn of 1965, things looked bleak again for our travelling heroes. The Beatles had spent the summer recording and filming *Help!*, touring France, Italy, France again, Spain, back to England, and then a hard put tour of huge stadiums in America. With their tiny Vox amplifiers and horrible sound systems, with the heat of the summer and the rigmarole of flying from city to city, it was no fun. They came back from America on August 31st and demanded (and received) six weeks off. Six weeks of not being Beatles which, apparently, also meant six weeks of not writing songs.

That six weeks must have been difficult to enjoy because they knew they were up against it when they came together in mid-October. There was that confounded agreement that they would record 2 albums per year. That meant that, by the set deadline of November 11th, they had to have16 songs (14 for an album and 2 for a single) written and recorded. Aside from writing and recording, this allowed two weeks to mix, publish, press and release it all. From a song-writing point of view alone, the situation looked dire. For one thing, they had determined to record only original songs.[1] Their time-off was well deserved, but it meant that they didn't begin recording until October 12th. Only four weeks to go. John and Paul later admitted the task in front of them was "very impossible."[2] Would it be as it had been in 1964 when it came time to record their second album of the year, and they just did not have the songs? Or would they somehow do the impossible and—in the space of a month—create a whole new Beatles' sound while writing, arranging and recording a whole new batch of songs? For the correct answer, pick the one that seems impossible.

Time to Record

Thankfully for the ages, the first and largest of the dramas was resolved when, on October 12, 1965, George Martin (complicated contracts worked out with EMI) walked through the doors of EMI Studios at Abbey Road as an independent producer for the group's upcoming sessions. The second worry, lack of material, would just have to be addressed as they went along.

It was time to make a Beatles album, and fast. And as it was a Beatles album, it had to be the best. Here, late in 1965, pop music had been advancing month by month. The Rolling Stones had cemented their place as equal rivals to the Beatles, and other British acts such as the Animals, the Kinks, the Searchers and even Herman's Hermits were in hot pursuit. Further, American acts had been fighting back after their total capitulation during the 1964 British wave. The Motown groups were back. The crooners (such as Frank Sinatra and Tony Bennett) were on the charts and demanding air time. There was the emerging folk-rock revolution (headed by Bob Dylan and followed by acts such as Simon and Garfunkel) to consider. The Beatles were excited about the emergence of the Byrds and continued to be impressed by what Brian Wilson was doing with the Beach Boys.

Whatever they did now had to capture as well as advance upon all of that and upon what they accomplished with their *Help!* LP. They had to do it all in their own style and all very quickly. They had standards. Somehow they did all this and more when their next album came out.

Wow! Listen to *Rubber Soul* again. Take note of how carefully each song was recorded. The heavy-acoustic-guitar-strumming-lots-of-noise wall of sound is gone. Instead, you'll find lavish space, lighter musical tones, breathy and beautiful harmony vocals, creative acoustic guitars, sitars, percussion, intriguing chord patterns (listen to "Michelle"), all laid down with careful production. Paul McCartney would take on a dominating role with next year's *Revolver*, but *Rubber Soul* was John Lennon's album.

These recordings seem to herald the end of the period where the group seemed to work together as a team in the studio. Before, the Beatles appeared to be a machine, spanking out fantastic records. Now there were contrasting sounds and ideas from the players and so—depending on your point of view—this emerges as a real positive.

Paul McCartney's Bass Playing on Rubber Soul

Rubber Soul marked the beginning of how the bass would be played and recorded through to the end of the Beatles. Interestingly, it was John Lennon who drove the change. He had been hearing American records with James Jamerson (Detroit's Motown) and Duck Dunn (Memphis' Stax) playing well up in the mix and loved it and who can blame him? He demanded that the Beatles have the same bass-driven sound. So it was only here that the decision was made to separate the bass from the drums in the recording to allow it to be elevated in the mix. This cure provided yet another benefit: it freed McCartney up to play around with his parts, to experiment with what had already been recorded. This behind-the-scenes change of recording scenery changed the sound of the Beatles for good.

Through all of these years, I was never much of a fan of *Rubber Soul*. A lot of this was due to the rather weak version we were handed in America (no "Drive My Car" for example). So, while preparing for this chapter, I went back and gave *Rubber Soul* a closer listen. My intent was to discover on which songs Paul played his old Höfner bass vs. his brand new Rickenbacker. Instead, what I discovered was that it was on this album, and not *Revolver* where McCartney really laid his claim on being not only on top of the rock and roll bass playing game, but just an all around top-flight bass player.

McCartney, throughout this album, is right on the spot. If a song calls for a solid underlying groove bass ("Drive My Car," "You Won't See Me"), then you've got it. If it is something that is needed to enhance a very pretty acoustic guitar part ("Michelle" and many others), then you've got that too. I was slow to realize Paul's bass mastery on this album because those "in the know" at Capitol Records in America decided it should be largely a folky album. But on the original British version throughout, the rockers are there and he has a new feeling of command with his playing. There is no doubt that getting a good new instrument inspires a musician to play better. In this case, the Rickenbacker 4001s with its longer neck providing more string tension allowed him to get much better tone and sustain (how long a note can hold a tone) than he had with the Höfner.

Paul and Ringo had developed an instinctive rhythm section that was rambunctious ("Drive My Car," "The Word," etc.) and extremely effective when needed (most of the album). And Ringo! A chapter can be written on his contributions to *Rubber Soul* alone. Along with the interesting percussive things he does, he had now developed a style that was not pushing the beat, but lying just slightly behind where the instruments want to go. Equate it with Al Jackson Jr. from Booker T.

and the MGs. The music wants to drive a little faster, but Jackson and Starr are holding the reigns. It creates a great tension in the music so that on a song like "Drive My Car" when Ringo gives the slightly rushed triple snare beats during the song, it is as if there is a release; the song has made it at last.

Here's a look at some of the songs on their amazing *Rubber Soul* album.

"Drive My Car"

This song was recorded on the second day of the *Rubber Soul* sessions.

When recorded where both instruments are clearly heard, the sound of a good rock guitar line with the bass following it an octave beneath it is pretty exciting. The guitar/bass parts in "Drive My Car" are a perfect example of this, and the lines are thanks to George Harrison who persevered against the will of Paul McCartney who wanted a different guitar line to be played. Listen to the way the bass works with the song, the way it works with the drums and under the guitar, the way he sometimes plays a simple line (verses) and the way he gets heavy at times (under "and maybe I love you"). This is a bass player having fun, and he's wielding an instrument that has the *power* in the band.

> "If Paul had written a song, he'd learn all the parts and then come in the studio and say 'Do this.' He'd never give you the opportunity to come out with something. But on 'Drive My Car'; I just played the line, which is really like a lick off, 'Respect'—you know—the Otis Redding version. I played the line on the guitar and Paul laid that with me on the bass."
>
> ~ George Harrison
>
> (*beatlesinterviews.org*, 1977)

"Besides the unsurpassed quality of the basic melody and beat, they provided all the extra features you could ask for. Start with George's tasty little lead guitar lick suspended out in front of the song, besides the solo (Note, the solo is Paul McCartney playing slide guitar). The close harmony vocals are to die for, at the end of the verses ('but you can do something in be-tween') and the end of the chorus ('beep-beep-a-beep-beep, yeah') especially."

~ Al Barger

(*email*, 2012)

"The song has the smooth bravado of a Jack Nicholson per-formance, grinning on the surface with wheels spinning like mad underneath. . . . The song's beat has a new freedom to it."

~ Musicologist Tim Riley

(*Tell Me Why: a Beatles Commentary*, 1988)

"The song shows that the practical philosophical lessons about the self and freedom they provide are philosophically substan-tive in that they show us how to be autonomous and happy agents. After all, the end or goal we have may very well be one of those 'external things' that remains forever outside our pow-er: 'I've got no car and it's breaking my heart.' But if we arrange our desires in such a way as to be satisfied with what is in our power, then the starting point may just be all we need: 'But I've found a driver and that's a start.' And how do the Beatles end this song? They do so with one of the most joyous affirmations one could hope for."

~ James South

(*quote from John Benjamin*, 2012)

"I got no car and it's breaking my heart This is Lennon endorsing the ideas of Meinongianism by the philosopher Alexius Meinong."

~ Marcus Rossberg

(*quote from John Benjamin*, 2012)

I disagree with those who are looking for philosophy in the lyrics. One of the great things about the song is that the words just sound good over the music. A lot like "The One After 909" (to which you could ascribe various philosophies as well). If you listen to the song from the bottom up (listen to the music and hear the words riding over the top), I think that's how the song works best. Because the music is fantastic. The song leads off *Rubber Soul* and rocks so well that my expectations are (every time I listen to the album) that it's going to be a great rock album. And it isn't. I almost wish they hadn't led the album off with that song.

It's pretty clear that Paul used his new Rickenbacker bass on "Drive My Car."

> "This is one of the songs where John and I came nearest to having a dry session."
>
> ~ Paul McCartney
>
> (*beatlesinterviews.org*, 1984)

Wow. Maybe they should have had more dry sessions!

"Nowhere Man"

The bass part to "Nowhere Man" with its bouncy ride around the neck was clearly recorded on Paul's new Rickenbacker. It was McCartney's task on this track to provide a lift to the song, and by the quick stride of his part, he found the best way to do it.

The sound of the song provided a stirring departure from the usual way of recording the Beatles. Their engineers did not allow that much high-end treble to come through in the final mix. The stand-out instrument in "Nowhere Man" is, of course, George's Stratocaster guitar, recorded as trebly as a guitar has ever been done. For ears that are used to the smooth sounding instrumentation of their recordings, the guitar can be almost an annoyance to the ears, especially during the solo. George's solo, by the way, is played out of chord positions instead of a straight lead line (and check out the delicate harmonic for the last note).

The vocals, as frequently done on Beatles records, were done in three parts but with some variances from the norm that are worth listening for. Paul, of course, sings the high tenor part with his usual grace. George and John begin the melody on the same notes ("He's a"). As John reaches up for ("real nowhere man") George stays, basically, on the same note. The end of the line has George right above John in a tight harmony.

It should also be noted that all three singers enunciate the words precisely together. This includes George who was never known for his diction or enunciation while singing. There clearly was a leader of the vocal section; someone who got the three together and worked the parts out to a specific arrangement. It is a very safe bet that any time you hear an outstanding vocal arrangement, George Martin is the one that should come to mind. It's clearly the case here.

> "Superficially, the melodic material of the song is straight away in the Major mode. However, one's interest in the tune is piqued on a more subtle level by a combination of the large number of appoggiaturas, the pseudo pentatonic nature of the bridge, and the prominent role given to the flat sixth scale degree (C-natural) in the backing vocals. The flat sixth also bears some influence on the harmony, 'forcing,' as it were, the appearance of one of John's much favored minor iv chords in the context of a Major key."
>
> ~ Alan W. Pollack
>
> (*Notes on ... Series*, 1989-2000)

By way of explanation, the song is in the key of E major. The verse goes to an A and then an A minor. While on the A minor, Paul sings a high C note (the third note in the A minor scale). The C is the minor (or flat) iv of the E major scale, to wit:

Paul	C# C B
Chord	A Am E
Lyric	"Making all his nowhere plans for nobody"

Clear as mud?

"Michelle"

Discussing the bass part to "Michelle" could be like discussing a fine wine. Observe the way the bass counters the guitar parts, subtly keeping the music interesting, yet remaining tastefully in the background so as not to disturb the superb vocalization. Ahhhh, priceless. Paul McCartney was understandably proud of his creation and the bass part.

> "I never would have played 'Michelle' on bass until I had to record the bass line. Bass isn't an instrument you sit around and sing to. I don't anyway. But I remember that opening six-note phrase against the descending chords in 'Michelle'—that was like, oh, a great moment in my life. I think I had enough musical experience after years of playing, so it was just in me. I realized I could do that."
>
> ~ Paul McCartney
>
> (*Paul McCartney - Bass Master - Playing the Great Beatles Basslines, 2006*)

Intro

The bass brings tension to the descending guitar line (played by both John and George) by simply refusing to conform to the root notes. And this is true right from the first chord (an Fm over C). This young man had discovered the power of the bass guitar in a group setting. Judging by the sound of the bass on the introduction, it is played with fingers and judging by the almost string-bass sound of the F (first note of the second bar), closer to the neck than the bridge.

The guitar changes to the intro are on the quarter note.

Guitar:	Fm	Fm(maj7)	Fm7	Fm6	Bm2	Bm7	C
Bass	C		E	F	C F		C

When listening, you'll notice that the bass and guitar really don't coalesce until the final C of the intro.

Experienced studio musicians frequently talk about the confidence that bands build as they spend years in the studio recording. From a listener's viewpoint, this was an extraordinary moment in the life of Paul McCartney. He had created an orchestrated bass part, separate from the guitars, that subtly, powerfully lifted the song. It may well have been this song that lifted his vision of the bass guitar out of the general mix of instruments.

Rubber Soul marked the beginning of this for him and he would explore it to even further extremes in the next few years.

> "Although I didn't really dig into the Beatles' material until about 10 years after this song first came out, it was Michelle that revealed itself to be the turning point for McCartney to my ears. The bass part isn't difficult, but it provides a very nice counter melody to what is already a great vocal melody. A notable feature is his use of non-root notes in the opening melody; the door was opening."
>
> ~ John Martin
>
> *(email, 2010)*

It's been substantiated by those in the process that George Martin arranged the beautiful background vocal parts. They provide the perfect mood for the song.

Speaking of vocal parts, John Lennon provided McCartney with just what was needed to drive the song from being a nice ballad to a full-flowered song. Paul didn't have a middle-eight and approached John for assistance who reached into his bag of tricks and pulled out an idea from Nina Simone's bad-assed version of Screaming Jay Hawkins' "I Put a Spell on You." There she wails "I love you, I love you I love you, I love you anyhow." The suggestion was for Paul to follow that lead.

How it is that John possibly connected one of the most hard, bluesy recordings ever to Paul's "Michelle" can only be speculated on. Paul's chord progression for "Michelle" had been around for years, played jokingly at parties. Maybe John had heard it enough to know that it needed a bluesy edge to make it a classic. And a classic it became.

In 2010, Paul McCartney gamely included "Michelle" in his set when he performed at the White House. As he sang, Michelle Obama (looking positively enraptured) mouthed along with the words while the president swayed back and forth and made quiet explanations to his daughter. At the conclusion, McCartney joked that he might be the first person to be "punched out by the president."

"You Won't See Me"

It was down to the last day and the Beatles needed two new songs to round the album out. Both John and Paul came through. John came in on the last day with "Girl" while Paul brought "You Won't See Me." Especially considering they were recorded in one day, both songs were nicely done with lush vocal harmonies. Paul's arrangement called for a myriad of sounds and merry making. You'd think he spent weeks considering his bass part. It counters the vocals here and there (walking down while the vocals move up) and moves the song along perfectly. It is heavily played, leading us to consider it as another candidate for being done on his new Rickenbacker.

John Lennon has his atypical pre-reggae 2 4 crash chords ("She's a Woman" "Taxman") that work every time. The piano, sounding like Paul's style, moves the rhythm well. Ringo is the man who really makes this song work. A very well recorded crash cymbal (the best sound of it to date), a lot of triplets on high hats and toms.

It's a great song all around, as is "Girl." As mentioned, both songs are well recorded, lush with vocals and all done in one day.

To recap *Rubber Soul*, it's amazing that the album is as enjoyable as it is. The writing and recording of it was sandwiched between major tours. It was done in a very short amount of time, and two of the best songs were crunched in on the last day of recording. And the record was influential. For example:

Brian Wilson said, "I give a lot of credit, a lot of it, for everybody's success, to the Beatles. They've had a tremendous, universal influence.

That *Rubber Soul* album was a great new contribution. It helped them reach a new plateau."

The Beatles were always a producer's dream. Need a hit? Here's one. But it's hard to say if they were an engineer's dream. Norman Smith? With George Martin gone from EMI, there was an opening for an A&R and Smith was in a position to move where he wanted.

"Back then, the sound engineers were judged—quite unfairly, in my view—by the number of hits they'd worked on. Consequently, once the Beatles broke through I was walking on water at Abbey Road and I could do no wrong, so I could more or less do exactly as I wanted.

The four boys, George and myself had formed a sort of family, and, as you can probably imagine, it was wonderful to be part of all that.

After the first LP in 1963, the following albums had been wonderful. But the *Rubber Soul* album was the most difficult one for me. It was much less enjoyable. I can't remember how long the gap was between *Help!* and *Rubber Soul*, but there certainly had been one hell of a change in the relationship between the boys—mainly between John and Paul. It was very noticeable, and it made me quite sad in actual fact. Something had happened between those two albums, but I'm not sure what it was. That was the beginning of the end, really. That's when it started."

~ Norman Smith

(*video interview*, 2006)

In the same interview, Smith describes further how demanding Paul had become especially with Ringo and George who bore a grudge over that until the end. Paul wanted things played a certain way and would ride the other Beatles until they got it the way he wanted or he would play the part himself.

The Beatles were no longer a well-oiled equal-parts machine in the recording studio. They were now becoming Paul McCartney's vision of the group. But, this was all behind the scenes and not public knowledge until relatively recently. I think the question we should ask ourselves is whether the product—the end result—was worth the behind-the-scenes tension which began with *Rubber Soul* and seems to have escalated through *Let It Be*. Without McCartney's influence, over-bearing or no, we wouldn't have had *Revolver* or *Sgt. Pepper* as they were. It's an interesting question to ponder. Did we enjoy McCartney's vision of musical perfection? When you consider that George and John were purportedly tired of being Beatles by 1966, the alternative is a little scary.

Norman Smith, faced with the internal tension of the Beatles, as well as a promotion, left his position as an engineer and moved up to a producer role. His first group: Pink Floyd. But for four years, he did a hell of a job at the desk for the Beatles. He had a good stint as a producer, a short recording career "Oh Babe, What Would You Say?" and as an author, *John Lennon Called Me Normal*. He died at age 85 in 2008.

Rubber Soul (track listing: UK and CD)

Side One	Side Two
1. "Drive My Car"	1. "What Goes On"
2. "Norwegian Wood (This Bird Has Flown)"	2. "Girl"
3. "You Won't See Me"	3. "I'm Looking Through You"
4. "Nowhere Man"	4. "In My Life"
5. "Think for Yourself"	5. "Wait"
6. "The Word"	6. "If I Needed Someone"
7. "Michelle"	7. "Run for Your Life"

"We Can Work It Out" (Single)
"Day Tripper" (A-side)
(Released December 3, 1965)

"Day Tripper"

Many times when we create something, we know what it should come out like, but those who sample the wares do not. Tell a good cook that their meal is delicious, and they will tell you that it's not quite what they wanted. The same is true with songwriting. I think "Day Tripper" is a brilliant song. Neither John nor Paul thought so because they had difficulty recording it.

> "Day Tripper was [written] under complete pressure, based on an old folk song I wrote about a month previous. It was very hard going, that, and it sounds it. It wasn't a serious message song. It was a drug song. In a way, it was a day tripper—I just liked the word."
>
> ~ John Lennon
>
> (*The Beatles Anthology* 1996)

> "That was a co-written effort; we were both there making it all up but I would give John the main credit. Probably the idea came from John because he sang the lead, but it was a close thing. We both put a lot of work in on it."
>
> ~ Paul McCartney
>
> (*Paul McCartney: Many Years From Now*, 1998)

Memory is an interesting thing. Paul's memory is that John sang lead, but the fact is that they employed the classic Lennon-McCartney voice blend for it. They're both singing lead. Also, by the end of his life, John's memory was that he had written the entire song.

> "That's mine. Including the lick, the guitar break and the whole bit. It's just a rock 'n roll song. Day trippers are people who go

on a day trip, right? Usually on a ferryboat or something. But it was kind of-you know, you're just a weekend hippie. Get it?"

~ John Lennon

(The Playboy Interviews With John Lennon and Yoko Ono, 1981)

Whoever wrote it, it's a classic. Paul decided to be a little fancy on this song. He doubles the fabled guitar line (starting on the 7th fret of the 3rd string) beginning the second time around, and the bass becomes a prominent part of the song.

The Beatles were, at last, deciding to tell the world that they were talented players, more than just skilled at coming up with perfect parts. Ringo had been doing it for years; now it was time for George and Paul to step to the fore as well.

As for the opening guitar riff, you know what song it is as soon as you hear the first guitar note.

"This is the first time that we come upon a Beatles song that bears the signature of an unforgettable guitar riff used to both open and unify the whole production. This kind of branding-by-riff may not be something the Beatles necessarily 'invented,' but there's no denying that it is one of several techniques by which they would be known."

~ Alan W. Pollack

(Notes on . . . Series, 1989-2000)

"We Can Work It Out"

Ah, but the Beatles were clever lads. Just like so many of their songs, this one sounds simple enough. Simple enough, that is, until you try to learn to play it. What's this? A shift from 4/4 to 3/4 on the bridge? And whose idea was it to have Paul's optimistic verses be in a major key while John's cynical bridges be in its relative minor? Notice the harmonium (the squeeze-boxy thing) played by John act as a harmony on Paul's lead vocal, and it works if you sing those notes as a high harmony.

The song rolls along so naturally that you might barely notice those things.

Though the music is subtle, the message surely is not. You have to wonder if that was Paul McCartney's style. See it my way, it will work. See it your way, it fails. By "we can work it out" he means, "we can work it out if you do it my way." If that was his style of arguing in 1965, it changed significantly by the *Let It Be* sessions. During those days, if Paul was confronted by a differing point of view, he would tend to say "I thought that way too, but then came to this realization." Either way, he tended to be the guy who got his way throughout the story of the Beatles. By the end of their years, it seems that John was growing tired of Paul always being "right." And while its too bad that Paul didn't lean on the experience of the other three more often, that's not a criticism because . . . well, look how the group turned out! Fairly successfully you might say.

The two songs for the single were to be "Day Tripper" and "We Can Work It Out." John wanted "Day Tripper" to be the A-side. The rest of the team wanted "We Can Work It Out." In this case, they did work it out. It was the first double A-side single ever released. Evidence shows "We Can Work It Out" was the more popular of the two singles.

Paul's Rickenbacker 4001S Bass

In 1965, McCartney got a free Rickenbacker 4001S bass guitar. According to research done by Björn Eriksson, it was built in January of 1964. As mentioned above there is considerable debate about what bass he played on what song on the *Rubber Soul* album. One thing is for sure, starting in 1966 he was recording steadily with the Rickenbacker. There are huge differences between the Höfner and the Rick and this meant an equally huge distinction in the style McCartney would employ on the bass from this time forward.

For one, the Höfner has a hollow body while the Rickenbacker's body is solid, and this changes the tone of the bass. The hollow-body is much more liable to feedback and will maintain a more hollow sound. The Höfner has a short-scale neck while the Rickenbacker is longer scale. This places the frets further apart which causes the player to work a little harder for each note. McCartney has smallish hands and was comfortable with the smaller neck, but certainly had no troubles playing the larger Rickenbacker. It's difficult to *groove* on a short-scale bass as well. Finally, the Höfner had difficulties with staying in tune with itself (poor intonation). All in all the longer neck and better intonation freed Paul up for what he was about to do for the next few years: expand. Paul McCartney was, truly, an emerging maestro.

In 1967, like just about every other bassist and guitarist, he gave the bass a psychedelic paint job. And in 1968, again like everyone, he sanded the paint job back off.

Notes

1. The idea of recording only original music began with *A Hard Day's Night*, all songs written by Lennon-McCartney. Out of necessity, they temporarily abandoned the idea for their next album, *Beatles for Sale*, returning to the agreement for *Help!* with John, Paul and George each contributing songs.

2. In the years since 1965, it has become standard procedure for producers to work at various studios. Back then, however, it was unheard of. Producers (A and R men) were tied to a company. It took the power of the Beatles to break yet another law of the recording world.

The Beatles in the Studio in the Early Days

The Beatles started their recording career at EMI's Parlophone Studio at Abbey Road in North London. With a few exceptions, they recorded all of their music there throughout their career. During these early days, Paul McCartney was playing his first Höfner 500/1 bass, the one he bought when he switched to being the bass player. This one was slightly different from the one we came to know as the Beatle bass later. The two pickups were positioned up towards the neck; at this spot on a guitar, the sound is bassier. He played through a Quad II/22 amp and a speaker cabinet with a 15" speaker.

Recording their music was to be a learning experience for all concerned. When they met, George Martin had not produced much by way of rock and roll, and the Beatles had not been in a professional recording studio before.

Let's take a peek behind the scenes at the way the Beatles would introduce a new song to George Martin at the studio in those early days. He soon developed a routine for listening to what John and Paul had brought to record:

> "I would meet them in the studio to hear a new number. I would perch myself on a high stool, and John and Paul would stand around me with their acoustic guitars and play and sing it—usually without Ringo or George, unless George joined in the harmony. Then I would make suggestions to improve it,

and we'd try it again. That's what is known in the business as a 'head arrangement,' and we didn't move out of that pattern until the end of what I call the first era. That was the era which lasted through 'Love Me Do,' 'Please Please Me,' 'From Me to You,' 'She Loves You,' and 'I Want to Hold Your Hand,' which were the first batch of recordings."

~ George Martin

(*All You Need Is Ears*, 1994)

This is an important point to understand when considering the Beatles early recordings. This was the Beatles' music making machine. In the early days (1962-65), they were so busy they didn't have a lot of time to spend in the studio. They became (obviously) very, very good at making a great song almost overnight.

"Nobody ever took stuff for their throats, or did scales, and we never rehearsed. It was very, very loose, but we'd been playing so much together as a club act that we just sort of knew it. It would bore us to rehearse too much. We knew the songs, so we'd get quite a lot done at those sessions."

~ Paul McCartney

(*Paul McCartney – Bass Master - Playing the Great Beatles Basslines*, 2006)

It's fascinating how the Beatles worked out these legendary songs, the ones we listen to until this day. They were not practiced by the band before they walked into the studio.

"Normally John and I would go in the studio, sit down with the guys and say, 'Right, what are we going to do?' . . . We'd show it to the band over the course of twenty minutes, possibly half an hour. Ringo would stand around with a pair of drumsticks which he might tap on a seat or a screen or a packing case. John and I would sit with our two guitars. George would bring his guitar and see what chords we were doing and figure out what to do. George Martin would sit down with us and then we would separate, go to each instrument and come out ready to fight. And we just did it, and within the next hour, we would have done it. We would have decided how we were going to play this song."

~ Paul McCartney

(Paul McCartney: Many Years From Now, 1998)

The Beatles got involved in the mixes:

"There was a period when we started realizing that you could go and remix it yourself. We started listening to them and started saying, 'Well, why can't you do that?' We'd be just standing by the board saying, 'Well, what about that?' And George Martin would say, 'Well, how do you like this?' In the early days, they just would present us with finished product. We would ask what happened to the bass or something. And they would say 'oh, that's how it is, you can't . . .' That kind of thing. It must have been a gradual thing."

~ John Lennon

(Rolling Stone, 1971)

In another account of the way the early songs were arranged, journalist Maureen Cleeve told about going to an early Beatles' recording and how she never had a clue that the song was being recorded. John was humming something to George, George Martin was playing the piano and then suddenly the song was finished. It obviously took a lot more than that to make a Beatles' record, but the story does lend credence to the idea that there was magic in the air when the Beatles recorded the music that is hashed out, analyzed, written about, sung, attacked and defended and universally loved to this day.

Master of the Studio
(1966)

1966 in Review

It's fairly common knowledge by now that 1966—though one of their best years musically—was a dastardly year for the Beatles logistically. It is here where their story changes completely from the excitement of being Beatles to one of abandonment and disillusion.

The year started nicely enough. In January, George married Patty Boyd with Paul as his best man. But in 1966, the Beatles experienced what had to be one of the worst world tours of all time. From Japan to the Philippines to America, they were treated shabbily. Oh how the mighty had fallen.

In Tokyo, they were hired to play at a martial arts arena and then heavily criticized by the press (and a lot of protesting civilians) for their choice of arenas. They were forced to stay in their hotels under heavy guard.

Later that month they went to the Philippines and failed to attend a President's Reception at the palace. This did not go over well with good ol' Imelda. In retaliation all police protection disappeared. After making their way to the Manila airport, they were shoved and punched and forced to give all of the money they earned back to the government.

John's comments about the Beatles being larger than Christ didn't exactly go over well in the American south and, in fact, it's my feeling that this was a trigger moment in his life. By that I mean that he learned that the slightest word given in one place in the world could trigger catastrophe on the other side. It doesn't seem that he was ever the same after that event. When they arrived in Chicago to start their tour of America, he "sort of" apologized to those who were offended. The band received death threats for their upcoming concerts. Welcome to America! To further their fun, the "butcher" cover for their album *Yesterday and Today* was found to be offensive to American record-buyers.

And the tour went on. And on and on. Violence at their concerts increased, and when they finally played their last stop at Candlestick Park in San Francisco on August 29th, it seems that the boys had had enough.

Who, listening to pop music in those days, will forget the sounds of 1966? Pop music decided to grow up that year, and it wasn't just the Beatles bringing the new sounds. There were fantastic songs full of great sounds coming from all directions. The music of '66 brought class as well as garage. From "Sunshine Superman" (which caught my ear) to "Cherish" to "They're Coming to Take Me Away" to "Daydream" to "Kicks" to "Wild Thing" to "Happy Jack" (have you listened to that song lately?), it was very good—in my opinion it was the best year for pop music ever. On top of all that great noise, "Paperback Writer" blasted out of our radio speakers with a sound that was fresh and a bit wild.

When the Beatles went to record what became the *Revolver* album, there was a huge challenge in front of them. They could very easily have hit a dry period, having long since grown completely tired of their lives as Beatles. Instead, Paul McCartney chose this time to shine and the Beatles rode the wave with him. In 1966, Paul was a part of the art scene in London and into some pretty far out stuff. It was his idea to bring the tape loops in that became such a huge part of Lennon's "Tomorrow Never Knows" (the banshee Indian sounds were taken from a guitar loop). While the other Beatles were wisely trying to spend their time resting, it was Paul who was listening to strange music and wanting to bring a new sound to the Beatles. *Revolver* has some great Lennon songs, there is no doubt. But it's Paul's songs and sounds that seem to define the sound of the Beatles in 1966 (just as it was John who seemed to define their sound in 1965).

Paul brought a certain classical influence to the album, and it showed itself in a number of ways. But also, he brought some surprising and dynamic bass playing. He was using his Rickenbacker 4001S exclusively in the studio now (even though he used the trusty Höfner on stage). With it, he created a new style of bass playing that—along with his playing on the white album—reverberates through the bass community to this day. People still talk in amazement about what he did on "Rain" and "Paperback Writer." He was on fire this year and it came through onto the *Revolver* album and R/PBW single in a huge way.

The recording of *Revolver* began in early April 1966. "Paperback Writer" was recorded on April 14th.

And all of this so far says nothing about what might be the best single record ever recorded, and it was done in 1966: "Penny Lane" / "Strawberry Fields Forever." John and Paul were at their individual best. What a year.

Paul's Bass Playing in 1966

At last, the bass was brought to the fore of the Beatles' records. In 1966, bass players were coming on strong and steady in England. Jack Bruce and John Entwistle both found stardom during the year. It's possible that McCartney was challenged by these usurpers to his throne. Compare his playing on *Help!* with *Revolver* and it's hard to imagine that the two albums were recorded one year apart. Considering how quickly he advanced as a bass player, it is also quite possible that he was only now realizing the power the instrument could have in a studio setting.

The *Revolver* sessions weren't the first time that he recorded with his Rickenbacker 4001S bass, but it was the first time he used it en masse.

With a new engineer, using new recording techniques and ideas, it was the first time Paul's bass came out to the front of the Beatles' sound (with minor exceptions, i.e., "I Want to Hold Your Hand").

When "Paperback Writer" was released in June of 1966, it was suddenly clear that the Beatles had a seriously good bass player.

And it wasn't only the sound that had changed. The instrument itself brought out a refinement of his style that he could not have accomplished with his beloved old Höfner bass. The neck was long-scale (vs. the short scale he was used to). You would think this would force him to play much simpler lines. Instead, he used his creative vision to bring the bass fully into the mix with soaring, rhythmic bass lines. And yet, as is so often claimed, he did not play lead bass. While he traveled up the neck frequently, he rarely ventured out of the role of his place in the rhythm section.

Beatle recording in 1966 didn't stop with the Revolver album or the "Paperback Writer" / "Rain" single. In November, they began working on what was to become the *Sgt. Pepper* album. During that year they worked on "Strawberry Fields Forever," "When I'm Sixty-Four" and— just before the year ended—one of Paul's best ever songs, "Penny Lane."

Paul McCartney's bass playing in 1966 (and beyond) is stamped in the playing that you hear to this day. He, along with a few others, defined what modern rock bass playing would be for decades to come. Well, let's see what a few famous bass players have to say:

"Paul's influence on bassists has been so widespread over numerous generations that there's no denying he's in everybody's playing at this point. We're all descendants. He played simple and solid when it was called for. But because he had so many different flavors to add to a song, he was able to take the instrument far beyond a supportive role. Paul taught the bass how to sing."

~ Will Lee (long time bass player on *The David Letterman Show*)

(*Bass Player magazine*, 1995)

"It's hard to separate McCartney's influence on my bass playing from his influence on everything else-singing, songwriting, even becoming a musician in the first place. As a child, I would play my Beatles albums at 45 RPM so I could hear the bass better. He's the Guvnor."

~ Sting

(*Bass Player magazine*, 1995)

The Emergence of Young Geoff Emerick

Geoff Emerick became the Beatles engineer after *Rubber Soul*. What would *Revolver* have sounded like with the outgoing EMI sound engineer Norman Smith? Perhaps a lot drier. More like *Rubber Soul*, maybe, but one thing's for sure; it would have sounded nowhere near like it did. Smith left either to pursue his own producing career (as per George Martin) or because he knew it was time to make it on his own (as per Norman Smith himself).

"*Rubber Soul* wasn't really my bag at all so I decided that I'd better get off the Beatles train."

~ Norman Smith

(*The Beatles Recording Sessions*, 1990)

Before the brilliant Mr. Smith departs, I think it should be pointed out that he was the engineer on some of the greatest moments of pop music of all time. The early Beatles records were fantastic, and hold up well to this day. Norman Smith was the engineer during the times when the Beatles had little time for recording their records. They would basically pop in, have a epic session and run out into the world again. He didn't have the technology available to him that the later Beatles engineers had. He did a fantastic job during his tenure.

This move, for whatever reason, is all-important in any consideration of the next Beatles records. To emphasize this major point, put *Rubber Soul* and *Revolver* into your player and just skip around between albums for a while. You'll see it wasn't just, as so often has been re-ported, that the Beatles had gotten better, it was also that the recording techniques went out of the universe in 1966. They were now using the compression techniques that are so evident on *Revolver*, *Sgt. Pepper* and *Abbey Road*. Norman Smith was great, Geoff Emerick was young and ready to burn.

> "'Paperback Writer' was the first time the bass sound had been heard in all its excitement. For a start, Paul played a different bass, a Rickenbacker. Then we boosted it further by using a loudspeaker as a microphone. We positioned it directly in front of the bass speaker and the moving diaphragm of the second speaker made the electric current."
>
> ~ Geoff Emerick
>
> (*The Beatles Recording Sessions*, 1990)

What a process—one that is used in some stereo systems today—created at Abbey Road for that song. Note that here Emerick doesn't claim specifically that it was the first time he used the Rickenbacker, which would have been an incorrect statement. Instead, he refers to it as a "different" bass. It might do well to keep in mind that Emerick's involvement on *Rubber Soul* (when Paul was first seen to have it in use) may have been minimal. It wasn't until the *Revolver* sessions that Emerick became the main engineer.

> "Geoff walked-in green but because he knew no rules he tried different techniques, and because the Beatles were very creative and adventurous, they would say yes to everything. The chemistry of George and Geoff was perfect and they made a formidable team. With another producer and another engineer things would have turned out quite differently."
>
> ~ Jerry Boys (Tape Operator)
>
> (*The Beatles Recording Sessions*, 1990)

"Geoff started off by following Norman Smith's approach because he'd been Norman's assistant for a while. But he rapidly started to change things around, the way to mike drums or bass, for example. He was always experimenting."

~ Ron Pender

(The Beatles Recording Sessions, 1990)

"Paperback Writer" (Single)
"Rain" (B-side)
(Released June 10, 1966)

"Paperback Writer"

It's a whole new bass player who emerged on June 10th, the day "Paperback Writer" and "Rain" was released as a single.

Reviews of "Paperback Writer," over the years, have tended to cast it off as being a fairly weak song. Better lyrics are demanded. But the reviewers miss the point entirely. It is not the lyrics that drive this song; it's the sound and the vibrating feel. It's the lead guitar riff, John's tremolo rhythm, Ringo's driving beat and the soaring bass playing. The sound of the song was quite completely different from anything else out in its day. The four musicians clicked together as a unit, each one completely holding his own and playing together with confidence.

To really grasp how powerful these songs were when they were released you have to go back in time and listen to what else was on the charts and playing on the radio in 1966 and 1967. There was nothing like it around. The bass work is at the same time heavy and flowery. An iron butterfly, if you will. It wasn't long after this that bass players in recording sessions and bands around the world found themselves facing the dilemma of having to "play like McCartney, man."

But Who Played the Guitar Riff?

It was my assumption for these past 45 years that George played the opening guitar riff and had made this claim on the website that was the precursor to this book.

> "[on your website] you said George played his Gibson SG on 'Paperback Writer.' Though George uses it in the video, at recent McCartney concerts I've been to Paul has said he played the riff on his Epiphone Casino. When you listen to it, this makes sense because the line is quite aggressive and more like Paul's style ('Taxman' and 'Sgt Pepper' solos) than George's more delicate playing."
>
> ~ Sean Farrel
>
> *(email, 2013)*

Thank you, Sean. I stand corrected. So we have McCartney playing the signature guitar line as well as the powerful bass parts on "Paperback Writer."

As for the recording, the mix of the two guitars really moves the song. The vocals are extraordinary; ingeniously arranged and recorded with flash and style. But, in the eyes of history, it's the bass that really cuts this song. Paul's bass fills leading into the verses are by now legendary. It was one of the first major hits—along with its flip side—that truly featured bass.

> "This song is definitely in the top tier of Beatles' hardest rocking cuts."
>
> ~ Alan W. Pollack
>
> *(Notes on . . . Series, 1989-2000)*

"Rain"

In its finished form, "Rain" was slowed down from the tempo at which it was originally recorded. This change was engineered to give the sound a warmer, almost dripping feel. But when you consider the fact that it is slower, think about how fast it must have been recorded. The first thing that comes to my mind is that Ringo played this track at a FASTER speed than the record.

Those who wish to hear *monster* bass playing, 1966 style, sit back and enjoy the show. Like so many facets of the Beatles' legacy, it's as alive today as it was then.

A lot of the song is played up the neck, but there are a number of lines where he moves from down the bottom end to up high quickly. Since the song comes out in G, it's my guess that they originally played it in A, allowing Paul to play the low open A and get up above the high G on the first string with relative ease. Listen to the bass line just after "Can you hear me? Can you hear me?" He gets from the low G to the high G just a little too quickly for it to be otherwise. If the song was not recorded, originally, in A, then the other possibility is that a capo was used.

Notes on the Single

The "Paperback Writer" / "Rain" (PPW/R) single is fascinating in many ways. It compares nicely to "Penny Lane" / "Strawberry Fields Forever" (PL/SFF) recorded later in the year. The songs from both singles were recorded during the making of their current album-in-progress (PPW/R during *Revolver* and PL/SFF during *Sgt. Pepper's Lonely Hearts Club Band*. Both feature incredible and previously unheard effects. Both feature strong songs by both Paul and John. Both singles show the Beatles at their united all-four-playing-well-together best and leaving their musical past far behind.

> "The subject matter, musical style, and recording technique of both 'Paperback Writer' and 'Rain' make them as qualitatively different from what we heard on the album which preceded them as they presage the album which was yet to follow. The release of 'Penny Lane' / 'Strawberry Fields Forever' as an antecedent to the *Sgt. Pepper's Lonely Hearts Club Band* LP is the

other major single of theirs to have this level of potent presci-
ence in terms of an album in progress."

~ Alan W. Pollack

(*Notes on . . . Series*, 1989-2000)

"By April '66, recording techniques had improved to the point
where the bass could truly have its own voice in a recording.
Damn if McCartney didn't make the most of it. He and Ringo
synch up fantastically on this one, and the speakers crackle with
the results. As usual, McCartney knew what a song needed, as
he heard a simple yet dense, droning guitar part and added just
the right amount of movement, stability and abandon to make
this one of his standout tracks."

~ John Martin

(*email*, 2010)

Revolver (LP)

Released
August 5, 1966

Cover Notes

The cover for the what may be the Beatles' best album was done by an
old friend from their Hamburg days, Klaus Voorman. If you look
closely at the top right of George's hair, you'll see Voorman's self-
portrait.

Klaus Voorman recalls "I nearly said no [when asked to do the
cover] because I hadn't had a pen or pencil in my hand for years."

Voorman went to the studio and heard "Tomorrow Never Knows"
and realized the cover should be avante-garde as well. The Beatles gave
him private photos for the montage. The photo of Ringo in the striped
shirt was from a magazine sent in by a fan, hence the funny angle.
Voorman drew the faces from memory, having difficulty getting
George's face to look right. That's why he put in cut-outs of his eyes
and mouth.

Revolver (LP)

Peak Position
Number 1

Number of Weeks on the Chart
77

Number of Days in the Studio
33

Almost twice as many days as they spent on their last album.

First Song Recorded for the Album
"Tomorrow Never Knows" on April 6, 1966

As was the case with most Beatles albums, the first song they set to work on was a strong John Lennon song. For Revolver, he wasted no time in trying to change the world of music. On April 6th, the Beatles began working the song with a working title of "Mark I," which would have been a great title. Lennon felt, however, that it needed something with some humor to it and so he borrowed a "Ringo-ism" and entitled it "Tomorrow Never Knows."

The first thing that should be written about *Revolver* is that the Beatles reinvented themselves their sound in the making of it. Not for the first time and most definitely, not for the last, but it may be that *Revolver* shows the biggest leap of all between albums. Were these the same four musicians who recorded the folk-rock based *Rubber Soul* only months before? *Revolver* is full of hard-rock sounding electric guitar. The recordings are slowed-down, speeded-up, recorded backwards and effects-laden. The lyrics show a new Beatles, love songs to the side. In fact the few love songs on the album are written with a decidedly non-poppish style.

Revolver is an incredible album, voted in many polls as the best album ever made. And it was made by men still playing the tired role of mop-tops but making music that left their old image far behind. They were in an experimental mood now, making music the likes of which had never been heard before. This was a case of the Beatles spending the last years under the yoke of publicity, recording, touring, generally having to be Beatles. Their creativity was generally stifled by the mere monstrosity of events they were constantly grinding through. Now, in 1966, they decided to let it all loose, take some time and make incredible music. They were hot and ready for new sounds and new styles. To top it off, EMI assigned them a young new engineer by the name of Geoff Emerick who did his best to toss out all the old rules. This was the first album he worked on as 1st engineer and what a magnificent job he did. If you think the superlatives I'm using to describe *Revolver* are overstating the case, let's see what thousands of other people—both inside and outside of the industry—thought.

Colin Larkin has written a series of books called *The All Time Top 1000 Albums.* He polled thousands of people to come up with the lists. In that series, Revolver has been in the top five, every time.

In 2003, *Rolling Stone* magazine polled hundreds of industry insiders to come up with a list of the 500 all-time greatest albums. *Revolver* came out [#]3.

"This album has taken longer than the others because, normally, we go into the studios with, say, eight numbers of our own and some old numbers, like 'Mr Moonlight' or some numbers we used to know, which we just do up a bit. This time, we had all our own numbers, including three of George's, and so we had to work them all out. We haven't had a basis to work on, just one guitar melody and a few chords and so we've really had to work on them. I think it'll be our best album yet. They'll never be able to copy this!"

~ Paul McCartney

(*beatlesbible.com*, 1966)

"We were really starting to find ourselves in the studio. We were finding what we could do, just being the four of us and playing our instruments. The overdubbing got better, even though it was always pretty tricky because of the lack of tracks (note: *Revolver* was recorded on a four-track recorder). The songs got more interesting, so with that the effects got more interesting."

~ Ringo Starr

(*Anthology*, 1996)

Ringo's point is a good one. It generally does take a while for a band to figure out how to work together in the studio. This was the first time they didn't rush through the creation of an album. In my opinion *Revolver* is one of the best pop albums ever. The sound of this entire album is unique. I know of no other that sounds close to it. Many fans and reviewers (and even George Martin) have referred to it as their favorite Beatles album. For this work, it was the sound that the Beatles sought to bring to the fore. Tracks were slowed down and sped up, parts were tracked backwards, all for the effect of the sound.

"*Sgt. Pepper* is a flamboyant, flowery thing; it isn't about a dark drug world. *Revolver* feels like an interior psychedelia. It deals with insecurity and death and uncertainty. It looks like the be-ginning—from here, anything was possible"

~ Wayne Coyne

(*Tell Me Why*, 2002)

"Taxman"

With a strangely recorded count-in (Lennon felt that the listeners would be interested in hearing what was on the tape), George's classic opens the album, and it's the only time a Harrisson song ever opened a Beatles' album. It was clear right away that the lovable mop-tops were a thing of the past. This was serious, and the Beatles didn't take long to show how powerful their rhythm section was going to be.

McCartney clearly had a great off-the-cuff approach to songs written by John and George. With George's "Taxman," Paul's contributions shine. His bass part is heavy and yet adapts itself to its surroundings as the song goes through it's various changes.

And then there's his guitar solo. Recorded on his trusty Epiphone Casino, it is probably the heaviest guitar solo on record by the Beatles.

"Taxman" is recorded at a fast tempo; one of the fastest songs by the group. The song is based in many ways around the flat seventh. As the song is in D, the note and chord C is just about the main feature point of the song structure. Further adding to the bluesy flavor of the sound, Lennon plays a D7 with a minor (flat) 3rd.

As with many of the Beatles' classic songs, "Taxman" features their almost casual way of starting off with one feel and building as the song went along. Each verse in the song adds something, seemingly subtle, to the mix so that by the end the song is pretty heavy.

The subtle machinations of the arrangement make a step-by-step analysis of the recording worthwhile.

Step-by-Step Analysis of Taxman

1st verse: Right at the start you have a solid groove: Ringo on drums, Paul driving on a slightly distorted sounding bass and John playing his rhythm guitar so hard that it sounds as if he might be banging it against the wall (perfect).

The bass line is interesting in that it is in counter-point to Lennon's guitar. At the outset of the line, it sounds as if he is going into a one-five mode in counter, but then decides to do a quick turn that ends abruptly. At the outset, Ringo is joining both forces. His bass drum (which now were to become a feature in the Geoff Emerick days) underlies the bass while his snare does the same with the guitar. He is restrained until it is time to signal the 1st chorus ("Cause I'm the taxman") when he does a delightful little snare roll.

2nd verse: Coming out of the chorus, right at 0:30, Ringo actually plays an old drummer's trick. He kicks his bass drum loudly one time to signal that the wild moment is over, and time to return to a more subdued form. It's equally possible that this was a glitch in the mixing stage. For verse two, the addition is a very subtly mixed tambourine played on the 3rd and 4th beats and an elevation in intensity of the bass and drums.

2nd chorus: The second chorus introduces a cowbell played on the quarter notes, and you'll notice that the tambourine is now up louder in the mix.

3rd verse: Verse three is another step up in intensity by all concerned. John, George and Paul's vocals are now in the lead ("If you drive a car, aaaah"). The cowbell and tambourine (now playing on beats 2 and 4 with the snare) are now firmly ensconced in the rhythm section. The rhythm guitar is sustaining a little longer. But the obvious indicator that we're heading towards a Beatles climax is the bass guitar. No longer content to provide a restrained groove, McCartney is pushing the beat and playing a line with more notes in it, and yet still somehow seems as if it should have one more note. This, along with the orchestrated build at the end of the verse and the nearly shouted "Taxman!" are the final straws that make us crave climax and release.

Guitar solo: And the release comes with McCartney's energetic, dazzling, rhythmic blast of a killer guitar solo (over a verse structure).

"Paul's guitar solo is hot stuff; fast triplets, exotic modal touches, and a melodic shape which traverses several octaves and ends with a breathtaking upward flourish."

~ Alan W. Pollack

(*Notes on . . . Series*, 1989-2000)

"I was pleased to have Paul play that bit on 'Taxman.' If you notice, he did like a little Indian bit on it for me."

~ George Harrison

(*Guitar Magazine*, 1987)

The several octaves Alan describes even happen right at the start of the solo. It starts on a low D and melds with a higher D by the ending of the opening assault. From there it just sounds like McCartney getting a powerful guitar sound and reacting to that by pulling out all of the stops, tossing in the "Indian bits" and coming to a sudden stop. The studio must have been on fire the day he recorded that solo.

3rd chorus: We're coming off a good high, so there was no need to add anything to the mix. A moment's respite. But . . .

4th verse: McCartney had such fun doing the solo that he can't stop now. His guitar line (somewhat) follows the bass line. The backgrounds are inspired in their admonishments of Messrs Wilson and Heath.[1]

5th verse: More tension mounting, if that were possible. You'll note that the tone becomes more somber, serious. The guitar line that invaded the 4th verse has picked up it's involvement and there is now also a very low voice (George's) added to the "Taxman" harmonies along with a higher and more prominent note from Paul's high notes there.

Last chorus and out. George Martin liked the guitar solo so much that he had his engineer (Emerick) splice a copy of it onto the end of the song, and this takes us to the fade.

The Beatles did not let George Harrison down.

Here is a note from Pierre Charron who wrote to me in December of 2007 to enlighten me about a detail of this song.

"In all the articles I've read or the bands I've heard, there is one detail that nobody seemed to take care about concerning the song 'Taxman.' If you listen carefully to the bass line, you will notice that McCartney doubles the high D note in his riff, right on the second beat instead of playing just one simple half note. Even if the kick and the bass aren't always tight together in this song, you can clearly isolate the bass and find that the combination of both instruments (with the heavy compression) gives a real punchy sound that makes us ask: Who plays what? I found this when, for my own pleasure, I decided to track 'Taxman' in my recording studio playing every part of the song. I have heard so many remakes of that song in different situations and never, never that second sixteenth note was played!"

~ Pierre Charron

(*email*, 2007)

"'Taxman' was when I first realised that even though we had started earning money, we were actually giving most of it away in taxes. It was and still is typical."

~ George Harrison

(*interview*, 1980)

"I remember the day he [Harrison] called to ask for help on 'Taxman,' one of his first songs. I threw in a few one-liners to help the song along, because that's what he asked for. He came to me because he couldn't go to Paul, because Paul wouldn't have helped him at that period. I didn't want to do it . . . I just sort of bit my tongue and said OK. It had been John and Paul for so long, he'd been left out because he hadn't been a song-writer up until then."

~ John Lennon

(*The Playboy Interviews With John Lennon and Yoko Ono*, 1981)

"George wrote that and I played guitar on it. He wrote it in anger at finding out what the taxman did. He had never known before then what he'll do with your money."

~ Paul McCartney

(*Playboy interview*, 1984)

"Tomorrow Never Knows"

Album placement of individual tracks is an incredibly important thing. George Martin was a master of this technique, and he had philosophies. Start the album off with the best, upbeat song on the album. Side one has to end with a song that will make the listener want to expend the energy into turning the album over and playing the other side. End the album with a song that will keep the listener wanting more.

"Tomorrow Never Knows" was placed at the end of the *Revolver* LP. It's always been my feeling that it was a bit of a (probably unintentional) disservice to this amazing track. The album is such a swirling roller-coaster (or helter-skelter if you prefer) of fantastic music that by the time you get to this last track, it's difficult to be ready for what may be the most experimental song they ever recorded.

But where else could the song have been placed? What if the opening to "Tomorrow Never Knows" was the first sound you heard when you put on this brand new Beatles album? It would have changed the entire feel of the album. If it was felt strongly that they would have lost a significant number of listeners from the opening, then perhaps it could have opened side two of the LP. Considering the times, in the end, the wisdom of the Beatles/Martin at placing it at the end makes sense but still I would like to hear this album with this song leading off.

"Tomorrow Never Knows" called for a droning rhythm on which to place the myriad of sounds. The drummer and bass player responded appropriately. Ringo's drum line stumbles on 3+ and McCartney, with high C hammering, follows the stumble on most measures. A stumbling drone is hard to conceptualize. The best guess is that the drum line was created first, and McCartney followed the rhythm with his bass.

The song, especially for it's day, was an amazing, impossible song. There was nothing like this in 1966.

"In 1965, the Beatles' recordings had been progressing quite nicely, thank you, but here was a quantum jump into not merely tomorrow but sometime next week."

~ Mark Lewisohn

(*The Beatles Recording Sessions,* 1990)

Did You Hear That?!

George Martin has said that "Tomorrow Never Knows" is the one song that could not be duplicated. That is because the various strange sounds that are heard on the track are all from little tape loops created by the Beatles, mainly Paul. The Indian war-whoops, for example, are from a guitar speeded up. There are many loops that spun continuously during the final mix, played on multiple tape recorders around the studios and fed into the main board where faders (volume controls) were lowered and raised to bring them in as desired. It was a live mix done incredibly well.

"Got to Get You into My Life"

1966 is the year that Paul McCartney really began to take his instrument seriously. He was at the forefront of a new breed of players, and he must have felt it was time for him to make a statement. His playing throughout the album, throughout the year, was at a peak. At times it was bold, at times tender. Sometimes quiet, sometimes loud; whatever the song called for.

"Got to Get You into My Life" was a tip of his hat to the Motown sound. When you think of Motown, you think of heavy, syncopated, dynamic bass playing. It's interesting, then, to hear that McCartney decided to keep his bass playing for this song extremely simple: mostly straight quarter-notes. As with "Taxman" the instrumentation for "Got to Get You into My Life" is sparse, perhaps even more so! This makes his decision to keep his playing simple even more interesting.

Let's not remove ourselves from this discussion without first mentioning that Paul's lyrics here are more powerful than his typical fair. He sounds as if he really means it when he sings "did I tell you I need you every single day of my life." Add his blast "Got to get you into my life!" to the mix and you have one of his better songs.

The song begins with a bass note (not unlike "I Feel Fine"), hi-hat and horns. Beginning at 0:04, especially noticeable on the CD, an extremely loud tambourine spices up the rhythm. Also (not unlike "I Want to Hold Your Hand") the intro is recorded in such a way that the verse starts one beat later than the listener might think. This is due to the horns playing what seems like the beginning of a new measure on beat 4.

Did You Hear That?!

Listen beneath the horns at around 0:06. Can you hear the sound of someone speaking? A voice that sounds a lot like George Martin, in fact.

At 1:50, you finally get the sense of why McCartney chose to play such a simple bass line. A guitar part (possibly double-tracked and sounds like him playing that, too) enters into the picture and stays there

Note: This was the first (but certainly not the last) Beatles song to use the aforementioned horns.

"Good Day Sunshine"

"'Good Day Sunshine' is a song that always made me feel good. This song alone could get me out of bad mood. The music and the lyrics are upbeat. Love it!"

~ Mary Andrade Crossthwaite

(email, 2013)

"Good Day Sunshine" is classic McCartney. It's a song that could only be done properly by a British group, with restrained British cool. It could really come off as a bubble-gum pop song if it was done any differently.

"And Your Bird Can Sing"

If you sit and listen to this song a lot, you come to realize that there are two forces at work. On one side, you have the wild and exotic twin (at least) guitar leads pulling the song along, kind of like the engine of a fast moving locomotive. Along with that are the strange and seemingly impossible to decipher lyrics. These lyrics are delivered with strength by John and then with powerful harmonies by Paul. Still on this same side of things, you have a strong and moving line by the seemingly newly liberated bass player. Underneath this all—the other side—you have a steady and plodding drum/rhythm guitar part. They sound as if they were recorded first: "Just lay down a steady beat Ringo and we'll think of what to lay on top of it." And it works!

The Beatles never recorded another song that sounds even close to "And Your Bird Can Sing," but you might say that the steady pulse is reminiscent of some of John's rockers from the white album.

Then, we have Take 2 (as heard on the *Anthology* album and what do we have here? A completely different, and yet maybe even more interesting version than the released one. The twin lead guitar part of this version of the song seems, in retrospect, as solid and interesting. The bass and drum parts—right from the intro—on this earlier version are certainly more prevalent, making the song more exciting. There is, however, a singular point of massive frustration about this version. If only we could hear this without the giggling John and Paul, we would surely have a new classic Beatles song on our hands. Why was it released with the giggling? I have no idea.

"I bought a copy of *Yesterday and Today* in '77 when I was about 14 and I wore that out. 'And Your Bird Can Sing' was my favorite track on that one. When I finally broke down and bought *Anthology 2* a few years ago I was just amazed at the alternate version; despite the common lyrics, these are two totally different songs. What is really impressive is the way McCartney approached each of these. Taking them chronologically, the 'Byrds' version from *Anthology* features a jangly guitar strum and a bass part that descends through the D Major scale, using the root as an anchor for each scale degree. Every line is a tasteful scalar approach to melody.

McCartney's work on the chorus here is similar to the orig-
inally-released version. For the original version, the Beatles
took the song up to the key of E Major and changed the guitar
part significantly. Now McCartney was presented with a cascad-
ing, descending guitar line and he responded with a rooted but
ascending bass line that became neatly juxtaposed to the guitar
line."

~ John Martin

(*email*, 2008)

"On *Revolver*, quite a few songs abandon chordal progression
in favour of the drone ('Tomorrow Never Knows,' even
'Taxman')—this would have dragged dreadfully with most bass
players, but McCartney lightens things up and provides melodic
interest. Get your average rock player to play one of these
songs, and listen to what happens, as the drone becomes a
dirge."

~ Richard Goodwin

(*email*, 2012)

"Your insight (on the website) into the impact of Geoff Emerick
stepping in between *Rubber Soul* and *Revolver* was spot on, and
his contribution can 'not' be understated. This was probably
one of the earliest examples of Emerick's work as the lead engineer, and I think his ability to bring the bass forward was as
much in response to the Beatles' demands to push in new directions as it was his own interest in, perhaps, making a name
for himself (using a bass speaker as a microphone, for example). What's the worst thing that would have happened? It
wouldn't have worked and they'd have gone back to what
they'd done before."

~ Michael Kimsal

(*email*, 2012)

As we say farewell to *Revolver*, I realize that it is difficult to comment only on a few of the songs from the album. There is so much to discuss. "She Said She Said," a great Lennon song, is one of the few Beatles tracks through their recording career that Paul McCartney did not play on ("Julia" being another). The vocals, which may include Paul, are the vintage Beatles mid 1960s sound. The Beatles do their usual nice turn of being casual about time signature shifts. "Here, There and Everywhere" is John and Paul's favorite Beatles' song and a beautiful recording. "I Want to Tell You" is another compelling argument against George's complaint that the Beatles did not put time into his songs. One of my favorite all-time Beatles songs is Paul's ballad "For No One."

Did they mess, yet again, with the album's song lineup in America? Oh yes! There was a massive cry for new Beatles material in the US and so Capitol Records decided to make an album of old and new material. Parlophone (EMI's subsidiary label) sent over three tracks from the *Revolver* album then in progress. All three were John songs ("And Your Bird Can Sing," "Doctor Robert" and "I'm Only Sleeping") and were put on the *Yesterday and Today* LP in the states. They were left off of the American *Revolver* album. The result of this maneuver was that we in America were not aware that John was still writing a lot of brilliant songs. All we heard on our version of *Revolver* was "Tomorrow Never Knows" and "She Said She Said." Two strange, but very cool songs.

Revolver (track listing)

Side One

1. "Taxman"
2. "Eleanor Rigby"
3. "I'm Only Sleeping"
4. "Love You To"
5. "Here, There And Everywhere"
6. "Yellow Submarine"
7. "She Said She Said"

Side Two

1. "Good Day Sunshine"
2. "And Your Bird Can Sing"
3. "For No One"
4. "Doctor Robert"
5. "I Want to Tell You"
6. "Got to Get You into My Life"
7. "Tomorrow Never Knows"

To Analyze 1966

Most people who work with a tool of any kind know that when you get a better tool, one that thoroughly outshines what you had before, it's easy to become more creative. It is true with most pursuits, and musical instruments are prime examples. For example, a beginner learning on a cheap instrument will be able to begin grasping the fundamentals of the instrument but will not attain a truly superb sound until they have upgraded to a higher quality model. People who get new musical instruments that sound better than before suddenly become many times better in their musicianship. Play a note and it sounds delicious; different. You find that you want to play different things, try different combinations. It's an exciting, magical thing to do to play a new top-notch instrument. Combining the Rickenbacker bass that Paul began using in 1965 with the studio techniques and sounds available to them during these years, 1966 and 1967 were banner years for Paul's bass playing and with songs like "Paperback Writer," took full advantage of his new range.

As for the Beatles, at the end of their final, harrowing tour in 1966 most of them had had enough. By all rights and by any measure of sheer sanity, the Beatles should have stopped being a group right then. In the past few months alone they had experienced the best and the worst. The best was their incredible album Revolver. No less a jazz aficionado than Ralph J. Gleason called them the greatest songwriters since Stephen Foster and called *Revolver,* "the best pop music album I have ever heard and is a remarkable performance." (*San Francisco Chronicle*, "On The Town" 1966) The worst was the tour they had just completed. From the mayhem in the Philippines to the riots in Munich to the Beatles are bigger than Jesus to the album burnings to nearly being electrocuted in Cincinnati, being a Beatle had become a nightmare.

When the final concert of their last tour was over and the Beatles were flying back to Los Angeles, George Harrison said, "So it's all over, I can stop pretending to be a Beatle now, people." John Lennon later said, "I was always waiting for a reason to get out of the Beatles from the day I made *How I Won The War* in 1966. I just didn't have the guts to do it." They had put more effort and energy into their careers during the last four years than you or I've put into a lifetime.

Paul McCartney, it seems, was the only one who wanted to keep the whole business going. It was him who led the Beatles for the next few years. The Beatles went back into the studio late in the year and began recording "Strawberry Fields Forever," "When I'm Sixty-Four," and "Penny Lane." Not a bad way to end the year.

Notes

1. Harold Wilson was the liberal leader of the Labour Party (and Prime Minister at the time). Sir Edward Heath was the leader of the opposition Conservative Party. He defeated Wilson in the 1970 election and Wilson returned the favor a few years later.

BETWEEN THE CHAPTERS

The Great Bass Players Discuss McCartney's Influence

The best compliments don't come from authors but from peers in the music industry. Let's take a look at what the best of the best think about McCartney's influence as a bass player.

"Paul definitely had an influence on my bass playing. Not so much technically, but more with his philosophy of melodic bass lines—especially as I hit my teens and the Beatles' records became more adventurous. On tracks like 'Come Together,' the bass line WAS the song. I've always liked that. The only other person I knew of who was doing that was James Jamerson. That was one of the reasons I was inspired to write 'School Days' so I could just play the bass lines and people would hear a whole song.

I had the honor of being contacted by Paul through George Martin to play on 'Tug of War' and I also appeared on 'Pipes of Peace' [both on Capitol]. Paul was very nice. He asked me to show him how to slap. During *Pipes* we got a groove going in a studio jam, and it ended up making on the album as 'Hey Hey' He graciously gave me a co-writing credit, and it's still a thrill to see my name next to his above the music in the song book."

~ *Stanley Clarke*

"It's hard to separate McCartney's influence on my bass playing from his influence on everything else-singing, songwriting, even becoming a musician in the first place. As a child, I would play my Beatles albums at 45 RPM so I could hear the bass better. He's the Guvnor."

~ Sting

"Growing up in Texas in the early 1960s I was so obsessed with the Beatles' music that I didn't feel like a fan, I felt like I was in the Beatles. About the same time I switched from drums to bass I became aware of who gave the band its charm and personality, from visual tunes like 'Penny Lane' to the group's repartee with the press. It was the same fellow who was able to take a poor-quality instrument like the Höfner bass and create magic on it.

I especially dug Paul's funky, Motown-influenced side, evident in the bass line from 'Everybody's Got Something to Hide Except Me and My Monkey,' or even in the syncopated part from 'A Day in the Life.'

Paul's influence on bassists has been so widespread over numerous generations that there's no denying he's in everybody's playing at this point. We're all descendants. He played simple and solid when it was called for. But because he had so many different flavors to add to a song, he was able to take the instrument far beyond a supportive role. Paul taught the bass how to sing."

~ Will Lee

"Paul was one of the most innovative bass players ever. And half the stuff that is going on now is directly ripped off from his Beatles period."

~ John Lennon

"There's no doubt that Lennon and McCartney were good musicians. They had good musical brains, and the brain is where music originates—it has nothing to do with your fingers. As it happened, they could also play their own instruments very well.

And since those early days they've all improved, especially Paul. He's an excellent musical all-rounder, probably the best bass-guitarist there is, a first-class drummer, brilliant guitarist and competent piano player."

~ George Martin

"The reason I got involved with music in the first place was because I saw the Beatles on *The Ed Sullivan Show*. I watched all the girls going crazy, and I figured this was the best business in the world to be in.

Later on, when I got more deeply into music, *Sgt. Pepper* was a break-through record for me. I must have listened to it several hundred times. What intrigued me was how totally musical every aspect of it was, especially Paul's melodic, fluid bass lines. When my band Talas was starting in the mid '70s, [the Beatles' tribute show] Beatlemania was big, and we used to play entire gigs of just Beatles tunes. I've learned so much from Paul about playing, writing, and playing and singing at the same time that I should probably start sending him checks.

Most bassists get into the flashy players, but I think the reason Paul is often overlooked is that what he was doing wasn't really obvious. It was so brilliantly woven into the context of the songs. One of my favorites is the bass line from 'Rain.' I still use it to test the low end of an amp. That Paul happens to play bass is a great boon to all of us, because he made us realize that there are no limitations to being a bass player."

~ Billy Sheehan

EIGHT

Creative Freedom
(1967)

"We're fed up with making soft music for soft people, and we're fed up with playing for them too."
~ John Lennon
(interview, 1967)

"We were fed up with being the Beatles. We really hated that fucking four little mop-top approach. We were not boys, we were men . . . and thought of ourselves as artists rather than just performers."
~ Paul McCartney
(Paul McCartney: Many Years From Now, 1998)

1967 in Review

1967 was another phenomenal year for the Beatles. This was the year they finally stayed home. And, free from the overwhelming burden of touring, they allowed themselves to put all of their energies into making incredibly creative music. In making *Sgt. Pepper,* these four men worked together in a tight-knit creative fashion as they never had before and never would again.

As they worked for months on end creating their psychedelic, era-defining masterpiece, the rest of the world had just about given them up for dead. We Beatle fans—as well as the press—learned a hard lesson during this period: we were going to have to wait for new music. What many of us discovered was that these endless months between albums caused *Sgt. Pepper* to feel more important when it made it into the stores at last. How many of us can forget seeing the cover of *Sgt. Pepper* in the shelves of the music store for the first time?

And that cover! It was as powerful as the music inside.

In 1967 they released "Strawberry Fields Forever" / "Penny Lane," possibly the best pop single ever made. Later that year they released *Sgt. Peppers Lonely Hearts Club Band*, the defining voice of the summer of 1967. Then, for good measure, they released "All You Need Is Love" recorded live with the Beatles representing England in the first ever satellite-driven world-wide tv show, watched by 350 million people. All this and these guys were all in their early (George was just 23) to mid twenties.

But, once those three epics had been released, an event occurred that is as controversial as it was tragic. In August, Brian Epstein, the man who had shaped the Beatles into the image that we all fell in love with, the man who handled all of their business affairs, died.

What were they going to do now? The Beatles had become more than massive by the late summer of 1967, able to get into any place they wanted just by being themselves, and for once they had the time to reflect on it. From now on, they would manage themselves. They would do everything.

The initial result: the TV special and EP, *Magical Mystery Tour*, released late in the year. They did everything in making this movie: they were the writers, producers, directors, chief actors and *everything* else (super italics on the *everything*). Having been sheltered from this side of things for so long, little did they know that there were business issues that had to be dealt with. What? You have to book a movie studio in advance? It takes longer than a week to edit a movie? Having a script is actually helpful? *Magical Mystery Tour* was finally shown in England on Boxing Day (the day after Christmas). And it was hated, lambasted by the press and public. For the first time, the Beatles crashed to earth, and you'd think they'd have learned that they weren't businessmen. It was a lesson not learned. In 1967, they soared to their highest of highs and landed with their lowest of lows.

Paul McCartney's Bass Playing in 1967

As McCartney had become the man in charge of the Beatles' studio by 1967, he was able to direct, in general, the way the songs were recorded. He clearly sensed that there was a revolution in pop music in terms of what the bass guitar could do for a record. He reinvented his playing style for the *Sgt. Pepper* sessions. Dynamic and driven in 1966, he was now melodic and thoughtful in his approach.

Being the main musical force, he was able to take a revolutionary liberty in the recording of the music. The Beatles began making their basic tracks lacking the bass. Then Paul would listen to the tracks on his own and develop the bass line from his imagination, without any limitations.

> "On *Pepper* we were using the luxury of utilizing one track for bass overdub on some of the things . . . We used to stay behind after the sessions, and Paul would dub all the bass on. I used to use a valve C12 microphone on Paul's amp, sometimes on figure eight, and sometimes positioned up to eight feet away. Direct injection wasn't used on the guitars until *Abbey Road* "
> ~ Geoff Emerick (1st recording engineer)
> (*The Beatles Recording Sessions*, 1990)

As the group dynamics allowed for more and more experimentation, Paul's bass playing became more innovative.

McCartney: It was much better for me to work out the bass later, you know.

Martin: I think it made it better.

McCartney: Yeah, I think it was . . . but the good thing about doing it later is it allowed me to get melodic bass lines.

Martin: All the bass lines were always very interesting.
McCartney: On this album I think that was one of the reasons.

~ Paul McCartney and George Martin
(*The Making of Sgt. Pepper. A Really Useful Group*, 1992)

Perhaps never before had a bass player in a band of such high visibility been given such leverage and time to come up with exactly the right thing to play on each song.

"As time went on, I began to realize you didn't have to just play the root notes. If it was C,F,G, then it was normally C,F,G that I played. But I started to realize you could be pulling on the G, or just stay on the C when it went into F. And then I took it beyond that. I thought, well, if you can do that, what else could you do, how much further could you take it? You might even be able to play notes that aren't in the chord. I just started to experiment."

~ Paul McCartney
(*Paul McCartney – Bass Master - Playing the Great Beatles Basslines*, 2006)

"Strawberry Fields Forever" (Single)
"Penny Lane" (B-side)
(Released February 17, 1967)

I throw down the gauntlet and ask anyone to name a better, more powerful single in the history of pop/rock music than "Strawberry Fields Forever" / "Penny Lane."

"Strawberry Fields Forever"

From Paul McCartney's standpoint, "Strawberry Fields Forever" was about far more than bass playing. Written by John Lennon while he was in Spain filming his role for the movie *How I Won the War* (starring the same Michael Crawford who was the most famous phantom of the opera of them all), McCartney's influence on the song becomes clear when listening to the steps of its development. Starting out as a melodic, strangely shaped ballad, it's Paul who is playing the flute tone on the Melotron that opens the track and guides us through the first minute.

The bass is vintage '66/'67, melodic and yet on beat. There is a chapter, towards the end of this book, on the mammoth recording of this song.

"Penny Lane"

If forced to choose my favorite pop song of all, it would be "Penny Lane." It comes gift-wrapped as a serious, very clean sounding, pop song. A more than casual listen, however, reveals a lot of little studio trickery. The song's moods are set, one after the other, by the bass and piano. Beneath the flourishes of brass, bells, vocals and all else, the beat drives on with the bass and piano firmly at the controls. There was a lot of effort put into getting the piano sound just right, and it was overdubbed many times by both John and Paul.

The interplay between the piano and bass is intriguing. At the beginning of the verses, the bass provides a happy-go-lucky feel, walking from chord to chord while the piano—with its well thought out inversions—provides an air of almost orchestral class. The two instruments are not necessarily at odds with each other, but the difference is interesting. It's where they come together that is really striking.

At the point where the word "know" is sung in the first verse, the chord shifts to a Gm. The bass stops its jaunty walk and falls in line with the piano. This chord change causes one of the biggest mood shifts of any Beatle song. While, a moment ago, we had been walking along Penny Lane on a bright and sunny day, greeting passers-by, suddenly a cloud has passed over the sun. We see deviousness in the people, and what's up with that weird barber? It's not until the "Stop and say hello" that the sun seems to re-appear.

There is a lesson for us here. One of the most effective things that can be done in a performance is to begin something and then suddenly remove it. In this case, it is the jaunty bass walk. Its removal, along with the major to minor shift and particularly emphatic striking of the piano chords, was all it took to do it.

"Penny Lane" has so much going on: so much musicianship, so much gamesmanship with the arrangement and yet it is all done under cover of a cool exterior.

Talk about lessons. The Beatles were learning them and using them to excellent advantage.

Did You Hear That?!

At 2:06, right when Paul sings the word "trim," the electric bass is dropped out and there is one note of a stand-up bass.

"I loved your assessment of 'Penny Lane'; for me it is simply the greatest single ever (because of 'Strawberry Fields'). Can I just say that in 'Penny Lane,' the tone of the bass from the first note got to me, and its first descending half dozen notes are like something an orchestral bass would do. Most bass players never achieve anything like this energy, joy and inventiveness in a lifetime. McCartney did it over and over, but never better (For No One is always very orchestral in its approach). The bass bubbles and pops around into and out of the song, much like the person in the song is popping in and out of the shops and locations in 'Penny Lane.' I understand that the bass was one of the last parts recorded (possibly before the piccolo trumpet, but after the 'rhythm' section had been laid down), so it is really freed from the kind of role Donald Dunn uses to ground the song in the root note of each chord (what a genius he is, too!). In fact, in this song, McCartney doesn't seem to be thinking chordally, the way guitarists do—he's just accentuating and underpinning the melody."

~ Richard Goodwin

(*email*, 2012)

"On first listen, the vocals are the only standout on this song. Listening again, it's almost impossible to not hear the unconventional interval leaps and melodic lines from McCartney. This one doesn't get mentioned enough in the context of McCartney's contribution to bass. Put the headphones on and hear it again for the first time."

~ John Martin

(email, 2008)

Sgt. Pepper's Lonely Hearts Club Band (LP)
(commonly known as *Sgt. Pepper*)

Released
June 1, 1967

Cover Notes

The *Sgt. Pepper* cover is one of the most widely imitated of all time, second maybe only to *Abbey Road*. The art-director was Robert Fraser. The designers were Peter Blake and Jann Haworth. It was photographed by Michael Cooper.

Each of the Beatles submitted a list of characters they would like to have on the cover with them. The cover, unsurprisingly, won a Grammy award.

Peter Blake said, "It was very mysterious. It was like a game or quiz to see if you could spot who everyone was, but of course nobody could. I think a kind of cult grew up around it."

Peak Position
Number 1

Number of Weeks on the Chart
175 (over 3 years!)

Sgt. Pepper's Lonely Hearts Club Band (LP)
(commonly known as *Sgt. Pepper*)

Number of Days in the Studio
55

This was a huge question in the world press as the Beatles spent months recording the album. It was assumed that either the Beatles had dried up or had broken up.

First Song Recorded for the Album
"Strawberry Fields Forever" on November 24, 1966

Yet another John Lennon classic to start things off.

The album was recorded between December 6, 1966 and April 3, 1967. The first song recorded for what was to become *Sgt. Pepper's Lonely Hearts Club Band* was John's new song, "Strawberry Fields Forever."

1967 seemed to be the year of hope. A time when "the people" could change the world for the better. Sad to say it all seems so trite now, but peace and love were more than words for the generation. Remember Wavy Gravy, the guy in Woodstock who said "What we have in mind today is breakfast in bed for 400,000!"

> **"I recall feeling that extraordinary things were about to happen and it felt as if we were at the centre of things, making them happen."**
> ~ Wavy Gravy
> (*It Was Twenty Years Ago Today,* 1987)

Sgt. Pepper was created to be a musical masterpiece, but somehow, without intention, it heralded that change in the world. It had a *huge* cultural impact, and e*veryone* was playing it that year. The Beatles were not impressed with the "hippie" reaction. George Harrison (along with his wife Pattie and Derek Taylor) flew to California and paid a memorable visit to San Francisco's Golden Gate park during the summer, hoping to find the real hippie story. He had hoped they would be a bunch of nice young people. Instead, he found them to be "hideous, spotty teenagers." In the *Anthology* videos, McCartney said that he felt that '67 being the "summer of love" was a bit soft.

Enough of culture. Back to the music, then, folks. Come along, everyone, no crowding. There are seats for everyone. Mind the gap.

"It's been 25 years now since it's been issued, and there aren't many records which really last in the memory for a quarter of a century. It evoked the spirit of the age. It was the turning point, something that will stand the test of time as a valid art form: sculpture in music."

~ George Martin

(*It Was Twenty Years Ago Today*, 1987)

"I remember track by track it was very exciting at that time. Nothing like that had ever been . . . We spent hours getting drum, bass and guitar sounds, then balancing them and then doing the take. That was, in effect, a backing track and then we later added overdubs."

~ George Harrison

(*It Was Twenty Years Ago Today*, 1987)

"That's probably the big difference is that people played it a bit safe in popular music. But I think that's when we suddenly realized that you didn't have to. . . . I think the big influence was *Pet Sounds* by the Beach Boys. That album just flipped me out. I thought, this is the album of all time. What the hell are we going to do? My ideas took off from that standard."

~ Paul McCartney

(*Musician Magazine*, 1980)

"It was colorful and it was peace and it was love and it was music.

With *Sgt. Pepper*, I felt more like a session man because we were interested in making an album with strings and brass and parts. Everyone says that record is a classic, but it's not my favorite album."

~ Ringo Starr

(*The Beatles Anthology video*, 1996)

"*Sgt. Pepper* is called the first concept album, but it doesn't go anywhere. All of my contributions to the album have absolutely nothing to do with this idea of *Sgt. Pepper* and his band; but it works because we said it worked."

~ John Lennon

(*The Playboy Interviews With John Lennon and Yoko Ono*, 1981)

"I was in a real big depression in [*Sgt.*] *Pepper*, and I know that Paul wasn't at the time. He was feeling full of confidence. I was going through murder."

~ John Lennon

(*Interview with Barry Miles*, 1969)

"We knew it was something special because the Beatles would ask other artists who were recording in the EMI studio complex to come in and listen to some tracks that we'd finished. Richard Lush, who was my assistant, and the boys were watching for their facial expressions. They were just amazed at what they were hearing because all those tracks were just mind blowing. No one had ever heard anything like these tracks, especially 'A Day in the Life.' We knew it was special but we never knew it would develop into what it developed into."

~ Geoff Emerick (1st recording engineer)

(*Lunchtime with Ira*, 2009)

"They were workaholics . . . They took a lot longer than before because they weren't on the road."

~ Neil Aspinal

(*It Was Twenty Years Ago Today*, 1987)

"The mirror of a culture. Everybody was primed to say, 'What's next?'—and wow, did they deliver."

~ James Taylor

(*interview*)

"*Sgt. Pepper* has been named on many lists of the best rock albums. In 1997 *Sgt. Pepper* was named the number one greatest album of all time in a 'Music of the Millennium' poll conducted by HMV, Channel 4, *The Guardian* and Classic FM. In 1998 Q magazine readers placed it at number seven, while in 2003 the TV network VH1 placed it at number 10. In 2005, the album was ranked number 1 on *Rolling Stone* magazine's list of the 500 greatest albums of all time. The publisher called it 'the most important rock & roll album ever made . . . by the greatest rock & roll group of all time.'"

(*Wikipedia*)

My son Paul, born in 1981, had no choice. Sort of like how some Christian parents give their children no choice about religion, I gave him no choice about being a Beatles fan. He was indoctrinated in the crib.

"I was talking with a friend the other night. Somehow *Sgt Peppers* came up (I don't really roll with people where this comes up) and instantly remembering listening to that album every morning before school on the stereo you bought me and tricked me into helping put together (jk)(but that was funny). It was 2nd grade. I remember really putting in an effort to listening to every instrument, and the different things they were doing, and then some songs like 'Lucy in the Sky with Diamonds.'

And now that I'm older, realizing that my imagination was doing things with that song that older people were taking hallucinogens to try to recreate. Good times."
~ Paul Alstrand

(*email*, 2013)

There are moments of absolute clarity in all of our lives; a point in time when something monumental suddenly makes total sense. Here is a perfect example of that.

"While I was learning the newly released *Sgt. Pepper* bass lines note for note on my violin shaped Teisco, a door opened up . . . the whole album just opened up and every song and every bassline made perfect sense. At that point it was a matter of going back to the past albums and filling in the gaps and eagerly awaiting what the Beatles were going to do next. It was an exciting time."
~ Rick McLay

(*email*, 2007)

Not only has so much been written about this amazing album, but the words "so much has been written" have themselves been written hundreds of times. Where do you start? To begin with, the album was on the charts for 175 weeks. It was a certified, roaring monster of an album. It's sappy to say, but it defined a generation. From the opening audience buzz to the resounding final chord of "A Day in the Life," it was monumental in its recording techniques (what album had songs go from one right into another before?), song-writing, and performance.

Notes on the Bass Playing on Sgt. Pepper

Most of his bass playing on this album was not ensemble playing. In fact, most of the music on this album was not ensemble playing. The days of the four lads standing and playing music together had passed under the bridge and, with certain exceptions such as "Yer Blues," would stay under that bridge.

The touring, smiling and waving Beatles were no more. It was time to find something new and—fortunately for us—John Paul George and Ringo decided to find it together. They now had time to sit back and relax with no worries about playing huge noisy stadiums any more. The sessions that became *Sgt. Pepper* started off on an incredible note—not unlike *Revolver*—and McCartney was ready to establish new styles and sounds with his Rickenbacker bass. While his playing on 'Paperback Writer" (on *Revolver)* was aggressive and very rock oriented, *Sgt. Peppers* was different. The expression is cool, a bit laid back, but creative and completely different than anything yet done. With some exceptions (most notably the reprise of the theme) the playing is a bit disconnected from the rest of the band. There's a reason for that. Aside from the above mentioned recording technique of adding his parts last, he lived nearby and was usually first and generally last at the studio and had time to play with his bass parts.

> "I got into more melodic bass lines. In fact, some of the best-paced bass playing I ever did was at that time."
> ~ Paul McCartney
> (*Paul McCartney – Bass Master - Playing the Great Beatles Basslines*, 2006)

Here are some collective thoughts on various selected songs from the *Sgt. Pepper's Lonely Hearts Club Band* LP.

"With a Little Help from My Friends"

> "On first listen, the vocals are the only standout on this song. Listening again, it's almost impossible to not hear the unconventional interval leaps and melodic lines from McCartney. This one doesn't get mentioned enough in the context of McCartney's contribution to bass. Put the headphones on and hear it again for the first time."
> ~ John Martin
>
> (*email*, 2008)

"I think the remarkable thing is (as you already mentioned) that Paul is far more inventive on the songs he doesn't sing than on the ones he sings. On this one, the bass sounds guitar-like in the verses as he plays very high on his Rickenbacker with the string blocker and he develops another melody than the main one. He used to do such thing on the songs he didn't write, like 'Lucy in the Sky . . .' and 'Something' for example. But very rarely on his own compositions. You can notice too that he uses a lot, on this song, hammers and glissandos on the bassline."

~ Phillipe Zarview

(*email*, 2013)

"Lucy in the Sky with Diamonds"

"Lucy in the Sky With Diamonds" is a bona fide Lennon/McCartney song. John wrote the verses and needed a chorus. Paul supplied the chorus ("Lucy in the sky . . .") to Lennon's lyrics (taken from a drawing his son had brought home).

A song such as "Lucy" needs something right at the start to help whisk the listener away to the magic land in which it resides. The keyboard intro, apparently composed by John Lennon, is the *perfect* vehicle. It is simple and beautiful. Recorded on an organ, it evokes similar sensations to the celeste in Tchaikovsky's "Dance of the Sugar Plum Fairy." The intro, here, was played by Paul McCartney on a Lowry organ.

The sound of the instruments on this song all have a floating feel to them and the bass is no exception. This is another example of a Beatles song that has a bass line completely different from what one might expect, and yet fits perfectly. It doesn't anchor the song to the ground; that is a role that the bass seldom plays on this album. But somehow it does hold it to some floating anchor and is probably the representation of *Sgt. Pepper* style bass playing. If the song comes from a different place, as "Lucy" does, then why not anchor it in that place in a tricky, bizarre and different way?

"On 'Lucy in the Sky with Diamonds' for example, you could easily have had root notes, whereas I was running an independent melody through it, and that became my thing. It's really only a way of getting from C to F or whatever, but you get there in an interesting way. So once I got over the fact that I was lumbered with bass, I did get quite proud to be a bass player. It was all very exciting."

~ Paul McCartney

(*Paul McCartney – Bass Master - Playing the Great Beatles Basslines*, 2006)

The verses in John Lennon's melody tend to feature one repeated note, changing key for the second part of the verse (sub-chorus). Beneath this subtle and simple melody interesting things are happening. Though the root of the first part of the verse is in A, there is no real chord structure until the end of the verse ("girl with kaleidoscope eyes"). The key changes to Bb for the next section of the verse and the transition from this to the chorus is also interesting. Wanting the chorus to be in G, they simply caused the end of the sub-chorus to go to the II, C major, then to the III chord, D, which—you guessed it—is the fifth chord to the new key of G.

Clearly, the song goes from a dreamy, floating feel during Lennon's verses into a heavy, wide-awake chorus. The transition is helped along by a number of things. To end the first two verses, John sings the word "gone" with more power than previously done. The three drum beats (snare with tom beneath) are the wake-up call. For being such a far-out song, the chorus is almost rock standard—G C D. The first time through the "Lucy in the sky . . ." is John's voice alone. The second time adds tension by that good old John/Paul mixed voice, singing as one. On the third, Paul moves—with added tension—to the harmony. A close listening to the voices indicates that the vocals were recorded slow and sped up. Lest we forget one of the most basic alterations between verse and chorus, the band slides (by way of the drum fill) from 3/4 to 4/4.

The transition back to the dreamy verse is achieved only by singing a harmonized "ahhh" and adding a phase shift. Simple! And those are the major ingredients to creating what is probably the best—if not archetypical—psychedelic song ever.

"Getting Better"

The title was taken from Jimmy Nichol who toured as drummer with the Beatles briefly in 1964. When asked how things were going, he'd say "It's getting better."

Paul went for the heavy-ended bass feel on this song and got it. "Getting Better" sounds like it fits best on *Sgt. Pepper* because of the sounds employed by the Beatles. Yet, unlike some of it's album brethren, with a different style of recording, it could fit on many of their albums. A classic.

"Being for the Benefit of Mr. Kite!"

More inspired bass playing here. On the verses, the bass starts out as an almost typical one/five bass line, but by the end of the verse has transformed into a melody that counters Lennon's lead line. The bass, in fact, seems to counter the rest of the recording. The keyboards and drums stand on one side, plodding along beneath the vocals, with the bass on the other.

This entire song, perhaps more than any other song on the album, required a commitment to creating a strange, acid-like circus visual. Visual, because the song seems to be meant to evoke images of strange old-fashioned circuses as seen through the eyes of someone under the influence. There are merry-go-round sounds, organ grinding, bits of recorded tape tossed in the air and taped together in random sequence and a story line that is pure 1967 Lennon. Seemingly "normal' until you start looking under the covers.

Sad to say it is a song that was rarely talked about by the Beatles. But George Martin discusses it at length in his book *All You Need Is Ears*.

> "When we came to the middle section of the song, where
> 'Henry the Horse dances the waltz,' we obviously had to go in-
> to waltz-time, and John said he wanted the music to 'swirl up

and around,' to give it a circus atmosphere. . . . (after recording
the organ parts) even when we had done it this new way, it still
didn't sound quite right. I found the answer. I got together a lot
of recordings of old Victorian steam organs—the type you hear
playing on carousels at county fair. But I clearly couldn't use
even a snatch of any of them that would be identifiable."

~ George Martin

(*All You Need Is Ears*, 1994)

So the two of them took the tapes, cut them up, threw them in the
air, picked them up, and spliced them all together . . . order did not
matter—backwards, whatever.

"It was an unreal hotch-potch of sound, arrived at without
rhyme or reason; but when it was added as a background 'wash'
to the organ and harmonica track we had already made, it did
give an overall impression of being in a circus."

~ George Martin

(*The Making of Sgt. Pepper. A Really Useful Group*, 1992)

"Lovely Rita"

McCartney is a clever lad when he picks up a bass guitar. On "Lovely
Rita," right from the start he moves the song with it. Under the opening vocals his bass is moving as in a dance. During verses he is foot
stepping in staccato eight-notes with the odd sustained note thrown in.

He shows here, once again, the benefit of having his bass part laid
down after most of the other instruments. He dances throughout the
song and when it comes back to the backing vocals (as in the introduction) he no longer does the swing line he did at the start. The bass
changes all the way through the song. It's a continuous, but ever changing dance.

"Perhaps not the most elaborate or technically difficult bass-line, but try listening to the song without the bass—the bass transforms it into a different song entirely."

~ Sue Smith

(*email*, 2009)

Did You Hear That?!

Listen to the outro of "Lovely Rita . . ." (from 2:10 to 2:55). Everything falls into an entirely different groove. The piano is funky and the bass is different than anything he's ever done. He plays a weird little line that repeats, measures after measure, eight times. To fully understand what was happening in this section, I sat down one day and listened to the section sixteen times in a row. It's difficult, at times, to listen to the section timed parts all together. The brain (my brain anyway) wants to listen to individual parts. It was only after repeated listenings that I began to notice the incredible interplay between the drums, bass and piano. Each instrument in no way anticpates the other and yet they all work as a unit. All of this may well be something you've never noticed because you're attention is taken by the piano and the strange breathing sounds (sounds like John).

One thing that makes this section all the more interesting is that the bass part was played improvisationally all through the song and then suddenly locked down into this ever-repeating, unexpected riff. An amazing little gem that has been overlooked throughout the years.

What about Ringo?

"Ringo throws together a very solid backbeat for 'Lovely Rita' with some subtle touches - notice how he lags behind the beat in the verses, then leans ahead of it during the last two bars into the refrain. And he shows admirable restraint during the

freak-out section at the end—other drummers would have
been all over the kit, but by sticking to the beat he allows this
regrettable exercise to pass without too much abuse of the ear-
drums."

(*Steve and Dennis and Abe's Record Reviews*, 2013)

"Within You Without You"

George Harrison's original contribution to *Sgt. Pepper* was "It's Only A
Northern Song." George Martin, mindful of the great contributions of
John Lennon and Paul McCartney, asked Harrison to go back and
come back with something stronger. He made that happen with "Within You Without You." Recording for one of his most memorable songs
began on March 15th.

"'Within You Without You' was a great track. The tabla had
never been recorded the way we did it. Everyone was amazed

when they first heard a tabla recorded that closely, with the texture and lovely low resonances."

~ Geoff Emerick

(*The Beatles Recording Sessions*, 1990)

"To me, 'Within You Without You' is a song that has grown in
stature, and has emerged as a masterpiece (though one of
many) in the Beatles catalogue. For George Harrison to have
absorbed Indian and eastern religion and culture at such a
young age, and write a song that espouses its philosophies and
spiritual themes so well was extraordinary. Imagine the wisdom
of someone then 24 years old, who had the world at his feet
able to see the reality 'and to see you're really only very small'—
it's one of numerous examples in which the Beatles proved
they were wise beyond their years. George wrote the song at
Klaus Voorman's home in London while playing a pedal harmonium. The song was brilliantly arranged using a variety of
Indian instruments, and George Martin was to say that he

worked closely with George Harrison on the scoring of the song. He was introduced to the dilruba, an Indian violin, which has a lot of sliding techniques when using it, and George (Martin) tried to get the string players (violinists, cellists) to sound like the Indian musicians in the bending of the notes. Simply a brilliant song and recording."

~ Ken Michaels (*Every Little Thing* radio show host)

(*email*, 2013)

"Fixing a Hole"

On February 9, the Beatles recorded the first session for EMI at a studio other than Abbey Road—Regent Sound in London. "Fixing a Hole" was begun there that day. The Beatles stepped out of their normal recording style, laying down rhythm tracks and vocals simultaneously. The tape of the second take from that day was brought to EMI and used as the basis for the final recording. Who actually played the harpsichord is lost to history, but a good guess would be George Martin himself.

As for the bass, this is another perfect example of "not playing" to perfection. The bass line continues to seem to go somewhere and then suddenly stops. Very untypical of a bass line, and very reflective of the mood of the song.

"Good Morning Good Morning"

The inspiration for this song was a Kellog's Corn Flakes® TV commercial, "Good morning, good morning, the best to you each morning" He also mentions "time for tea and Meet the Wife," a TV show. John's formula is simple: take mundane things and write great songs about them. As for the strange-yet-natural odd time signatures, George Martin is convinced that Lennon had no idea. For example, for the sub-chorus ("nothing has changed it's still the same, I've got nothing to say but it's okay"), the bars count as 3/4 2/4 4/4 2/4 and 4/4 . . . and it sounds perfectly natural.

On this song, Paul and Ringo began using a one beat technique that they kept in their repertoire through *Abbey Road*. At the end of the

verses, they add an exclamation point by slamming the beat home together, the bass starting at one note and sliding downward. In fact, the
whole song showcases the rhythm section to great effect. The song
opens with a galloping rhythm and there are sections in the song where
Ringo's bass drumming rolls at a super-fast rate.

If you'd like to hear how good Paul and Ringo were on "Good
Morning Good Morning," give a listen to the version that was included
on *The Beatles Anthology 2.* The horns have been removed and the instruments you hear are Ringo, Paul and Lennon's smashmouth guitar.
This is the Beatles rock and roll rhythm section at its best. I like it better than the released version, but then of course I would: I'm a bass
player. Say no more. Ringo SHINES!

> "'Good Morning Good Morning' is another drummer's head-
> ache—it varies between 4/4 and 6/4 (or it's in 5/5), but he
> smoothes out the rhythm by sticking to a strident soul-style 4-
> to-the-bar pattern. When he switches to the hi-hat during the
> bridge it's a nice way to lighten the atmosphere."
>
> *(Steve and Dennis and Abe's Record Reviews,* 2013)

And the ending, for the trivia buffs out there, includes all animals
who are capable of devouring or frightening the one before it (at least
that was the original idea) . . . rooster, chick, cat meow right into a
barking dog, pack of dogs, horse, goat, lion, pack of hunting dogs with
horn, whinnying horse, hunting dogs again who fade nicely into the
famous clucking chicken who whoops right into the first guitar note
of the *Sgt. Pepper* reprise. John's idea. Weird. Off the wall. Somehow
perfect.

"Sgt. Pepper's Lonely Hearts Club Band (Reprise)"

There's one of my all-time favorite Beatles' tracks. Put that reprise on
with the bass turned up all the way. There's Paul counting off . . .
there's the four bars of drumming, and then on the final eighth note of
the fourth measure, Paul gives the intro note and slams it into gear.

From there, it's full speed ahead and rock solid, and John must have been proud. McCartney's playing on this song is actually a portent of styles to come. When the beat needed to be laid down, McCartney did it.

Unfortunately, the song comes and goes so fast. Thanks to the advent of the CD, however, it's very easy to start the song over right up to the point where the instruments come in, time after time. According to George Martin in his book *With A Little Help From My Friends*, the idea for a reprise was Neil Aspinall's idea. They worked hard on making it sound live and it is incredibly live sounding, and very powerful.

"A Day in the Life"

> "'A Day in the Life'—that was something. I dug it. It was a good piece of work between Paul and me. I had the 'I read the news today' bit, and it turned Paul on. Now and then we really turn each other on with a bit of song, and he just said 'yeah'— bang, bang, like that. It just sort of happened beautifully."
>
> ~ John Lennon
>
> (*Rolling Stone*, 1971)

I've heard this called a "museum piece" lately. Horrifying. Take some time to reconsider this song. If you were not around in 1967, try to put it into the context of the time. If it is somehow possible, listen to the song against the backdrop of what sort of music was out on the charts in mid-summer of 1967. If you were around, try to remember how you felt when you first heard it. "A Day in the Life" may be *the* most stunning song ever released by anybody.

For me, when I heard the song, even at 12 years old I recall coming to the conclusion that the Beatles had made their last album. How could they possibly make anything to follow this?

McCartney plays bass and piano on the track (and conducted the orchestra!). Having heard it for so many years it has become normal, the way bass and piano should be played against Lennon's acoustic guitar. But, as should often be done when considering parts to songs, think about what you'd do if the guitar player in your band played the song. What would you have come up with? McCartney's piano playing, especially, is the perfect complement to the song. It builds and drops, goes loud and goes soft, always there, sometimes in the background and sometimes leading the way, especially at the end when the piano chords lead the way to the final orchestral buildup.

The bass is creative and moving. Like the piano, it floats in and out of the consciousness of the listener. Especially when it plays against those incredible, heavily reverberated tom parts that Ringo elected to play. Almost monstrous, they're fully *in* the consciousness of the listener every time. It was one of those songs, as did the entire album, that required something different, something more, something that added to the power of the track. Ringo's tom work is a huge part of why "A Day in the Life" is such a monumental recording.

"Well I think he is vastly underrated. The drum fills on 'A Day in the Life' are in fact very, very complex things. You know you could take a great drummer from today and say 'I want it like that' and they really wouldn't know what to do."

~ Phil Collins

(*The Making of Sgt. Pepper. A Really Useful Group*, 1992)

"On 'A Day in the Life' he breaks every convention of drumming, in that his lines serve no rhythmic purpose whatever— they're merely obbligatos designed to play against the melody. It's either insane or brilliant, but this time it works in spades. The fills themselves are quirky in their timing, leaving lots of spaces between the notes, then a flurry of tom hits. The beauty of his new calfskin heads is expressed particularly well here."

(*Steve and Dennis and Abe's Record Reviews*, 2013)

The Orchestral Climax

Recorded on February 10, 1967, a whole book could be written about the recording of the amazing orchestral climax of "A Day in the Life."

> "For the 'I'd love to turn you onnnn' bit, I used cellos and violas. I had them playing those two notes that echo John's voice. However, instead of fingering their instruments, which would produce crisp notes, I got them to slide their fingers up and down the frets, building in intensity until the start of the orchestral climax.
>
> The climax is something else again. What I did there was to write, at the beginning of the twenty-four bars, the lowest possible note for each of the instruments in the orchestra. At the end of the twenty-four bars, with reference points to tell them roughly what note they should have reached during the bar."
>
> ~ George Martin
>
> (*All You Need Is Ears,* 1994)

Martin and McCartney did not want them to play smoothly together. It was difficult at first to get these trained musicians to play separately from the others, especially the violins who are so used to matching each other.

> "How they got there was up to them, but it all resulted in a crazy crescendo. It was interesting because the trumpet players, always famous for their fondness for lubricating substances, didn't care, so they'd be there at the note ahead of everyone. The strings all watched each other like sheep. You listen to those trumpets. They're just freaking out."
>
> ~ Paul McCartney
>
> (*It Was Twenty Years Ago Today,* 1987)

The Beatles made a party of the recording of the orchestral climax. All of the musicians were handed masks, gorilla paws, etc, to give it a carnival atmosphere. Many of their friends were invited, and this was the first inkling to anybody outside of the Beatles' circle as to what they were up to. A carefully thought out maneuver. To those who witnessed the recording of that climactic orchestration, some felt that there was no way they could ever come close to creating what the Beatles had. But there was a final, crashing moment to consider before the album could close.

> "One part of me said, 'We're being a bit self-indulgent . . .' and the other part of me said, 'It's bloody marvelous. I think it's fantastic.'"
>
> ~ George Martin
>
> *(All You Need Is Ears,* 1994)

The Final Chord

It was not known at the time of the orchestral recording how the song would end. On that evening, a group of musicians hummed the final note: a purposeful letdown. The idea was quickly scrapped. How could they follow the incredible climax of the orchestra? On February 22, John, Paul and Ringo (on the same piano) and Mal Evans sat at 3 pianos and, simultaneously hit an E Major.

> "It took nine takes to perfect because the four players were rarely able to hit the keys at precisely the same time . . . It was take nine that was considered 'best' so it was overdubbed three more times, with George Martin compounding the sound further on a harmonium, until all four tracks of the tape were full. The resultant wall of sound, which lasted for 53 ½ seconds was the perfect ending."
>
> ~ Geoff Emerick
>
> *(The Beatles Recording Sessions,* 1990)

And it was the perfect ending to an album for the ages.

Sgt. Pepper's Lonely Hearts Club Band, due to a clause in the Beatles new contract, was not modified for the American market.

It was released on June 1st in England and June 2nd in America.

"Three bars of "A Day in the Life" still sustain me, rejuvenate me, inflame my senses and sensibilities."

~ Leonard Bernstein

(*The Beatles,* 1979)

"I was reading the paper one day and noticed two stories. One was about the Guinness heir who killed himself in a car. That was the main headline story. He died in London in a car crash. On the next page was a story about four thousand potholes in the streets of Blackburn, Lancashire, that needed to be filled. Paul's contribution was the beautiful little lick in the song, 'I'd love to turn you on,' that he'd had floating around in his head and couldn't use. I thought it was a damn good piece of work."

~ John Lennon

(*The Playboy Interviews With John Lennon and Yoko Ono,* 1981)

"The verse about the politician blowing his mind out in a car we wrote together. It has been attributed to Tara Browne, the Guinness heir, which I don't believe is the case, certainly as were were writing it, I was not attributing it to Tara in my head. In John's head it might have been. In my head I was imagining a politician bombed out on drugs who'd stopped at some traffic lights and didn't notice that the lights had changed. The 'blew his mind' was purely a drugs reference, nothing to do with a car crash."

~ Paul McCartney

(*Paul McCartney: Many Years From Now,* 1998)

Did You Hear That?!

There are a lot of little things in this song that are audible if you listen to each side of the stereo separately. My favorite little piece is barely heard over the orchestration. It's a spooky little part that happens at 3:02, you can hear what sounds like an owl . . . wayyyy in the background, hooting twice. The only problem is that I seem to be the only one who can hear it.

And, by the way, who do you think it is that is singing that part? For years I thought it was John. Now, after listening very carefully, I hear it being Paul.

More Notes on the Bass on Sgt. Pepper

"Once you realized the control you had over the band, you were in control. They can't go anywhere, man. Ha! Power! I started to identify with other bass players and talk bass with the guys in the bands . . . So I was very proud of being the bass player. As it went on and got into the melodic thing, that was probably the peak of my interest."

~ Paul McCartney

(*Paul McCartney – Bass Master - Playing the Great Beatles Basslines*, 2006)

Yes, the bass style on the album is a very cool Paul McCartney, poised and confident. The judgment on whether it was his top stuff is completely up to the listener. It certainly was revolutionary. It certainly fit the music and that's the main thing. In the author's opinion, it's his most creative and melodic, but not his most influential. That was yet to come.

The Role of the Producer

The quotes from all but John Lennon are taken from the TV special *The Making of Sgt. Pepper. A Really Useful Group* (1992). Interestingly, all of the Beatles seemed to want to talk about the early years with Martin. But it's in the later years where Martin made an even more indelible stamp. He knew when to back away, and he knew how to score for them.

"The role of the producer had changed over the years. When we started in 1962, my job was really an organizer, to get them into some kind of shape, make sure they were tidy in the studio. Musically, I mean. Gradually, that changed. By the time Pepper had come along, I suppose I was a realizer of their ideas so that if John wanted something really weird, I had to try to provide it for him. Or if Paul wanted some extraordinary orchestration, I had to try to find out what he wanted."
~ George Martin

"[in the early days] he would translate . . . if Paul wanted to use violins he would translate it for him. Like 'In My Life' there is an Elizabethan Piano solo in it, so he would do things like that. We would say 'play like Bach' or something . . . He helped us develop a language, to talk to musicians."
~ John Lennon
(*Rolling Stone Interview,* 1971)

"What I think his great skill THEN was, was to allow us to do what we wanted. So his role changed from really deciding what was done to allowing us to do it."
~ Paul McCartney

"I think the role with George became easier because at first to us we were kind of frightened because we were nervous kids and he was like this big school-teacher sort of person who we had to find and have a relationship with."
~ George Harrison

"George was like the big cheese. He would come in as the producer. We were all a little, not afraid, but we knew he was The
Man. And he was very good. And he was very humorous so
that's how George really got into our good books because we
were very tight . . . very seldom did we let anybody in."

~ Ringo Starr

"And I think we just grew through those years together, him as
the straight man and us as the loonies. He was always there to
interpret our strangeness."

~ George Harrison

Sgt. Pepper's Influence

Talk about influence . . . suddenly, every album—even bubble gummy
pop albums—had to have a psychedelic cover (or sleeve, if you please)
with the members wearing hippie clothes. Thinking back, almost all
music had to have psychedelic undertones, overtones, incomprehensible words ("*Incense and Peppermint*") and the players had to look
much more serious when on TV.

The dichotomy is that *Sgt. Pepper* chiefly heralded those things and
yet was not really much of those things. The sleeve was different, but
not the psychedelia that permeated later albums. The lyrics were not
incomprehensible, at least in retrospect, but in some cases presented in
a very strange way. This album influenced almost everything about the
entire music industry for about a year, but the Beatles were used to
that, having done the same thing in January of 1964.

Sgt. Pepper's Lonely Hearts Club Band
(track listing)

Side One	Side Two
1. "Sgt. Pepper's Lonely Hearts Club Band"	1. "Within You Without You"
2. "With a Little Help from My Friends"	2. "When I'm Sixty-Four"
3. "Lucy in the Sky with Diamonds"	3. "Lovely Rita"
4. "Getting Better"	4. "Good Morning Good Morning"
5. "Fixing a Hole"	5. "Sgt. Pepper's Lonely Hearts Club Band (reprise)"
6. "She's Leaving Home"	6. "A Day in the Life"
7. "Being for the Benefit of Mr. Kite!"	

For once, the American album was "virtually" the same as it's British counterpart, a first for Capitol Records. The album was released on June 1st, 1967 in the UK and June 2nd 1967 in America. There was one difference between the two. At the very end of the UK version, in the runout groove, there is heard some Beatle gibberish. Capitol disdained this. (By the way, if you get a chance to hear the bit of gibberish backwards you might be surprised at what they say they'll do to you like Superman.) All in chance, claims engineer Geoff Emerick.

"All You Need Is Love" (Single)
"Baby, You're a Rich Man" (B-side)
(Released July 7, 1967)

Throughout their years, the Beatles shrugged their collective shoulder to pressure, even on a world-wide scale. It was time to come through with a song that would represent their homeland to the planet and John Lennon came up with an anthem. Not for the first time, the recording owes a lot to the arrangement of George Martin. From the brassy catchy opening intro to "La Marseillaise" (there's some irony in using this song to open "All You Need Is Love" as it was the rallying song of the French Revolution and was so named because it was first sung on the streets by troops from Marseille) through the interesting cello patterns to "Greensleeves" a Bach two-part invention and the introduction to Glenn Miller's arrangement of "In The Mood."

But the underlying song was complex (weren't they all?). The verse itself follows a pattern, bar by bar, of 7/4 (played as 4/4 3/4) 7/4 4/4 4/4 7/4. Lennon always claimed that he was unaware of his strange time signatures (as in "Good Morning Good Morning") but in this case you have to wonder how he could create something that complex without *some* idea. The Beatles, as always, were casual about the fluctuating time signatures.

Another Mystery to Solve

"We just put a track down. Because I knew the chords I played it on whatever it was, harpsichord. George played a violin because we felt like doing it like that and Paul played a double bass. And they can't play them, so we got some nice little noises coming out. It sounded like an orchestra, but it's just them two playing the violin and that. So then we thought, 'Ah, well, we'll have some more orchestra around this little freaky orchestra that we've got.' But there was no perception of how it sounded at the end until they did it that day, until the rehearsal. It still sounded a bit strange then.**"**

~ John Lennon

(*The Beatles Anthology video*, 1996)

As Lennon correctly remembered, George played a violin and Paul an upright double bass on the original track. Lewisohn shows that McCartney recorded another bass track on a later date but is not clear which was used in the final mix. So just which bass was used then?

The bass on the record sounds a bit like a double bass but has the feel at times of an electric bass. No answer there. Discovery! You can hear the original instrumentation at the start of their spot of the *Our World* telecast. With no orchestration added yet, you can clearly hear Harrison fumbling on the violin as well as McCartney's double bass which, tonally, is very much like the record including similar slides. However, the patterns played are different. In the end, we can only guess and it's mine that the finished song has Paul McCartney playing a double bass.

> "The BBC had suggested the idea of using new satellite relays to connect the national television networks of countries across the world, to make a live link-up on a scale previously unknown. The Beatles were the natural choice to represent Britain, and they decided to compose a new song especially for the broadcast."
>
> (*beatlesbible.com*, 2009)

> "We were big enough to command an audience of that size, and it was for love. It was for love and bloody peace. It was a fabulous time. I even get excited now when I think about it."
>
> ~ John Lennon
>
> (*The Beatles Anthology video*, 1996)

> "Lennon wrote this as a continuation of the idea he was trying to express in his 1965 song The Word. He was fascinated by how slogans effect the masses and was trying to capture the same essence as songs like 'We Shall Overcome.'"
>
> ~ Joel Benjamin
>
> (*Beatle Song Profiles*, 2010)

"All You Need Is Love" represents the pinnacle of the Beatles unquestioned and (seemingly) uncompromisable status as the most famous group that ever existed. The sheer audacity of them taking on the challenge (apparently in stride) of representing Britain to the entire world for the first ever "live world-wide broadcast" and then coming through with nothing short of a full scale anthem and doing it without breaking a sweat . . . well, it's just mind blowing to me. The show happened just a few weeks after *Sgt. Pepper* was released, so their confidence was at an all-time high.

If you watch the film of their performance, you can see how cool they are about the whole thing. John is chewing gum and sitting on a stool singing the song to the world.

"When John was repeating love is all you need over and over, and then Paul called out 'all together now,' pop music never had a finer moment."
                              ~ Derek Taylor
                              (*It Was Twenty Years Ago Today*, 1987)

"It was not until 1983 and the publication of the book *John Lennon: In My Life* that it was revealed that John Lennon was the primary composer of the song. It is typical of Lennon: Three long notes ('love—love—love') and the rise of excitement with at first speaking, then recital, then singing, then the climax and finally the redemption. This as opposed to McCartney's conventional verse, verse, middle part, verse or A, A, B, A. Lennon felt that a good song must have a rise of excitement, climax and redeeming."
                              ~ Johan Cavalli
                              (*Beatle Song Profiles*, 2010)

It occurs to me that the Beatles had jumped so many walls and scaled so many world-wide mountains that nothing could faze them. But, it's the flip side of this song that has the killer bass playing on it so let us not tarry!

"Baby You're a Rich Man"

As far as Beatles' songs go, "Baby You're a Rich Man" is a forgotten piece. And yet it is to me one of their best ever songs. The vocals, melody, the strange lyrics, the weird instrumentation and fantastic low-end bass guitar all come together to make a fantastic song whose chief crime was that it was relegated to the B-side of their monumental "All You Need Is Love." On May 11, 1967, The Beatles started recording the song that brought the sonic boom to bass playing: "Baby You're a

Rich Man." This was recorded at Olympic Sound Studios and engineered by Keith Grant. It may be one of the many that qualify for "the most unique Beatles' record." Its sound is almost communal, not so much a rock song but a rock congregation.

To hear the bass on this song in its full glory requires a fairly good speaker system, one that can handle extreme low end. Of all the Beatles' records, Grant got the deepest bass end. It resonated with pure sound, pure low end feel. With that sound, the bass became a powerful motivating force in the song. "Baby You're a Rich Man" along with "Everybody's Got Something to Hide Except Me and My Monkey," "Come Together" as well as all of the playing on *Wings Over America* stand as McCartney at my most favorite on the bass guitar.

> "Paul says his dad liked to play boogie-woogie on the piano, which is interesting when you look at Paul's own development into one of the world's great bass guitarists. In a boogie-woogie piano tune, the bass line, played by the left hand, produces a strong contrapuntal melody, rather than just a rhythmic thud. Paul's own bass guitar playing is of course the most melodic ever. He set a standard no one has ever reached. Sometimes he even composed songs around a bass line melody. Paul's bass line on 'Baby You're a Rich Man' is a good example of what he can do."
>
> ~ George Martin
> (*With a Little Help from My Friends*, 1995)

Magical Mystery Tour (EP)

Released
December 8, 1967

Peak Position
Number 1

Number of Weeks on the Chart
91

Number of Days in the Studio
33

First Song Recorded for the Album
"Your Mother Should Know" on August 22, 1967

"*Magical Mystery Tour* was terribly badly organized and it's amazing that anything ever came out of it. They were into their random period—they said 'If Laurence Olivier walks in this room we'll record it and it'll be great.' It was chaotic, the coach tour itself was dreadful, apparently, but I didn't go on that. I tended to lay back on *Magical Mystery Tour* and let them have their head. Some of the sounds weren't very good. Some were brilliant but some were bloody awful. 'I Am the Walrus' was organized—it was organized chaos. I'm proud of that. But there was disorganized chaos that I'm not very proud of."
~ George Martin
(*The Beatles Recording Sessions*, 1990)

"There was something lacking about *Magical Mystery Tour*. It wasn't going to be another album, or another single, it was probably going to be a film. It was a funny period."
~ Geoff Emerick
(*The Beatles Recording Sessions*, 1990)

"Your Mother Should Know"

The Beatles were last in the studio on June 25th to record "All You Need Is Love" for the live satellite hookup. They had scaled the heights, had recorded another world-wide hit album (*Sgt. Pepper*) as a seemingly airtight unit. What could they possibly do now? And why would they want to jump right back into things?

John, George and Ringo were content to rest in their gardens. According to the other Beatles, McCartney was ever the driving force during the years 1966 and '67. He got them back into a new studio (Chappell Recording Studios in London) on August 22nd and 23rd to begin recording songs for their planned TV special *Magical Mystery Tour*.

The song they worked on was Paul's "Your Mother Should Know." It's been said that it is similar to "When I'm Sixty-Four," but if so it is only because it is one of those great old-style melodies that go well with a ukulele.

I include the song here to point out, not so much the tasteful bass playing (which it was), but the cleverness and subtlety of Paul's piano themes. Listen to the song with an ear towards the single note repetition he does with the left hand. It is incessant while it lasts, and builds tension in the song. The tension is released during the instrumental section.

This clever and effective subtlety was explored much further and deeper on side two of *Abbey Road* two years later. "Your Mother Should Know" is a beautiful song and it was the last Beatles song Brian Epstein ever heard them play.

The Beatles' manager did not attend too many recording sessions, especially in these later years.

The Death of Brian Epstein

"He [Brian Epstein] came in to hear the playbacks looking extremely down and in a bad mood. He just stood at the back of the room listening, not saying much."

~ John Timperley (1st engineer at Chappell Recording Studios)

(*The Beatles Recording Sessions, 1990*)

He was the man who brought us the Beatles. If Brian Epstein had not taken them on and believed in them, we might never have heard of them as a group. But he did take them on and made them a world-wide sensation that has never been and can never be equalled.

He died on August 27, 1967. More information and thoughts about him can be found in "1967 in Review" (see page 180). I'd just like to add "Thank you, Brian Epstein."

"I Am the Walrus"

After the death of Epstein, the Beatles made the monumental decision to carry on and manage themselves. Their next task was to continue with their new piece of randomness, the incredible "I Am the Walrus."

Stop what you're doing. Put this book down and run to your computer or CD player and play this song. Turn your balance away from the side of your stereo that has the (great) cellos, etc. You'll be able to listen to "I Am the Walrus" with the Beatles' rock and roll rhythm section. Listen to the (yes I'm going to use the word just this once) awesome chord structure, the drums and bass, everything you can.

Are you back? Did you enjoy that?

"I Am the Walrus" was John Lennon at his 1967 best. If he was not confident during *Sgt. Pepper* (as he claimed), he surely was for this song.

According to Lennon, the song was written mostly on various acid trips. The lyrics don't discount this as a possibility.

> "He'd written down another few words that day, just daft words, to put to another bit of rhythm. 'Sitting on a cornflake, waiting for the man to come.' I thought he said 'van to come,' which he hadn't, but he liked it better and said he'd use it instead."
>
> ~ Hunter Davies
>
> (*The Beatles*, 1968)

"I Am the Walrus! I just love the nonsensical lyrics. As a kid I had a hard time understanding most poetry and that song took the cake. Then I learned it wasn't supposed to mean anything and was very relieved that I wasn't just a total dumbass."

~ Bob Kirk

(*email*, 2013)

"There are expressions here that have some relation to reality. Semolina Pilchard is Liverpool slang for sardine. Yellow matter custard is a reference to Eric Burdon's penchant for breaking eggs on the torsos of female groupies. At least that is the story I have heard. This song is a major masterpiece not a minor masterpiece because there is nothing else quite like it lyrically and musically. Listening to it now, Walrus still amazes me with its audacity."

~ Joseph Brush

[*responding to a referral to the song as a minor masterpiece*]

(*email*, 2009)

"The walrus came from 'The Walrus and the Carpenter.' *Alice in Wonderland.* To me it was a beautiful poem. Later I realized that the walrus was the bad guy in the story, and the carpenter the good guy. I thought, 'Oh shit, I picked the wrong guy.' I should have said 'I Am The Carpenter.' But that wouldn't have been the same, would it?"

~ John Lennon

(*The Playboy Interviews With John Lennon and Yoko Ono*, 1981)

A Quick (and Non-Magical) Tour of the Rest of the EP

The song, "Magical Mystery Tour" seemed to me for years to be a lot of bluff and flash. Now, listening to it again, I realize . . . that my mind hasn't changed. Don't get me wrong, it's *catchy!*

"Flying" is a nice song. The only instrumental that they made.

"The Fool on the Hill" is another example of McCartney's extreme cleverness with piano and melody.

Finally, if "Blue Jay Way" had never been released, I don't think my life would have been altered much. No, that's not true, I might have listened to the whole album more often. I think it's a dreary piece of boredom and—in the movie—having George wearing an orange suit playing a keyboard drawn on the floor seems somehow fitting. Amazingly, he doesn't even begin to smirk and I guess you have to hand it to him for keeping a straight face through the whole thing.

I told my wife Sandi, "I can just picture George telling the other Beatles 'We'll sing *please don't be long* about 40 times and then switch to *don't be long* for another 30 times.'"

She replied, "well, if they were stoned it would be normal to be doing it over and over."

Magical Mystery Tour (EP) (track listing)

Side One	Side Two
1. "Magical Mystery Tour"	1. "The Fool on the Hill"
2. "Your Mother Should Know"	2. "Flying"
3. "I Am the Walrus"	3. "Blue Jay Way"

To Analyze 1967

There was positive hope in the world. It was an amazing, colorful year and the Beatles, having dropped the mop-top image, seemed to be at the helm of the ship.

Paul's bass playing wasn't as flashy as it was in 1966, but he explored new avenues of melodic-ness [MS Word doesn't think "melodiousness" is a word] that inspired . . . many . . . bass players. Including, very much, the one who is right now sitting at a computer typing these words. I'd go as far as saying that the influence of his playing during this year is only out-shone by what he did in 1968 when he reinvented himself and played in a style that is in just about all of the rest of us to this day.

One last story about 1967. I had cut out the mustache from the *Sgt. Pepper* album and had that in my nostrils and was playing a guitar along with the album when suddenly I heard the stroke of doom. The bedroom door had opened and my Beatle-despising Dad was standing there looking extremely disappointed. He thought for a while and said, with scorn, "You're going to be a musician, aren't you?" Twelve years old, I stood there for a while with the fate of my future hanging in the balance.

It would be very easy to say "no" and make him happy. But I decided to stand up to him for once. I told him "yes" and waited for the worst.

He just shrugged his shoulders, said "Okay" and closed the door. My point is that I probably wouldn't have become a musician had it not been for the Beatles and for Paul McCartney, and I certainly do not stand alone with that thought.

Paul's Bass Playing
on John and George's Songs

There has been some discussion over the years about how different a musician Paul McCartney was when playing on his own songs vs. playing on John or George's songs.

In the *Playboy* interview, amongst the last of his life, John mentions that when it came time to record his songs a looser air came over the studio. He felt that he would be called paranoid for this, but there is no doubt that his feelings were correct and true right from the start of the Beatles Parlaphone recording career. Taking a listen to various Beatles' recordings, he's absolutely correct! On Paul's own songs, his bass parts are controlled and (usually) perfected while on John's songs they are more inventive and spontaneous; his playing is *more fun* on John's (and George's) songs than on his own.

Many have referred to this as a purposeful thing on McCartney's part as if his aim were to sabotage Lennon's songs. But I decided to give it some more thought. McCartney himself has said that the Beatles did not rehearse before going into the studio. They had gotten so good at playing with each other after so many hours of doing so in Germany and on tours that rehearsal was an unneeded commodity. There isn't much doubt about the type of songwriters McCartney and Lennon were. Paul would get a song and flesh it out in his head. He would hear musical parts and what sort of instruments should play those parts and how they should be played. It was an intellectual approach. John, by *all* (and I mean ALL) accounts would bring his song and let the boys work their parts out themselves. George and Ringo have both said that it was more fun playing John's songs and if you listen to the bass parts on Beatles albums from the earliest to the last (give a listen to "I Want You (She's So Heavy)" and "Come Together" from *Abbey Road*) I think it's safe to say that Paul joined in on the fun as well. His bass parts were more daring and less precise on John's songs.

This is an interesting point to ponder as we go through the Beatles' catalog. In the early days, when John had most of the hits and more control of the group, the Beatles style was spontaneous and a lot of fun. In the days around *Revolver* and *Sgt. Pepper*, when Paul had more control of the group, the style was intellectual, maybe a bit more controlled, but very nice sounding. Then in the later years, it was more of a mix of styles and you'd have a single like "Hey Jude" / "Revolution" which showed Paul and John at their strengths.

In an interview with Tony Bacon, Paul discussed 1967, saying that being the bass player was "my only job." His point was that after some years of doing a million things a day, all they had to worry about now was recording music.

By 1966, John and George wanted to take time off and stop being Beatles for a while. Paul knew that the Beatles could make their best music yet and '66 and '67 became his years as the chief motivator and songwriter of the band. By late 1966 until the time Brian Epstein died, being a recording artist for the Beatles *was* his job. He didn't have to worry about a whole lot else and so we have *Revolver* and *Sgt. Pepper*. A more controlled feel to the albums, but in my opinion some of the best music they ever made.

> "When someone else is singing, I'd realize my role was to play a bass part to complement what he's singing . . . I would think it's because someone else is singing, I see my role as the bass player and I'll come up with something inventive. When I'm singing, I think, 'Well, all you've gotta do is just play a bass part, mate,' and I might not think, 'Ooh, I've gotta pull it out the bag.'
> Yeah, so what's some good bass parts? 'Taxman' was good, that

was George . . . 'Something.' That was good; that was George. 'Come Together' was good; that was John . . . Yeah, it's probably true!"

~ Paul McCartney

(Paul McCartney – Bass Master - Playing the Great Beatles Basslines, 2006)

My final point on this topic is that the Beatles, all four of them, were fantastic sidemen. They knew how to make a song work. Paul was one of the best sidemen ever and if a song called for some wild and uninhibited bass playing, then he would be there making it happen in a big, big way.

NINE

The Artist
(1968)

1968 in Review

For the Beatles, 1968 was a year of divergence in a number of ways. They diverged in their recording methods (working endless hours on songs and allowing their women into the studio), from their public image of being a close-knit unit and, most alarmingly, from each other.

On one hand, almost everyone involved with the recording of the white album says that they were pretty tense with each other. On the other, they spent more hours—by far—working together to make that album than any other.

The year started off in a positive way. They had been buckled into the London scene for years now and, being their own managers, decided to clear off their calendars and head to India to take up Transcendental Meditation with the Maharishi Mahesh Yogi with plans on staying until late April. But, being the enterprising lads they were, they knocked out four new songs before leaving: "Lady Madonna," "The Inner Light," "Across the Universe" and "Hey Bulldog."

The Beatles had finished recording "Lady Madonna" and planned to have themselves filmed acting as if they were recording it the next day. Instead, with the cameras rolling, they created, recorded and mixed "Hey Bulldog."

Unbeknownst to us, this was a crucial session. This was the first time Yoko went to a Beatles' session. The Beatles, especially John and

Paul, were having a lot of fun recording the track, as you can hear. Upon leaving the session, John was full of himself and asked Yoko what she thought about the song. She told him she thought it was childish and that he could do a lot better than that (the above was told by John and Yoko separately).

Those of you who have been in bands for long probably heard a loud dissonant piano chord when you read that. The women in the lives of male musicians tend to see only their man when looking at a band; the others merely in the way. Yoko saw John for what he was; a man who had a lot more to give as a solo act than what he could as part of a group, even if that group was the most famous that ever existed.

The Beatles went to India. Ringo came back after 11 days. George and John stayed for two months and ever afterward George mocked Paul about leaving as quickly as he did. And yet he was there for a month. It's most likely true that George and John were trying to shed their musical careers, something that Paul hasn't done to the time of this writing [*January 2013*].

Once back on their home turf, the problems and divisions they were easily able to overcome in 1967 became more pronounced and difficult to avoid. This was largely due to the re-emergence of John Lennon into a leadership role, in large part due to the prodding of Yoko. Instead of waiting for Paul to call him to action, he was in action again now with Yoko attending all the sessions. Now, instead of the four musicians playing off of each other, they had a fifth (albeit unwelcome) voice presiding. What was good for John, what he needed, was the same thing that began tearing the Beatles apart. And that, dear reader, is enough about that for this book.

The group went into a massive recording frenzy that began on May 30th (recording "Revolution") and did not end until a marathon two-day session on October 17/18. For that 24 hour session, John and Paul (along with producers and engineers) put together the rules and running order for the album.

Meanwhile, music was also being prepared for the *Yellow Submarine* album.

If 1968 was a year of tension between the Beatles, maybe that wasn't a bad thing. "Because," said John Lennon, "it obviously worked."

Paul's Bass Playing in 1968

If 1966 was the year that McCartney emerged as a bass master, 1968 is the year he created a style of bass playing that is heard on through today. During the sessions for this year and the next, he complemented his trusty Rickenbacker 4001S with a sunburst 1966 Fender Jazz bass (the 1966 identification is based on the shape of the tuners). There is a fair bit of discussion in various books about what songs he played the Fender on. Walter Everett claims that he used the Fender on "Yer Blues," "Glass Onion," and "While My Guitar Gently Weeps" from *The White Album* and "Sun King" and "Mean Mr. Mustard" on the *Abbey Road* LP. If his conclusions are correct, it's interesting to note that the three songs listed from the white album do sound similar in their sound of near dead-stringed trebleness. Compare the full rich bass tone employed on "Dear Prudence" with the following song "Glass Onion" and you'll hear the difference immediately.

Paul McCartney was in a unique situation throughout his career as a bass player. From 1961-1965, he followed the trend of all the best players of the day to come up with just the right bass parts to elevate the ensemble. There was just not much thought given to making the bass guitar stand out. By 1965, the bass was emerging as a powerful instrument (a huge about-face from just a year or two before). James Jamerson's work at Motown Records was becoming influential to the extreme and the Beatles, Lennon especially, were keen to have it up in the mix. As the bass became more important in the world of pop and soul, McCartney must have felt the need to expand his bass horizons, and he clearly did. 1966-67 were years of exploration and separation from the song. No longer would McCartney think only of using the bass to underly the rest of the song. During those years, he was unleashed, out front. By 1968, he brought a two-edged sword to the instrument. He no longer felt the need to be in a lead situation with his instrument. But he wanted it to sing with the rest of the song. His approach became heavier and, frequently using a Fender Jazz bass, the sound of his pick hitting the strings became more prominent. The cut of his sound became his focus. As the bass players of the world began to rub their eyes and revolt against the yoke of their guitar player overlords, McCartney seemed to be right with the best of them.

And, in the magnified world of Beatle-dom, he led the rest of us down the path of bass attack. Such was always the case with the Beatles. They didn't necessarily do things first, but when they did them, everyone was going to notice. In the world of bass players, the picking techniques, the palm-muting, the sustained notes during breaks and the way McCartney's bass was mixed in 1968 are all heard to this day from many of the rest of us.

Take some time and listen to the Beatles' output from this year and see if you don't agree. This was the big year for the evolution of rock bass playing.

"Lady Madonna" (Single)
"The Inner Light" (B-side)
(Released March 15, 1968)

On March 15th, with the Beatles in India, the "Lady Madonna" / "The Inner Light" single was released. By now, psychedelia had gained a fairly firm foothold in the music industry and people were waiting for the Beatles to come out with the monster of all *psychedelicness.*

Surely, their next record would be the one that would be beautiful, wondrous and mind-bendingly strange. Instead, we got "Lady Madonna," a song based on a very cool blues record, "Bad Penny Blues," by Humphrey Lyttelton and recorded with his band in London on April 20, 1956 at EMI studios. The Beatles must have remembered hearing Lyttelton's track back in the day because now they came to the studio wanting to make a record that sounded very much like that one. "Bad

Penny Blues" was unique in that it had a solid, old sounding, boogie style piano with a heavy left hand (played by Johnny Parker) and brush-stick style drums. Ringo especially wanted to capture the drum style for "Lady Madonna" and so George Martin gave him a brief lesson in using brushes.

They had to experiment to get the piano sound that permeates the track, using various microphones and double-tracking the piano. If you've heard "Lady Madonna" on the radio, you'll remember that the piano wastes no time in grabbing your attention. That mission was well accomplished. Note, also, that if the piano is double-tracked,[1] then Paul did a great job of doing it. It does not sound like two piano parts.

As for the bass, McCartney had done it again; it's a good bass line. Close inspection of it reveals some choppiness in the playing and he tends to miss slightly on some notes, but it was clear that by 1968 McCartney was in a luxurious position. He could spend time laying down the best sounding performance on bass and then let the engineers hide the flaws. And, in fairness, the flaws were minimal on "Lady Madonna."

Most importantly, McCartney's bass follows the piano bass to a large degree, and it had to as there is a prominent piano bass featured on the track, to fall astray from that would have muddled up the sound.

The piano part, while relatively simple to play, is so well constructed that you know upon hearing the first note what song it is. If the bass part were to run astray from it too much, the song would be frustrating to listen to. Instead, it follows the piano bass from A to C to D and then, while the piano bass continues to ride on the D, it completes the typical rock and roll bass line, riding up to the F# and A. It is a very prominent aspect of the song, and it works. My memory of the song when it came out was that, once again, everyone thought Paul McCartney was a hell of a bass player.

Give credit where due for "Lady Madonna." Giving a lot of effort, George Martin and Geoff Emerick made the piano sound fantastic, and this may be the Beatle track that sounds the most different from any other.

"Hey Jude" (Single)
"Revolution" (B-side)
(Released August 30, 1968)

Where do we start with this? "Hey Jude" was immense. It is possibly the biggest record of all time; clearly it is the biggest Beatles' single ever. It is at the top of a number of all-time-great-song lists. To discuss "Hey Jude" and give it the credit it deserves would require a full chapter and, upon reading this section, it just about does.

Sometimes as a writer, it's difficult to come up with words to describe something that is extreme in popularity. That was the case with this classic (or "masterpiece" as John Lennon referred to it). So you can guess that I was happy to discover that Allan W. Pollack, whose scholarly look at every Beatle song recorded (you can find his *Notes on . . . Series* on the web) had a similar issue.

> "'Hey Jude' is such a monumental favorite, I'm almost dissuaded from touching it because of the pressure to say something profound. I'll go for it nonetheless, even if I do get everything wrong, because it's such a good illustration of two compositional lessons—how to fill a large canvas with simple means, and how do use diverse elements such as harmony, bassline, and orchestration to articulate form and contrast."
>
> ~ Alan W. Pollack
>
> *(Notes on . . . Series,* 1989-2000)

By simple means, he refers to the lack of intricate parts in this song. Paul's lead vocal is, straight from the outset, relaxed. His piano part appears to be fairly straight forward but, as was so often the case with his piano, was extremely clever. It fulfills two roles. 1) It drives the rhythm and 2) underpins the lead vocals in a number of spots.

The Beatles instrumentation on the song begins subtly and builds towards its epic ending. Let's follow the song straight through to the finish.

Note: If you're at all "game," it's worthwhile at this point to listen to the song a number of times and concentrate on each instrument separately. Paul, John and Ringo are all filling musical roles very nicely and becoming more energetic as the song moves along. And it all builds so subtly that, unless you're consciously listening to the changes, you hardly notice they've happened.

1st verse: lead vocal, piano (right side). Everything here is straightforward with no real hint of what's to come.

2nd verse: lead vocal, piano, acoustic guitar (enthusiastically played by John and mixed to the left side), tambourine (playing half notes). Halfway through the verse, harmony vocals ("ahhhh") are added and beneath the harmonies you will hear soft drum beats, especially under the word "better."

A drum fill brings the song to it's first bridge. It's always been my feeling, contested by many, that Ringo came to the end of his fill too soon (no innuendo intended). He rolls over the toms, hits a ride cymbal and then—realizing there was more time before the bridge starts—deftly adds another half bar of drum fill.

1st bridge: ("and any time you feel the pain") We now have the Beatles' rhythm section in place.

Listening to Paul's bass part, I'm reminded of the style he used on the Beatles' previous masterpiece, "A Day in the Life." Laconic, and very much on rhythm.

His role on the instrument here is to keep the song in time, unrushed, and (for the moment) cool. The end of the verse features a nice little piano line that is heralded by a subtle and effective hammer note on the bass.

3rd verse: The Beatles' innate sense of how to build a song towards a climax shows itself here. The tambourine is now playing sixteenth notes while the background singing has dropped out for a moment. It returns with John harmonizing beneath Paul.

2nd bridge: Yet another rule is broken by these rascals. The words to the second "chorus" here are completely different from the first. This is not a lyrical effect that was used often in those days. The underlying music continues to move, especially Ringo shaking things up on the drums. Paul's vocal parts are now frequently double-tracked, adding more power to the singing.

4th verse: What stands out to me at this point of the song is not so much the instrumentation but the total and complete confidence the Beatles have as they push the song along. They may have had their tensions and disagreements, but when they got behind a great song, such as "Hey Jude," there was no denying that they could play together with the best of them. You can hear the joy in their voices and in their instruments.

Million-mile Singalong: And now we reach the epic climax we've been shepherded towards since the beginning, the moment (at 3:07) when the song shifts dramatically to the singalong section. But listen closely; this is all extremely well orchestrated.

As the music pauses during the transition, Ringo pops a nice little note on the hi-hat and we're off to new lands. Allan Pollack points out that the "na na" line is repeated no less than nineteen times and is, somewhat surprisingly, one minute longer than the entire first section.

Beginning with the second round of "na na" there occurs, way down in the mix, a sound that I've never heard discussed in all of my Beatle-book ramblings. There is what sounds like a fuzz guitar, bass or maybe even a distorted trombone, that is playing sustained notes on the root of each chord (F / Eb / Bb / F). It is even more audible during the 3rd round.

It's at the 4th round where George Martin begins his entry into the arrangement, adding low (very slightly out of tune) horns that follow the chords. And then Paul is back singing his heart out. If there is any doubt that Paul has one of the best rock voices ever, he dispels it with his contributions to this section.

And so it goes for the rest of the song. But I'd be willing to bet that you've never heard the violins playing a high C, beginning at 4:45. The song begins to fade out at 5:00. You think the song has reached the end, but there is still over two minutes to go. As the song fades to its final breaths, the engineer lowers the faders on all of the instruments but leaves the vocals higher in the mix. Accidental? Possible, but the Beatles and the recording staff were always good at turning accidents into gold.

Notes On "Hey Jude"

It is the longest song ever for a hit record. I recall looking, back in 1967, at how long "Within You Without You" and "A Day in the Life" were and was amazed to see that they were both just over five minutes long. Unheard of! And now, here comes "Hey Jude," clocking in at over seven minutes!

Backed by John's classic rocker "Revolution," the single is one of the best ever.

Interestingly, for those who keep track of such things, this song was not engineered by Geoff Emerick. The recording was made in the midst of *The White Album* sessions where the Beatles took to taking so many hours to create a record that Emerick opted out of being their engineer (not returning until *Abbey Road*).

Other comments:

"The song resonates, it holds you captive from the beginning to the end. Gives me chills literally every time I listen to it. Oh if only I could have been a fly on the wall in the studio when they cut this song!"

~ Dawn Carlson-Kingsley

(*email*, 2013)

"the older I get, the more convinced I am that the main message here is to be found in the first half—the 'imperative' to now pursue one's destined love the minute either you have found her, or she has found you. Yes, I do believe that once you internalize that much, the transcendent, blissful joy of the second half falls right into place."

~ Alan W. Pollack

(*Notes on . . . Series*, 1989-2000)

McCartney has claimed all along that the song was written for John's son Julian. John and Cynthia had just divorced, and Paul felt that he didn't want to throw away the years of friendship between Cynthia and him. So he drove down to see them one day to show support; an act that touched Cynthia deeply. On the way down, he wrote the beginnings of the song, singing "Hey Jules."

Julian Lennon discovered the song had been written for him almost twenty years later. He remembered being closer to McCartney than to his father.

> "Paul and I used to hang about quite a bit—more than Dad and I did. We had a great friendship going and there seems to be far more pictures of me and Paul playing together at that age than there are pictures of me and my dad. It's very strange to think that someone has written a song about you. It still touches me."
>
> ~ Julian Lennon
>
> (*otscotsman.com*, 2009)

> "Hey Jude is Paul's. It's one of his masterpieces . . . I always heard it as a song to me. If you think about it . . . Yoko's just come into the picture. He's saying, 'Hey Jude-hey, John.' I know I'm sounding like one of those fans who reads things into it, but you can hear it as a song to me. The words 'go out and get her'—subconsciously he was saying, Go ahead, leave me. On a conscious level, he didn't want me to go ahead. The angel in him was saying, 'Bless you.' The devil in him didn't like it at all, because he didn't want to lose his partner."
>
> ~ John Lennon
>
> (*The Playboy Interviews With John Lennon and Yoko Ono*, 1981)

> "If the song is about self-worth and self-consolation in the face of hardship, the vocal performance itself conveys much of the journey. He begins by singing to comfort someone else,

finds himself weighing his own feelings in the process, and finally, in the repeated refrains that nurture his own approbation, he comes to believe in himself."

~ Tim Riley

(Tell Me Why, 2002)

"'Hey Jude' is one I listen to over and over. It always cheers me up, and reminds me of my brother [East Hawai'i disk jockey Darrin Carlson]. Growing up with him and his eclectic music tastes has had a big effect on me. So this song brings him to mind and makes me feel closer to him."

~ Dawn Carlson-Kingsley

(email, 2013)

I think it would have been interesting if "Hey Jude" was the last song the Beatles ever recorded and released (but then I thought that about "A Day in the Life" too). This is the Beatles at their absolute power. It is stunning, climactic and shows them playing together like we wish they always had. Because of that, "Hey Jude" is the Beatles' dream song.

Did You Hear That?!

At 2:12, between the words "perform with" and "don't you know that . . ." there is either a vocal part with strange phasing or an instrument that is heard only once in the song.

The Beatles (LP)
(commonly known as *The White Album*)

Released
November 22, 1968
Five years to the day after *With the Beatles*

Cover Notes
The cover was designed by Richard Hamilton. The conceptual all-white cover may have been as shocking as *Sgt. Pepper* had been a year before.

Peak Position
Number 1

Number of Weeks on the Chart
155

Number of Days in the Studio
An incredible 73 days were spent in the studio.

You keep hearing how tense things were, but they sure spent a lot of time together.

First Song Recorded for the Album
"Revolution" on May 30, 1968

The usual Lennon classic, the album version. The recording was about 10 minutes long, huge chunks of which were used for "Revolution 9."

A study of pop and rock music shows that a group will always have an extremely difficult time following up on an album that either sells particularly well or achieves immense critical acclaim and cultural influence. By 1968, due to a combination of all of the above after the release of *Sgt. Pepper's Lonely Hearts Club Band*, the Beatles had the world at their feet. By dint of that album alone, they were everywhere and influenced just about everybody, to wit:

> "*Sgt. Pepper* constituted a historic departure in the progress of music—any music."
>
> (*Time magazine*, 1967)

> "I declare that The Beatles are mutants. Prototypes of evolutionary agents sent by God, endowed with a mysterious power to create a new human species, a young race of laughing freemen."
>
> ~ Timothy Leary
>
> (*Timothy Leary: Biography*, 2007)

> "When you have a big selling album, everybody wants to do everything. Everybody wants to do everything."
>
> ~ Don Hendley
>
> (*TV interview*, 2008)

There are few groups who can handle following up a huge success, and many have fallen apart trying to do it. It was no longer an issue of going into the studio and having fun creating music. It was now a matter of four men trying to answer the question asked by the world, "What will you do to save us?"

Of those four men, one of them had enjoyed being at the helm for the last two albums and—due to their tremendous success—wanted things to stay that way. One of them, prompted by his new love, had reawoken from a two-year sleep and wanted his place in the order of things. One of them found that he, too, was a gifted song-writer and wanted a new foothold in band politics. And one of them had been finding those same politics—as well as the endless hours spent on recording—tiresome.

Contradictions: both Ringo and 1st engineer Geoff Emerick quit the process during the making of *The White Album* and yet it has also been called many times the most honest album they made. The Beatles have said that times were very tense in the studio, and yet Emerick's replacement, Ken Scott, remembers it as happy times.

> "I was afraid that my memory might be clouded . . . and that whole thing of having a good time making the white album was something I wanted to make sure it wasn't just me. So I spoke to Chris Thomas (who produced 'Piggies'), I spoke to John Smith who was my second engineer almost the entire time and we all said almost the same thing: There were moments that there was tension but a majority of the time we had a lot of fun. It was great! I have worked on projects that it took two weeks to record the album. Someone at some point during the two weeks will blow up. There will be an argument. You're dealing with artistic temperaments . . . so when you take a six month one like the white album was, its gonna happen more often than once. Yes we had a couple of those but we also had a blast. It was so much fun."
>
> ~ Ken Scott (Beatles producer)
> *(Ken Michaels' Every Little Thing radio show, 2012)*

Electric Light Orchestra leader (and later Beatles producer) Jeff Lynne met the Beatles during the making of *The White Album*.

> "To be in the same room as the four of them caused me not to sleep for, like, three days."
>
> ~ Jeff Lynne
>
> *(Q Magazine, 2007)*

Notes on "The White Album"

The four Beatles met at George's house in Esher (Kinfauns) on May 30th and recorded 23 demos there. All but a few were destined for *The White Album*.

Songs That Were Recorded in Esher But Not Included on The White Album

"Child of Nature"

A Lennon song that, with the lyrics changed, became "Jealous Guy" on his *Imagine* LP.

"What's The New Mary Jane"

Was a strange, almost-make-it-up as you go song that can be heard on *The Anthology* album. It was performed by John, Yoko and trusty roadie, Mal Evans. It's similar to the strange song stylings that John and Yoko produced on their later records, generally released as the B-side of the Plastic Ono Band's B-Sides. The long ending has John repeating "What a shame Mary Jane had a pain at the party," over bells and pianos and Yoko.

"Circles"

A haunting Harrisong played on a very harsh sounding organ that day. If you have a chance to listen to it, remember it was a demo, never meant to be heard by the general public. Listening to the interesting chords, melody and lyrics, it's intriguing to consider what the song might have sounded like with a Beatles' treatment,. It's my feeling that "Circles" may have been a better song to include than "Long Long Long."

"Sour Milk Sea"

Was yet another good George song that was left off of the LP. The song was a rocker later recorded by Jackie Lomax for Apple Records.

"Not Guilty"

Another George rocker, an excellent one, and a song for which the Beatles recorded over 100 takes!. Looking at the lyrics, it's somewhat easy to guess that one of the reasons for its absence from the LP as it's pretty clearly a song about George having to sit and wait in the wings while John and Paul strut their stuff in the studio. George had apparently had enough of being third banana.

"Junk"

A song Paul worked on for *The White Album* as well as for *Let It Be*. The song, one of Paul's prettiest, was clearly unfinished during those times. It was finally placed on his first solo album.

If you can find these songs (check YouTube for "Esher demos") and listen to them, you might wonder what was going on in the four Beatles' heads that day. This was not just a session to blithely listen to what the others had to offer for the new album. This was, as it always was with the band, the place where they had to sell their songs to the group. As they recorded their prospective songs, each one must have been thinking about how they were going to interject themselves into the power-structure as they began making their album.

As they recorded their demos, it must have been clear to all four that they had a lot of really good songs all waiting for the Beatles' treatment. Considering how competitive the Beatles were with each-other, each song recorded that day had to be a statement. John, who had been somewhat missing from the competition for the last two albums, was there to make sure that the others—especially Paul—knew that he was back. George, always shunted to the background while recording the albums, entered the proceedings knowing that it was not going to change. He made that point by recording "Not Guilty," a clear jab at John and Paul's firm control over things. He also made the point that he had some excellent songs ready for them to work on. Paul, who had shone most brightly and confidently on *Revolver* and *Sgt. Pepper*, must have been at least somewhat taken aback by the songs his bandmates had brought along. Ringo? Well, Ringo was the one that everyone liked. Not an easy role! I would make a confident guess that if he wanted to continue to be the friend to all, he knew that he had a long, hard road ahead of him as shifting band politics were about to hold sway in the recording studio.

> "It was a relaxed place, away from the city. The musicians were bursting with material . . . now, hunkered down together with Harrison's Ampex four-track tape machine rolling, the four worked up acoustic versions of song after song . . .taken together, the "Kinsfauns demos" constitute the juiciest Beatles bootleg set of the band's career, and possibly the greatest 'unplugged' session in pop-music history."
>
> ~Tim Riley
>
> (*Tell Me Why,* 2002)

After their meeting in Esher, it was time to get into the studio and mash their many songs into a sellable LP. As the Beatles worked, there were rumors floating around everywhere that they were busy working on the greatest psychedelic album ever. So many questions. What would the cover be like this time? Would they record the bible? *The Lord of the Rings?* No one outside the inner circle knew what they were doing, or if they did they sure weren't telling. The only thing for sure was that it would be the most stupendous, incredible flash of psychedelia produced yet. It's a relatively safe statement to make that few people expected an all white album cover and some of the most blatant rock music they had ever done.

Hard rock was a new commodity in 1968 and the Beatles, especially John Lennon, approached it with an unadulterated vengeance. As with *Sgt. Peppers* there was a collage of music styles; Hollywood show tunes, dreamy ballads, Beach Boy-type harmonies, a little bit of soul, country western; it was all there.

It is called the album of solo tracks. Engineer Ken Scott maintains that this is because *The White Album* was going to be the first Apple Records album release. They had to have a date that it would be ready by, and so they worked separately frequently.

If the Beatles weren't getting along, they surely did not show it in the log books. They worked for far more hours on this album than any other they had made. Perhaps it was a nice break for each one to get away from the other three for a while.

And yet, there was a real difficulty in working with the group. Their expectation was that the engineer would sit and wait for hours at a time while they worked out how their songs would be recorded. They could not leave for meals; they must be ready at all times to begin recording. So, in that sense, it's hard to blame 1st engineer Geoff Emerick for deciding he had had enough.

Geoff Emerick Departs

It happened on July 16th, 1968. The Beatles 1st engineer for *Revolver* and *Sgt. Pepper* had had enough of the fighting and decided to leave. Ken Scott took over the engineering reins for the rest of the way.

In researching this book, I found an interesting sidelight to this fact. Following is a listing of the songs on *The White Album*. The following table shows the songs engineered separately by Emerick and Scott.

Engineers for Songs on The White Album

Songs engineered by Emerick:
1. "Revolution I"
2. "Don't Pass Me By"
3. "Revolution 9"
4. "Blackbird"
5. "Everybody's Got Something to Hide Except Me and My Monkey" (*Begun*)
6. "Good Night"
7. "Ob-La-Di, Ob-La-Da"
8. "Revolution"
9. "Cry Baby Cry"

Songs engineered by Scott:
1. "Helter Skelter"
2. "Sexy Sadie"
3. "Don't Pass Me By" (*Completed*)
4. "Everybody's Got Something to Hide Except Me and My Monkey" (*Completed*)
5. "While My Guitar Gently Weeps"
6. "Hey Jude"
7. "Not Guilty"
8. "Yer Blues"
9. "What's The New Mary Jane"
10. "Rocky Raccoon"
11. "Mother Nature's Son"
12. "Wild Honey Pie"
13. "Back In The U.S.S.R. "
14. "Dear Prudence"
15. "Helter Skelter" (*Completed*)
16. "Glass Onion"
17. "I Will"
18. "Birthday"
19. "Piggies"
20. "Happiness Is a Warm Gun"
21. "Honey Pie"
22. "Savoy Truffle"
23. "Long Long Long"
24. "I'm So Tired"

The breaking point between the two is interesting. The music after the change tended to be more raw and rock-ish. Whether this was due to the change in engineers or because they were heading in a new direction anyway, or whether it's because "Helter Skelter" happened to be the next song they were going to record is impossible to say. But a definite change took place.

Let's take a listen to some of the songs from this amazing album.

"Back in the U.S.S.R."

The old George Martin rule applies here: open the album with a catchy rocker. Have you ever tried to write a rocker like this? Most songwriters will tell you that it's one of the more difficult things to do. McCartney seems to have been born with the ability because here's yet another one, a "potboiler" as George Martin called them. There are two interesting things to note about "Back in the U.S.S.R." First, this was one of the songs (along with "Dear Prudence" up next) that was recorded during the time Ringo had split from the group. So that's McCartney on drums. As for the bass, which is largely inaudible in the mix, Mark Lewisohn suggests that its possible that both remaining Beatles had their hand in on the line.

The sliding vibrato style and bends of the guitar solo sound like McCartney playing that as well. Seems like he played most of the best guitar solos through the Beatles' catalog. Not a bad way to open an album. Makes you want to listen to what's coming next.

"Dear Prudence"[2]

And next up is a nice Lennon song, "Dear Prudence" which utilizes a tricky finger-picking style taught to John by Donovan while in India. The song, with just the guitar and vocal, stand by themselves as a good ballad. But John wanted the Beatles' treatment here. To put that into perspective, let's play a little game here. Pretend that you're Paul McCartney and your job is to figure out what you would do on John's great new song. Listen to the demo recorded at George's house to get an idea of what you've been given to work with; a very nicely constructed song, pretty vocal and nicely executed finger picking by John on acoustic guitar. Now it's time to lay down not only the bass but the drums as well (Ringo's gone for a few days). What would you do? Listening to the demo, I feel that melodic, sometimes soaring bass lines and scant percussion would fit the bill nicely.

The real Paul McCartney decided to construct a solid drum/bass feel that really moves that song without getting in its way at all. At the outset, he determined to stay away from the descending acoustic guitar line, but to begin with one note bass parts and for the drums to follow the bass at the end of the verse. The background instruments build, build from there. The second verse features a full drum/bass rhythm section.

I just know, without looking, that Alan W. Pollack will have some interesting comments about this introductory section of the song and how it builds towards the bridge. Let's go see:

"The impressive accomplishment is that such a satisfying build up of tension and its release is achieved In Spite Of All Stasis :) The challenge is to create a sense of build up without relying much at all on either harmony or melody. Instead, the strategy is to carefully sustain an atmosphere within which texture and dynamic crescendo are developed over the long run."

And, as for the bridge itself:

"[The Beatles] add the unique appearance of male chorus in background singing a mantra at first in imitation of the lead vocal, but which in the final phrase becomes block chords sung in a glissando with the lead."

~ Alan W. Pollack

(*Notes on . . . Series*, 1989-2000)

Speaking of the bridge, you'll notice that it doesn't really sound very much like the Beatles' voices singing the "look around round round" mantra. This may be partly due to the inclusion of the voice of Jackie Lomax on that part.

"Dear Prudence" is, as a matter of opinion, one of the better Beatles recordings, from Lennon's excellent guitar and vocals to the rhythm and tasteful background vocals. It moves from mood to mood, and by the end, if you're listening closely enough, you're breathless, without consciously realizing how many changes the song just went through. It has risen to nice heights and comes back down to a neat descending guitar line that fades out and, uh oh, the record's moving along and it looks like it's time to rock again.

"Glass Onion"

"Glass Onion" is a fascinating bit of wordplay from John Lennon, with some well orchestrated madness from George Martin. Those of you familiar with the notes I made on the website will recall that I didn't have much positive to say about the tones of the bass and snare drum. I defend that only by saying I was looking for something to write about that for once wasn't written from a sense of awe. I was not inspired at the time.

But, after listening to the version on the *Love* album, the song took on a new sense of life. There are a lot of interesting recording techniques, including the recorder played after the mention of "The Fool on the Hill," the contrapuntal sounds of the cellos vs. the twangy and trebly rhythm guitar, the quickly faded piano bass note that sustains at the end of the second verse, the always-handy buildup during the bridge ("oh yeah . . . oh yeah"), and the achievement of perfect silence for a split second at the end of the bridge which is followed by the usual rhythm pattern, but this time with no bass guitar. Finally, listen to the way the piano is recorded. At times it sounds almost as if it was recorded and played backward. McCartney played his Fender Jazz bass on "Glass Onion" giving it a very trebly sound.

"Helter Skelter"

Ken Scott's first session was "Helter Skelter," but a different version than the one heard on *The Beatles*. The song was much more relaxed in its early stages of life and with its sparse instrumentation, sounds very much like a Lennon solo record.

The released version that we've come to know and love took on a life of its own. McCartney had read an interview with Pete Townshend who claimed "I Can See For Miles" was the loudest, rawest, dirtiest song the Who had ever recorded. Listening to it, Paul felt that it was a pretty straight record and that it would be fun for the Beatles to make the wildest record on record (ignore the pun). It was time to set the studio ablaze and make sounds that had never been heard before.

It is most likely that John Lennon played bass on this song while Paul McCartney was busy playing the heavy-handed rhythm guitar.

As you listen to the bass, you can hear a high very trebly sound doubling it. Most likely this was achieved by putting the bass into two separate channels and mixing one with treble. However it was done, it creates a wild effect, adding to the mayhem. I believe the reason for this effect is to allow the bass to stand out from the droning guitars. One of the more difficult things to do is to get bass to cut through guitars—especially more than one that are playing low bar chords.

By using this effect on the bass, Scott was able to achieve this and more. The bass actually stands out in the forefront of that song once it gets rolling. The guitars were recorded quite well, made to drone and create more of a "noise" than a clear-cut guitar chord, yet done in a clean enough way to where you can hear the chords. The way the drums are played and recorded is designed to do the same thing. It sounds as if Ringo is basically riding on his crash cymbal and tossing in the snare/tom fills at will.

The guitar droning effect is something that later day heavy metal engineers should listen to. Too often, these engineers will go for the same effect with the rhythm guitars and take the easy way out by having them sound purely and simply like white noise. If they want to create mayhem, they should sit down with this record, play this song and find out what George Martin and Ken Scott did to get those sounds.

There's so much happening on this album that it's almost difficult to keep the discussion purely to the bass playing on it, and this is mainly due to the fact that McCartney had very nicely answered John Lennon's challenge. Lennon wanted to be a hard rocker now, and credit goes to all the band members for making the change to this new hard rock music. The only piece of the puzzle that I think falls a bit short is the sound of the drums on *The White Album* and "Helter Skelter" is a prime example. Had a fuller sound been used on the drums, this song would have been the most devastating rock song—of ALL time. It may be anyway.

> **"**The version on the album was out of control. They were completely out of their heads that night. But, as usual, a blind eye was turned to what the Beatles did in the studio. Everyone knew what substances they were taking, but they were really a law unto themselves in the studio.**"**
>
> ~ Brian Gibson (*Technical Engineer*)
>
> (*The Beatles Recording Sessions*, 1990)

"Everybody's Got Something to Hide Except Me and My Monkey"

Another mystery! What is difficult to determine, and it's really unfortunate, is when the bass part to "Everybody's Got Something to Hide Except Me and My Monkey" was recorded. Was it before or after Ken Scott replaced Geoff Emerick in the booth?

The Beatles Recording Sessions by Lewisohn indicates that only drums, two different lead guitars, a vigorously shaken hand-bell and a chocalho were recorded during the session that Emerick worked and that a new lead vocal, backup vocals and handclaps were added on July 23rd A.E. (After Emerick). There is no listing of when the bass was recorded.

In any discussion of the evolution of rock bass playing, this song is all-important. It is nothing short of superb both in its execution and recording. As you listen, the initial probe of the bass line played under the verses shows what at first seems to be a rather simple blues type line. Further listening shows something else completely. It's an eight-note line and a good one that starts at the first beat of the measure on the root note. It then drops down an octave and walks its way back up time and time again to that root note. There is a lot involved in making this line work.

> ❖ The final four notes of each run of the line are the most noticeable. Once the second note is played the line drops slightly in its presence but by the time the fifth note is hit

(partly because the notes are getting higher and partly because he's switched to another string) it's right back in your consciousness again. It crescendos up to the root note and drops again.

❖ The line is played again and again and again, and many times is played slightly off meter. This is probably the most important aspect of the line. The best way I could describe it, visually, would be to illustrate a child on a rocking horse swinging back and forth with total abandon. Not always right on a meter, but the same thing happens over and over again, close to the meter.

❖ The bass is a perfect counterpoint to John Lennon's strange and insane rhythm line, a guitar part that commands an article all to itself (another kid on a stranger rocking-horse). Meanwhile, those hand bells could be the alarm the kids have set off in the local firehouse. The bass counters all this.

After the verse has been established as described, it's time for Lennon to have his music follow his usual rule of building towards a climax and then giving a release. "Take it easy!" He shouts, clearly meaning he wants just the opposite approach. Now, the Beatles are locked solidly on the chorus. "Take it easy!" He shouts again, sounding even less as if he means that. And then the release: "Everybody's got something to hide except for me and my monkey." Finally, here comes those strange chord changes, lead lines, and drum breaks. The bells have left us for a moment. But not for long.

This is pure Beatles' genius, and a method they weren't using for the first time. As far back as their second single they employed it, when on "Please Please Me," John would shout "Come on," building up to the "please please me" explosion of vocals. At that point in PPM, the bass line comes back with its rhythmic pounding. Here, they've done it again. Pounding the bells/bass/guitar, etc., into your brain for so long, they take it away for the big buildup. Just when you realize it's gone, here it comes again—with a vengeance.

Of course, let us not forget to make note of The Great Bass Part, occurring towards the end of the song. The guitars all stop and John and Paul start doing their crazy "C'mon c'mon c'mon c'mon . . ." and then that bass line.. You can sing it—it's even double-tracked to add emphasis—ba pa bubububoom ba bump pa.

What I wouldn't give to have been there when they put this song together, taking it from John's original acoustic guitar/vocal demo to the hard-screaming, pile-driving powerhouse it became. This is classic Beatles.

"I would love to see video of Paul recording this bass part. You can feel the energy, joy, intensity and blistering sexiness of the man in that sound. Well, I can, anyway. Closest thing available to an aural orgasm."

~ Sue Smith

(*email*, 2007)

"[I] especially dug Paul's funky, Motown-influenced side, evident in the bass line from 'Everybody's Got Something to Hide Except Me and My Monkey.'"

~ Will Lee

(*Bass Player magazine*, 2006)

"Why Don't We Do It in the Road?"

This was one of McCartney's early "one-man-band" ventures; all of the instruments with the exception of the drums (Ringo) are played by him. The drums, piano, guitar and vocal really do the job nicely. But the bass part? It is a bouncy little line that would befit something like "All Together Now" more than this song. In the recording world, even with the time given to make Beatles' albums, there isn't always time to think every little aspect through. The bass playing on this song may be a victim of that fact. McCartney did show a tremendous aptitude for playing good blues bass, as shown on songs like "Yer Blues" and "I Want You (She's So Heavy)," so let's just move on.

"I Will"

As if there had not been enough innovation already on this album, a new idea was put into place: Paul doubles the bass with a vocal part. Listen closely and you'll hear it.

Regarding the acoustic guitar: It's a style that Paul developed and dropped all too soon. He used it at the end of "Mother Nature's Son" and for a good bit on the *McCartney* album but rarely afterward. Mostly powering the non-picking fingers or the "playing fingers" does it (in Paul's case, his right hand). With each note, his right hand fingers react strongly and with a quick shake vibrato.

"I Will" could have been recorded in 1964. It's one of the few post moptop songs that could have fit in any of their eras.

"Mother Nature's Son"

My feeling is that this is one of the most beautiful songs Paul ever did, and yet you rarely heard the song mentioned, and never hear it on the radio.

The voice seems to gently float down from the hills. Trombones are skillfully employed (who would have thought of that?). The guitar part is well constructed. All in all, a very nice song.

"Yer Blues"

This is Lennon's version of the blues, and the best part of it is that they recorded it, all four, together. These are some hard blues, and the band responds accordingly making one consider it too bad that they didn't record all together more often. Paul, most likely playing his Fender Jazz bass, provides a somewhat new definition for blues bass playing. Instead of the usual walking line, he syncopates his part, which provides a nice undercurrent to the whole feel. His sound is trebly, far more so than most blues bass players. Overall, its a nice effect. As for the band, it's joyful to listen to, knowing that all four were playing it together, just like many of us imagine the Beatles always should have been. The title,

"Yer Blues," according to John Lennon, was a play on words similar to McCartney's *Rubber Soul*. Instead of American blues, it's British, hence the "yer."

"Savoy Truffle"

"Savoy Truffle" is interesting in its recording. The opening electric piano part does a neat skid/stop that brings the vocals in. The guitar (George) is recorded in a somewhat sloppy, but catchy, fashion (isolate the guitar and listen again). The rhythm section (bass and drums) takes care of this by standing right out front, fighting it out with the saxophones. This driving style was used again in a later Harrison classic, "Here Comes the Sun." It's bouncy and lively and moves the song along, all in all a very well structured bass line. No better line might have been played by the Beatles' bass man. The song moves!!

The Beatles always made George's songs sound good. Put them on, one after the other, and the point is made just by listening. Why would he argue about how they backed him up on that one as well as "Think for Yourself," "Taxman," "Love You To," "I Want to Tell You," "It's All Too Much," "While My Guitar Gently Weeps," "I Me Mine," "Here Comes the Sun" and "Something," let alone the mighty groove they gave him for "Savoy Truffle." Fantastic!

> **"I love 'Savoy Truffle' from *The White Album*.** The intentional over modulated horns has such a cool texture to it and I love how it duets with George's guitar during the middle part. I'm surprised it's not a more popular song. It's a short tune but it totally lights up the pleasure center of my brain. LOL."
>
> ~ Darrin Carlson "DC" (*Disk Jockey*)
>
> (*email*, 2013)

Yeah?! Why isn't that song more popular? It's the Beatles at their best. But what the heck do those lyrics mean anyway? You came to the right place.

"'Savoy Truffle' on *The White Album* was written for Eric [Clapton]. He's got this real sweet tooth and he'd just had his mouth worked on. His dentist said he was through with candy. So as a tribute I wrote, 'You'll have to have them all pulled out after the 'Savoy Truffle.' The truffle was some kind of sweet, just like all the rest—cream tangerine, ginger sling—just candy, to tease Eric.**"**

~ George Harrison

(Interview, 1977)

The name Good News is used in the song. This was the name of the candy assortment, made by MacKintosh, that included the various candy types mentioned in the song.

"Piggies"

How is it humanly possible that one could get one's bass guitar to sound like a pig? If you ever get a chance to talk to Paul, ask him. The song was produced by Chris Thomas who also arranged and played the harpsichord part. I think this is yet another example of the Beatles with their producers and engineers taking a fairly good George Harrison song and making it a fantastic song.

"I'm So Tired"

The main point that stands out regarding "I'm So Tired" is the excellent dynamic flow of the musicians and vocalist. Providing the perfect undercurrent for the singer is vital and there are some points in this song that indicate that this aspect had become second nature to the band.

Musical goings on just before the second and final chorus offer a good, if not subtle, example. Just after John agonizes "and curse Sir Walter Raliegh, he was such a stupid git!" They let you know something big is coming. The music had been building up to this line, creating tension driven by all the instrumentation. The bass is walking up through the chords. Lennon's rhythm is slapping chords on the three count and when the word "git" is sung, one of the guitarists starts playing little falling notes while the bass steps back a bit to let it all happen. Then, seemingly out of the blue: "You'd say it wouldn't be wrong . . ." The Beatles are back in gear here, but restrained. The bass and drums are fluid, and a buildup is starting all over again—yes in the atypical Lennon style—punctuated by the great line "I'd give you everything I've got for a little peace of mind!" Listen to the band behind these lines as they are sung. They drive the song forward, there is the sudden stop, a drum fill, and the line again. The sudden stop again, a drum and organ fill and the line one final time. This is ensemble playing by all the Beatles, and Paul had long ago learned the lesson of laying back when most effective is put into play. After all, as Sting points out, space—musical silence—is the most effective weapon a musician has.

"Ob-La-Di, Ob-La-Da"

"Much like 'And Your Bird Can Sing,' 'Ob-La-Di, Ob-La-Da' is revealed by the Anthology releases to be a song that evolved greatly over the course of the studio sessions. I've never been a huge fan of the version released on *The White Album*, but I went nuts when I first heard the Version on *Anthology 3*. The bass line on the *Anthology* version really captures the spirit of ska that was the basis for this song. Allow me to disagree with the Beatles here: the alternate version is far superior to the version selected for *The White Album*; thanks in large part to McCartney's bouncy bass line."

~ John Martin

(email, 2008)

I completely agree with John's disagreement. I wouldn't have even written about the song without the nice *Anthology* version. The released version is the most fun to play while sitting at the piano at parties, but the *Anthology* version works well.

"Happiness Is a Warm Gun"

"Oh, I like that. One of my best, I had forgotten about that. Oh, I love it. I think it's a beautiful song. I like all the different things that are happening in it."

~ John Lennon

(*Rolling Stone*, 1971)

I think they call songs like this a tour-de-force. But then I've never really known what the phrase means. A quick look-up on the web shows it to mean "An impressive performance or achievement that has been accomplished or managed with great skill." Seems like that aptly describes the song. John Lennon had certainly emerged from his shell. He may have been persona non grata on *Revolver* and *Sgt. Pepper* but he was back and giving his best now. His songwriting talents may have been "only sleeping" for a few years, but no longer. And this one might have been the best of the bunch. Further, the other Beatles, not just Paul, seem to glorify in backing him up on his music. This song is in three parts, a suite of good old fashioned rock and roll inspired by a gun magazine with the title *Happiness Is A Warm Gun In Your Hand.*

With its time-shifts, changing meters, outstanding background vocals, hot Fender amp driven guitar solos, how—while recording thirty-two songs—did they have time to learn and play songs like this? Did they have a never-ending supply of energy? Were they born to record with each other? (Well that probably goes without saying.) The main problem with *The White Album* is that there are so many good songs that the bar is raised too high to continue appreciating them.

"Happiness Is A Warm Gun." What the heck do the words mean? Some people think they have the answers. I don't know where they get these, but they're interesting. All of the following quotes come from a collection by the excellent Beatles' writer, Joel Benjamin.

"'She's well acquainted with the touch of the velvet hand' was inspired by a meeting Beatles publicist Derek Taylor had with a person in a bar on the Isle of Man who had a fetish about gloves and sex and said to him: 'I like wearing moleskin gloves, you know.'"

~ Steve Turner

(Beatle Song Profiles, 2010)

"The lizard on the window pane was a recollection from Taylor's days living in Los Angeles. The line 'The man in the crowd with multi-colored mirrors on hob nail boots' is a reference to a Manchester City football fan who had been arrested for inserting mirrors on his shoes so that he could look up girls skirts."

~ Joel Benjamin

(Beatle Song Profiles, 2010)

Okay . . .

"The hands busy working overtime weren't about masturbating, [it] refers to another man who would place fake plastic hands on public counter tops and with his real hands would pick the pockets of the people standing at the counter beside him."

~ Joel Benjamin

(Beatle Song Profiles, 2010)

Hmmmm . . .

"A soap impression of his wife which he ate and donated to the National Trust. The National Trust was the name of the English national park system and it was not uncommon in England to step in people's poop when walking through public parks in England."

~ Denny Somach

(Beatle Song Profiles, 2010)

Well now!

> "The song relies on plural perspectives, based on multiple nar-
> ratives, which generate discourse between the reader and the
> text, because when a text does not explicitly spell out its mean-
> ing, a place develops for the reader to contribute to the produc-
> tion of meaning."
>
> ~ Brad Hurvitz
>
> (*Beatle Song Profiles*, 2010)

I think Brad's on to something, actually. Lennon was good at that.

> "Any even semi-notorious musical group endures hours upon
> hours of studio time, constantly bringing all of their new ideas
> to the table, recording non-stop. We as the audience hear only a
> fraction of a bands recordings through their albums. There are
> countless songs out there like this one in regards to the fact
> that they exist as several different ideas/melodies construed at
> different times."
>
> ~ Joel Benjamin
>
> (*Beatle Song Profiles*, 2010)

Another good point.

Okay, we have a song with three distinct parts, each impossibly different than the last. How the heck does that work?

> "[It] represents a most intriguing formal experiment, one that
> you might describe as a 'teleological medley.' The individual
> components are quite fragmentary and rely heavily on immedi-
> ate repetition of a single idea to establish any sense of formal
> autonomy. There's not quite enough substance in any of them
> to stand on their own. The primary force that holds it together
> and prevents it from otherwise sounding like a random grab-
> bag is the modulated development of intensity and mood

created by the specific sequencing of the sections; each new section builds on what has preceded it while adding something new."

~ Alan W. Pollack

(*Notes on . . . Series*, 1989-2000)

According to *The Beatles Recording Sessions*, this song took a long time for the others to learn and play, and you can see why. John was looking for and achieved (with the help of his bandmates and a sympathetic engineer) was a 1950s sound laid on top of some modern (for 1968) musical expressions. Right to the very last sound of chords being held and a drum lick played, the recording sounds like the 1950s. It sounds like a record, and that's what the Beatles loved.

"Not Guilty"

It's unfortunate that the Beatles' version did not get placed on this album. It has since, of course, been included on the *Anthology* album. It is very dynamic and well played. With their apparently new style of beginning a song right in the studio and calling each rehearsal of it a take, this song went over 100 takes! This was the most takes for any Beatles recording. Perhaps they tried too hard and too long to perfect it and got tired of it because it was scrapped in the end. It has an excellent hook, the six beats played just before the "I'm really sorry for your . . ." That little break is like a car screeching to a stop and is played to perfection by Paul and Ringo. Through most of the rest of the song, the bass is played in excellent British New Orleans rock style.[2]

"While My Guitar Gently Weeps"

The bass part was done on Paul's Fender Jazz bass. At various times during the song, the bass part is doubled. This song, saved for last in this discussion on this amazing album, may contain the heaviest of all the bass playing to be found throughout it. Here is yet another example of the Beatles making a George Harrison song sound fantastic.

"When we laid that track down, I sang it with acoustic guitar with Paul on piano, and Eric and Ringo—that's how we laid the track down. Later, Paul overdubbed bass on it."

~ George Harrison

(Guitar Player Magazine, 1987)

"A great tune that evolved from an acoustic demo and benefited greatly from Eric Clapton's contribution, it would be folly to ignore the importance of McCartney's often chordal bass line. This is another departure from the past, but his use of a lefty Fender Jazz adds a nice grindy tone to the mix. Whenever I hear this song I crank it up because McCartney's counterpoint is both stilted yet rich that's beautiful and dirty at the same time. If that isn't what R&R is all about, I've been missing something for some 40 years."

~ John Martin

(email, 2008)

At one point, while listening intently to this song, it occurred to me that the bass part might be doubled. There are sections where it sounds as if two basses are in the mix. I asked John Martin's opinion and here's his response.

"There is some element that suggests a doubled bass part, almost akin to 'Think for Yourself.' The difference being that all of these recordings speak to me of a Fender jazz bass being used for a pedal tone supplemented by upper register chords. While I cannot eliminate the possibility that someone may have played a simple bass line and someone else added the upper licks, I'm 99.9% inclined to believe that Macca did it all in one take. The double-stops are too perfect to have been done in separate takes, and the growl of the bass is so very Fender Jazz."

~ John Martin

(email, 2008)

Recapping the Bass Playing on
The White Album

To recap, it's fairly clear that the bass playing on *The White Album* was revolutionary for its time. To this day many bass players' styles don't sound all that different than the style Paul McCartney created on *The White Album*. It went from no holds barred madness ("Everybody's Got Something to Hide . . .") to excellent ensemble sound and style ("Honey Pie") to very pretty ("I Will"). With the possible exception of *Led Zeppelin II*, there may have never been an album that had more of a long lasting effect on rock bass playing than this one.

Sgt. Pepper had made Paul McCartney known as a formidable bass player; a peer amongst an extremely talented pool of bass players in Britain at the time. *The White Album* might have shoved him over the top.

Notes on the Layout of Tracks on
The White Album

As mentioned in the notes for "Not Guilty," John and Paul (along with George Martin, Ken Scott and John Smith) spent about 24 hours mixing, editing and creating the track placement for *The Beatles*. According to Mark Lewishon it was the first and only 24 hour session. It was a frantic session.

> "Even working to the tried and trusted George Martin formula of opening each side of vinyl with a strong song, and ending it with one difficult to follow, the 31 songs were just too varied and wide-ranging in styles to slip easily into categories."
> ~ Mark Lewisohn
> (*The Beatles Recording Sessions*, 1990)

The Rules Followed for Putting The White Album's Songs in Order (as per Mark Lewisohn)

❖ The heavier rock songs are mostly on side three.

❖ George Harrison's four songs ("While My Guitar Gently Weeps," side one; "Piggies," side two; "Long Long Long," side three; "Savoy Truffle," side four) were distributed, one song to a side.

❖ No composer had more than two songs in succession.

❖ Each side lasted between 20 and 25 minutes.

❖ Most of the songs are linked by a crossfade or straight edit.

❖ Probably as a joke, the songs with an animal in the title ("Blackbird," "Piggies," "Rocky Raccoon") were placed on side two.

Thoughts on The Beatles at This Stage

In the past, the Beatles had worked as a cohesive unit in the studio. Now they had all the time they needed to make music. They had grown from a hit-making powerhouse to an all out musical creation machine. Each Beatle had, during *The White Album*, taken the lead with his own songs. This fact has been referred to in a negative way by various writers, but I contend that it was a natural phenomenon. Each one had finally grown in ways apart from the others. The best way to handle the situation would be to let each one take a leadership role on their songs.

The amount of time spent making *The White Album* is staggering, by far the most of any Beatle album. For example, they recorded over 100 takes for "Not Guilty" alone. 100 takes! (I'm stamping my foot while writing this.) They may have let their differences blow up full-scale, but they kept on doing what they now did best: recording great music. The behind-the-scenes power struggle was now up-front. Paul McCartney had led the group through a fantastic period (1966-67). Now John Lennon was back, and the tension was palpable. We could not expect the four men to keep being the same old charming, lovable boys who did everything together.

No, now we could expect them to get together and create some of the best music they ever did. And they were far from finished. It should be pointed out that John and George particularly have since referred to these times as very unenjoyable, they sure didn't sound like that during their interviews from back in the day.

Well, there you have it: 38 pages on the Beatles doings and recordings in 1968. It was a daunting period of time of which to write, and one that I found myself shrinking from as I made it through the chapters, year by year, towards this one.

Notes

1. "Dear Prudence" was written in India as a hopeful ballad to get Prudence Farrow (Mia's sister) to come out of her bungalow. There was, apparently, a good bit of competition amongst the party to see who could become the most cosmic and Prudence (according to John) got to the point to where she wouldn't even come out "to play."

2. There is another possible explanation for leaving "Not Guilty" off of the album. When it came time to take all of the recordings and assemble it an album, George left the country. In a 24 hour marathon, John and Paul went through everything and created the running order, a *massive* task. The exclusion might have been due to his absence, a little "f*** you," if you will.

Capitol Mash-up

I grew up in America where the Capitol Beatle albums (up through *Revolver*) were really different from their UK Parlophone counterpoints, a fact I wasn't even aware of until the early 1970s when I happened across these strange UK Beatle albums at Tower Records.

The disparity was for a few reasons:

❖ In 1964, when the Beatles broke through in America, they already had a large backlog of songs released. Capitol Records naturally wanted the opportunity to sell those songs too. Fair enough.

❖ The use of instrumental tracks by United Artists on *A Hard Day's Night* (due to ownership issues of the other songs from the UK album) and by Capitol on the American *Help!* LP allowed for more surplus.

❖ LPs in England usually contained 14 tracks and as a rule did not contain singles. LPs in America usually contained about 11 and contained as many singles as they could stuff in. There will be many examples of how this was of great benefit to Capitol Records in this chapter.

Fasten your seat-belts, folks . . .

In 1963, EMI's American Subsidiary company, Capitol Records, didn't buy this "Beatles" thing and refused to distribute their records. Their reasoning was that no British musical entertainer had done well here. There were attempts to give songs to other companies ("She Loves You" to Swan Records) but there were few sales.

Vee-Jay Records was given the rights to songs from the British LP *Please Please Me* and some other records. Sadly for them, they ran into financial troubles (that's putting it in a gentle way) and were unable to put any money into promotion for the Beatles.

Then, in late 1963 and into early 1964, the Beatles started to break through the American "Iron Curtain." The men in charge at Capitol Records realized at last that they were losing out on big dollars and were amazing in their ability to toss albums together and get them on the market. At around the same time—to further confuse matters—Vee-Jay Records put out their *Introducing . . . The Beatles* LP.

By my count, EMI/Parlophone (in the UK) had released 37 Beatles songs by 1964. The rights to 12 of those songs were owned by Vee-Jay Records, making 23 available to Capitol.

> "By this time the news from England and Europe was over-whelming. They were a hit group and they (Capitol Records) had to take them more seriously than they'd done before. And also, the Swan and Vee-Jay labels were making inroads. They were selling by this time. So Capitol were forced to release 'I Want to Hold Your Hand.'"
>
> ~ George Martin
>
> (*All You Need Is Ears*, 1994)

Here is how the American Beatles' Albums were put Together

Meet The Beatles

January 20, 1964: Capitol Records released the LP *Meet the Beatles*. They took the photo from the cover of *With The Beatles*, shaded it blue and weren't completely forthcoming with the claim "The First Album."

To make *Meet The Beatles*, Capitol Records used the following	
Song Title	**British Release**
"I Saw Her Standing There"	*Please Please Me* LP
"I Want to Hold Your Hand"	British Single
"This Boy"	*With The Beatles* LP
"All I've Got to Do"	
"All My Loving"	
"Don't Bother Me"	
"Little Child"	
"Till There Was You"	
"Hold Me Tight"	
"I Wanna Be Your Man"	
"Not A Second Time"	

The Beatles' Second Album

April 10, 1964: Capitol released *The Beatles' Second Album*, using songs from many sources, creating my favorite album of all from the early days. It rocked from start to finish.

Notes: Interestingly there is only one song on it with a lead vocal by Paul McCartney.

Also, a lot of reverb was added to the mix of these songs in America. Hence, when many of us heard the true releases for the first time, they sounded dry. Conversely, when people used to the British releases hear these American versions, they sound ridiculous.

To make *The Beatles' Second Album*, Capitol Records used the following	
Song Title	**British Release**
"Thank You Girl" "I'll Get You" "She Loves You" "You Can't Do That"	British Singles
"Long Tall Sally" "I Call Your Name"	*Long Tall Sally* EP
"Roll Over Beethoven" "You've Really Got a Hold on Me" "Devil in Her Heart" "Money (That's What I Want)" "Please Mister Postman"	The five remaining tracks from the *With The Beatles* LP

Something New

July 20, 1964: It had already been three months since the last Beatle album had been issued by Capitol—this related to eons in "Beatle-time" in 1964. The movie *A Hard Day's Night* had come out. The soundtrack to the film was owned by United Artists. Since there were 8 new songs used therein, they released the album in America with those 8 songs along with four instrumentals (including the first ever sitar on a Beatles album, the instrumental version of "A Hard Day's Night"). This meant that the 5 songs recorded to fill out the UK release were available to Capitol (and 3 others from the movie, somehow). So was born a new U.S. Beatles album.

To make *Something New,* Capitol Records used the following	
Song Title	**British Release**
"I'll Cry Instead"	*A Hard Day's Night* LP
"Things We Said Today"	
"Any Time at All"	
"When I Get Home"	
"Tell Me Why" *	
"And I Love Her" *	
"I'm Happy Just to Dance with You"	
"If I Fell" *	
"Slow Down"	The two remaining songs
"Matchbox"	from the *Long Tall Sally* EP
"Komm, Gib Mir Deine Hand"	From the German sessions in early 1964

* It's completely unclear as of this writing how Capitol Records got the rights to these three songs that were clearly in the movie

Beatles '65

December 15, 1964: The Beatles had a new album out in England (*Beatles for Sale*) and there were new singles to "capitolize" upon. Time for a new album, the fourth released by Capitol in the year.

The album was such a hit and stayed popular for so long that 1965 saw the release of *Sinatra '65* by Frank Sinatra, *Ellington '65* by Duke Ellington on Reprise Records, *Trio '65* by jazz pianist Bill Evans on Verve Records, and *Brasil '65* by Sérgio Mendes.

"I Feel Fine" and "She's a Woman" were physically drenched with reverb, so much so that these American versions we were so used to are difficult to listen to now.

The cover was one of the least interesting covers ever to adorn a Beatle album.

This left a number of songs still available from *Beatles for Sale* and so a new album was conceived.

To make *Beatles '65*, Capitol Records used the following	
Song Title	**British Release**
"No Reply"	*Beatles for Sale* LP
"I'm a Loser"	
"Baby's in Black"	
"Rock and Roll Music"	
"I'll Follow the Sun"	
"Mr. Moonlight"	
"Honey Don't"	
"Everybody's Trying to Be My Baby"	
"I'll Be Back"	*A Hard Day's Night* LP
"She's a Woman"	British Single
"I Feel Fine"	

The Early Beatles

March 22, 1965: Capitol Records had tried to stop Vee-Jay from releasing their *Introducing . . . The Beatles* LP but were unable to. All they had to do, now, was to wait until October of 1964 for Vee-Jay's license to the rights to those songs to expire.

It did not chart well for Capitol Records, perhaps because everybody already had Vee-Jay's version of the same songs.

The cover was from the back of the British *Beatles for Sale* LP.

To make *The Early Beatles*, Capitol Records used the following	
Song Title	**British Release**
"Love Me Do"	British single and
"P.S. I Love You"	*Please Please Me* LP
"Please Please Me"	
"Ask Me Why"	
"Anna (Go to Him)"	*Please Please Me* LP
"Chains"	
"Boys"	
"Baby It's You"	
"A Taste of Honey"	
"Do You Want to Know a Secret"	

Beatles VI

June 14, 1965: Not including *The Beatles Story* this was the 6th Capitol Beatles album released in a year and a half. Two of the songs written by Larry Williams, "Bad Boy" and "Dizzy Miss Lizzy" were recorded specifically for the American market and recorded on Williams' birthday (May 10, 1965). Two songs were pulled from the upcoming *Help!* LP.

To make *Beatles VI*, Capitol Records used the following	
Song Title	**British Release**
"Eight Days a Week" "Kansas City/Hey-Hey-Hey-Hey!" "I Don't Want to Spoil the Party" "Words of Love" "What You're Doing" "Every Little Thing"	*Beatles for Sale* LP
"You Like Me Too Much" "Tell Me What You See"	*Help!* LP
"Bad Boy" "Dizzy Miss Lizzie"	Specifically for the American market. "Dizzy Miss Lizzie" ended up on the *Help!* LP while "Bad Boy" wasn't released in the UK until 1966's *A Collection of Beatles Oldies*.
"Yes It Is"	B-Side of "Ticket to Ride" single.

Help!

August 13, 1965: It had been a full two months since Capitol had released a Beatles album. It was time to get to work and this time they were able to put some songs into the bag for later use. Following United Artists' gambit of only putting movie soundtrack songs onto *A Hard Day's Night*, Capitol Records followed suit with *Help!* Seven actual Beatle songs were taken from the British *Help!* LP. Five instrumentals from the soundtrack were added.

To make *Help!*, Capitol Records used the following	
Song Title	**British Release**
"Help"	*Help!* LP and singles
"Ticket to Ride"	
"The Night Before"	*Help!* LP
"I Need You"	
"You've Got to Hide Your Love Away"	
"Another Girl"	
"You're Going to Lose That Girl"	

Rubber Soul

December 6, 1965: Folk-rock was big in America and Capitol Records wanted to capitalize on this trend with the new *Rubber Soul* LP. So, they removed "Drive My Car," "Nowhere Man," "What Goes On," and "If I Needed Someone" and replaced them with folky songs left off of the *Help!* LP. There was a method to their madness.

Aside from the song changes, for the first time, Capitol used the same album title AND cover for a Beatle release.

To make *Rubber Soul,* Capitol Records used the following	
Song Title	**British Release**
"I've Just Seen a Face"	*Help!* LP
"It's Only Love"	
"You Won't See Me"	*Rubber Soul* LP
"Norwegian Wood (This Bird Has Flown)"	
"Think for Yourself"	
"The Word"	
"Michelle"	
"Girl"	
"I'm Looking Through You"	
"In My Life"	
"Wait"	
"Run for Your Life"	

Yesterday and Today

June 20, 1966: It had been six months since Capitol had released a Beatle album It must be assumed that the market had saturated. There were songs from various previous releases at the ready but, most interestingly, three songs from the yet to be released *Revolver* LP! The three songs from that LP were strong Lennon songs, leaving only two by him on the American *Revolver*!

The original cover, the "Butcher" cover, was controversial and was quickly pulled from the market. Quite a few had the new, bland cover patched over the old. You could tell by looking at your album at the spot where Ringo's black t-shirt bled through. Kids like me then tried to remove the new cover and ruined the butcher cover underneath. There is a lot of information available about these various covers and their worth.

To make *Yesterday and Today*, Capitol Records used the following	
Song Title	**British Release**
"Day Tripper" "We Can Work It Out"	British single (both sides)
"Yesterday" "Act Naturally"	*Help!* LP
"Drive My Car" "Nowhere Man" "If I Needed Someone"	*Rubber Soul* LP
"I'm Only Sleeping" "Doctor Robert" "And Your Bird Can Sing"	*Revolver* LP

Revolver

August 8,1966: With their issue of *Revolver*, Capitol Records got even closer to the original release. However, passionate American Lennon fans ought to have been furious over the evisceration of some of his best songs. As told above, Capitol got hold of three songs from the British *Revolver* LP and put them onto their compilation *The Beatles Yesterday and Today*. The loss of "Doctor Robert," "And Your Bird Can Sing" and "I'm Only Sleeping" was huge. The resulting two Lennon songs were "Tomorrow Never Knows" and "She Said She Said." They're both great songs but, standing alone on an album full of some of McCartney's most brilliant pop songs to date, they seemed strange.

To make *Revolver,* Capitol Records used the following	
Song Title	**British Release**
"Taxman"	*Revolver* LP
"Eleanor Rigby"	
"Love You To"	
"Here, There and Everywhere"	
"Yellow Submarine"	
"She Said She Said"	
"Good Day Sunshine"	
"For No One"	
"I Want to Tell You"	
"Got to Get You into My life"	
"Tomorrow Never Knows"	

Sgt. Pepper's Lonely Hearts Club Band

June 2, 1967: Aside from some minor differences (the removal of the dog whistle and play-out groove gibberish) Capitol—under strict orders—at last kept a Beatle album as it was meant to be.

Magical Mystery Tour

November 27, 1967: *Magical Mystery Tour* came out as a six song EP in England. EPs didn't sell in America, so Capitol rubbed their hands together and realized that they could farm those songs and some of the recently released singles that had not been included on the British albums by those whacky Beatles.

The cover was similar to the British EP, but more colorful.

To make *Magical Mystery Tour*, Capitol Records used the following	
Song Title	**British Release**
"Magical Mystery Tour"	*Magical Mystery Tour* EP
"The Fool on the Hill"	
"Flying"	
"Blue Jay Way"	
"Your Mother Should Know"	
"I Am the Walrus"	
"Hello, Goodbye"	Various singles
"Strawberry Fields Forever"	
"Penny Lane"	
"Baby, You're a Rich Man"	
"All You Need Is Love"	

The Beatles
November 25, 1968 — no change from the British release

Yellow Submarine
January 13, 1969 — no change from the British release

Abbey Road
October 1, 1969 — no change from the British release

Three albums in a row, all just like their British counterparts.

Hey Jude
February 26, 1970: This one just never felt like a Beatles album. Could it possibly be because you just can't shove "I Should Have Known Better" on the same album as "Hey Jude"?

To make *Hey Jude,* Capitol Records used the following	
Song Title	**British Release**
"Can't Buy Me Love"	Various singles
"I Should Have Known Better"	
"Paperback Writer"	
"Rain"	
"Lady Madonna"	
"Revolution"	
"Hey Jude"	
"Old Brown Shoe"	
"The Ballad of John and Yoko"	

Final Thoughts on the Capitol Mash-up

From a purely business standpoint, you can't blame Capitol Records for messing with every album the Beatles made up to and including *Sgt. Pepper*. After all, they made a lot more money the way they did it. But that's not how I feel about it.

As this book has tried to point out, the Beatles put their blood and sweat into making their albums. They were released with just the right songs in just the right order and with 14, generally, instead of 11 songs. It's not difficult to guess how they must have felt when they saw what was happening to their albums in America. Not only were the songs different, but most of the covers were nothing short of lame (see the cover for *Beatles '65*).

If forced to pick the album that Capitol did the worst job with, I'd go with *Revolver*. By removing those three excellent Lennon tracks, they destroyed the balance of what may have been the best album they ever made. Running a close second—and not far behind—would be *Help!*. While I still enjoy the instrumental introduction to the album, it ends there. Replacing Beatle tracks with instrumental music from the movie was asking a lot for us to sit through. Nobody was going to listen to those movie tracks more than once, and it became a pain in the ass having to continually pick the needle up to skip to the next Beatles' track.

On the other hand, I love what they did with *The Beatles' Second Album*. So, as McCartney and Stevie Wonder said, "there is good and bad in everything."

TEN

In Spite of All the Danger
(1969)

1969 in Review

It didn't take long for the tenseness that began manifesting itself in the previous year to come 'round the mountain again. Or, more precisely, stay right where it was.

What were the problems? Well, Yoko was there all the time and telling people what to do, which rubbed three of the Beatles the wrong way. Paul continued to be his bossy self, especially to George who—having seen some fab work done by The Band making their initial album—had come to realize that things didn't have to be so dictatorial. Ringo, as he has since revealed, had a drinking problem, and this brought along the inherent tendencies of not wanting to work too much. John was into revealing to himself and others that his life was full of pain, especially with what he saw as an open attack on his bride-to-be.

Paul was aware that another long slog in the studio would not work well and made the suggestion that the Beatles record a television show of them rehearsing for and then performing their new songs. Because of the tensions within, the tv show became a movie with the climactic Rooftop Concert to end it all.

Bicker, bicker, bicker. The effects of the loss of Brian Epstein in 1967 now reared its ugly head. Allen Klein, who had managed the Rolling Stones for a time, got John Lennon's ear and convinced him to try to convince the others that he should manage the Beatles. He would have their existing recording contract torn up and replaced by a far more lucrative one. This had been a serious issue for the Beatles since they had signed their last one in 1967, and since then had seen other bands were making a lot more money from their contracts. Why should the biggest selling band of all time be treated so? McCartney had heard about Klein's less than above board business dealings and wanted the others to go with his wife's father and brother. It was so much more involved than I even want to get into here, but this split was a driving nail into the coffin that was, by the end of the year, to house the Beatles.

And yet, in the middle of all this, the four men came together one last time and recorded what many people feel to be their finest album: *Abbey Road*. It was the next year that the *Let It Be* recordings made their appearance, but that (for our purposes) was the end of the line for the Beatles until the mid 1990s when the four of them magically got together again and recorded/released "Free as a Bird" and "Real Love" along with their *Anthology* albums.

Yellow Submarine (LP)

Released
January 17, 1969

Peak Position
Number 2
The only Beatle album not to hit number 1

Number of Weeks on the Chart
25

Number of Days in the Studio
18

The recording of the album was completed in 1968, but the release was set to January of 1969. Well, this album is as close to being forgettable as the Beatles could manage. They were not involved with the film aside from the section at the very end and the songs they sent were mainly the bottom of the barrel ("It's All Too Much," "Only a Northern Song") along with old singles, etc. One song, recorded early in 1968, merits mention.

"Hey Bulldog"

For an album that provided four new titles: "Only a Northern Song," "Hey Bulldog," "All Together Now," and "It's All Too Much," it's clear the Beatles didn't buy into the project. Aside from the great feedback intro in "It's All Too Much," only "Hey Bulldog" stands out.

On February 11th, the Beatles were to make a promotional film for "Lady Madonna" and instead John pulled a song out of the hat, and they finished writing it in the studio.

> "There's a rare number of days each one of us is given, even if you're a Beatle, that are impossible to plan for, but on which all matters, manners, and influences just seem be fall in place, 'so perfectly well timed.' For my money, this song happened on one such day."
>
> ~ Alan W. Pollack
>
> (*Notes on . . . Series,* 1989-2000)

"Hey Bulldog" is just a great song all around. The piano moves the song, the lead solo is inspiring and beneath it all, sometimes right up there with it all, is the good old Starr/McCartney rhythm section showing how to play *right in the beat* with each other.

The piano line starts the song. The second time through, the choppy drums lift the song. The third time, Paul's bass comes in an octave higher than you might expect. Frequently when bass players play up high, a lot of the solid rhythm is lost. Not so here: it lends an element of excitement to the song, a bit brash sounding. I think "Hey Bulldog" is a top notch Beatles record, but don't ask John Lennon. While he obviously had fun making it, he sure didn't think much about it later. He was embarrassed, he says, that they would do something so simple and mundane for Yoko's first visit to the studio. This was an unfortunate turn of events because, to the outside observer, the Beatles seemingly rarely had as much fun in the studio again.

"This song needs no hype nor twist of fate in order to deserve attention. Compositionally it's got something for everyone. Musically, it creates a paradoxical mood equal parts kick-ass and jumping-jittery; quite uncannily in sympathy with the helluva mixed message delivered by the lyrics. Do you really believe the protagonist is interested in talking to you if you're lonely?"
~ Alan W. Pollack
(*Notes on . . . Series,* 1989-2000)

Alan also has some extremely interesting thoughts about the hilarious outro. I had never even come close to considering these things, but I could make similar comments about a lot of Allan's excellent work. The following is long but extremely worthwhile.

"While it remains less infamous than, say, 'Strawberry Fields [Forever]' or 'Helter Skelter,' the ending of this song is part of a pattern that could rightfully be called yet another Beatles 'trademark . . .' This penchant for making an outro the ultimate focal point of a track, to leverage it as an opportunity to further develop material heard earlier, or to surprise us with some McLuhanesque F/X germane to the medium of recorded sound has had a lasting impact on the way we perceive the form and proportions of the so-called pop song down to the current time! I dare say it bears some analogy to what Beethoven did for the coda section of Sonata form; the latter, kind of outro of its own kind . . . but where are the roots of this idea? We're more used to finding the deepest innovations of the Beatles in their synthesis of techniques and gambits taken from other artists and genres, rather than in pure new invention per

se. Yet, can anyone out there put examples of extended, tricky outros on the table that are antecedent to those of your Own Sweet Boys? It's good topic for a term paper . . . or longer!"
~ Alan W. Pollack

(Notes on . . . Series, 1989-2000)

Yellow Submarine (track listing)

Side One
1. "Yellow Submarine"
2. "Only a Northern Song"
3. "All Together Now"
4. "Hey Bulldog"
5. "It's All Too Much"
6. "All You Need Is Love"

Side Two
Seven soundtrack instrumental cuts by the George Martin Orchestra

Let It Be (LP)

Released
May 8, 1970

Peak Position
Number 1

Number of Weeks on the Chart
59

Number of Days in the Studio
13

First Song Recorded for the Album
"Dig A Pony" on January 22, 1969

Notes on Let It Be

The finished *Let It Be* album was a heroic salvaging job. It was recorded during some extremely trying times (George quit halfway through the making of it) and there were endless hours of noodling and mistakes on tape. Glyn Johns was given the tireless and thankless job of poring through all of this material and coming up with a saleable product. He eventually did come up with an album that was going to be called "*Get Back with Don't Let Me Down and 13 Other Songs.*" This album can be found on YouTube, and when you listen to it you might find yourself wondering if they actually considered releasing it. The marching orders for the producer were clearly that he was to include a vast amount of banter amongst the Beatles.

> "I had thought it would be good to let the shitty version out because it would break the Beatles, break the myth. It would be just us, with no trousers on and no glossy paint over the cover, and no hype: This is what we are like with our trousers off, would you please end the game now?"
>
> ~ John Lennon
>
> (*Rolling Stone Interview*, 1971)

Then, in 1970, after all of Johns' effort, Phil Spector was called in to make new sense out of the madness. Spector is the one who orchestrated "The Long and Winding Road" and "Across the Universe."

The album did eventually come out and was made to sound better than it was.

For the filming and recording of *Let It Be*, Paul adhered to his custom of switching back to his Höfner violin bass when the Beatles were being filmed. This had been the case, also, during the filming of the "Revolution" video. Paul has since maintained that people expect to see the Höfner—that it has become like Charlie Chaplin's cane.

Listening to the *Let It Be* and *Abbey Road* albums, the sound of the bass is certainly different. But then, truly, the sound of the whole band is different. Comparing McCartney's Höfner bass sound on *Let It Be* with *Rubber Soul*, the last time we heard the instrument, shows that recording techniques had come quite a long way in a few short years. They were able to bring his bass much higher into the mix, and it did sound good. He did not appear to be limited by the older instrument.

Although it was not released until 1970, the album *Let It Be* was recorded during the month of January, 1969. Many years later, a much better version of the album was released, entitled *Let It Be Naked*. This version of the album does not have the jam-alongs such as "Maggie Mae" or "Dig It" and Phil Spector orchestration has been removed (hence the "naked"). I recommend this version of the album, and if it had come out in this way, it would have been a far better Beatles album we came to know.

Here is some discussion on just a few selected tracks from the album *Let It Be*.

"Dig a Pony"

We all know how tense the Beatles had become with each-other. We've been hearing for years about how they couldn't pull it together anymore. It may be true that they weren't getting along but when a song was counted in, the Beatles could play and this song proves that point.

Recorded during the rooftop concert, you can hear them having nothing but fun playing "Dig a Pony." The song is an excellent example of how a bass player can best underscore a guitar heavy composition. At times, the bass is following the guitar lines, and at times it plays counter to the guitars. It's a personal preference of mine, but (as noted on "If You've Got Trouble" and "Drive My Car") I love hearing a guitar line with the bass playing an octave below. So, here it is again with all it's glory on "Dig a Pony." For the opening riff, Paul is doubling the guitar (an octave below). And he does it on and off throughout the song, at times playing straight rhythm and at times following the guitar.

If you get a chance to watch the movie *Let It Be*, you will see the Beatles having some fun and when they're on the rooftop. John and Paul are having a great time, especially on this song. They are using all of their energy to drive the point home, all together now.

Also, as you watch the movie, you'll note that there was a serious cut made to the released song. Before John begins his verse, he and Paul forcefully sing "All I want is . . ."

> "The *Let It Be* album track of this song is taken from the Rooftop Concert of 1/30/69, though Phil Spector misguidedly opted to edit out the same complete musical phrase from both the Intro and Outro sections. I don't get his motive: if he felt the track runs too long (which might be a point well taken, I'll grant), then the cut is not sufficiently large enough to make a difference. And in the meanwhile, he winds up eliminating an element from the original that helps reinforce set the obsessional tone of the piece."
>
> ~ Alan W. Pollack
>
> (*Notes on . . . Series*, 1989-2000)

"I Me Mine"

Listen closely to "I Me Mine" whenever you get a chance. Tucked away in the middle of one of the Beatles' least popular albums, you find that the song is magnificent. The song captures your attention right from the opening organ/guitar lead. George sings the song well, and the playing amongst the three musicians is high-standard Beatle quality. Three musicians? Well, here is an interesting side-note you may not have been aware of. "I Me Mine" was recorded on January 3, 1970 with only Paul, George and Ringo in attendance. According to Mark Lewisohn, the last time all four Beatles were in the studio at the same time was on August 20, 1969. But this was the last Beatles recording session.

George playfully read a press-statement to those in the studio, saying "You all will have read that Dave Dee is no longer with us. But Micky and Tich and I would just like to carry on the good work that's always gone down in number two." An intriguing announcement and it gives us three of their nicknames. Dave Dee is clearly John, Micky is Paul and Tich is Ringo.

The reason for the recording session was because of a rule that was being followed. If even a hint of a song was played in the movie, it would be on the album. There is a short sequence in the movie where George plays "I Me Mine" on the acoustic guitar for Ringo, so the three remaining Beatles came together on January 3, almost exactly one year after the *Let It Be* project (originally entitled "*Get Back*") began.

Another note of interest about the song is that it was originally about half as long as the released version. Phil Spector added a copy of the chorus to the end of the original song.

The song is in a fast ¾ waltz time. The bass is following George's acoustic guitar through much of the song which provides an interesting effect. There is an electric guitar added sparsely for further effect. As I had not heard the version on the *Let It Be* album in some years, I put it on to prepare for this paragraph and was surprised to hear the orchestration and choir added by Phil Spector.

But the lyrics! There are many who claim (and I believe it to be so) that how we see the rest of the world is a reflection of what we're like inside. Here, George is seeing the people of the world as selfish crybabies. Sort of like "Piggies," "Not Guilty" and so many of his songs. Here is a man who was relegated to third position by possibly the two most successful songwriters in history and had a hard time with the role. And he complained about it for years after the Beatles were long through. On the other hand, as proved by the Traveling Wilburys, George was extremely good in a situation where there was a balance of power between all of the writers and performers.

"The One After 909"

This song, aside from being great fun, is interesting to listen to by way of comparison to the previous versions. The first one, done at Paul's house in 1960 is worth listening to for historical purposes. The Beatles are enthusiastic and playing the song very fast. Then there is the take they recorded at Abbey Road back on March 5, 1963. That was hoped to be the B-side for the "From Me to You" single but, as they could not produce a full version of the song, it was scrapped. Until January 28, 1969, that is.

John and Paul had been discussing bringing one of their old hits back for the project. "I Want to Hold Your Hand" was considered, while George lent strong support to "Eight Days a Week." In the end, it was decided to bring this blast from the long past out and dust it off. Listened to today, it sounds like one of the more fun recordings they ever made. John and Paul are singing together with great spirit. The comparison to be made with the previous attempt is in Paul's bass playing. In 1963, he attempted (unsuccessfully) to drive the rhythm by hammering eighth-notes. In 1969, he went for a much easier one-five bass style with the occasional walking line. Another point of comparison is the inclusion of Billy Preston's Fender Rhodes piano on the new version. It's a brilliant song with great lyrics and what Frank Zappa would call a dynamo hum. Play that one again!

For a more detailed history of the song, let's turn to our musicologist.

"The song must have been written during the late fifties. Lewisohn's *[The Bealtes] LIVE[!]* book lists it as a staple of the fledgling Beatles stage act starting somewhere between 1957 - 1959 and all the way through 1962. The earliest known recording of it is on the so-called 'Quarrymen, Spring 1960' tape (some tracks of which, but not this song, appeared on *Anthology volume 1*). They took it into the studio with them in early 1963, thinking to possibly turn it into an official release, only to quietly pack it away. After this one recording session, there is, in fact, no evidence that they performed the song in concert or for broadcast ever again until they suddenly were to whip it almost six years later out for the *Get Back* sessions of January 1969."

~ Alan W. Pollack

(*Notes on . . . Series*, 1989-2000)

"The Long and Winding Road"

This song was recorded the day after the Rooftop Session, and you can see in the movie that Paul is at the helm of the ship on this day. He's at the piano and the others are seated around him.

This is a good example of a song that sounds much better on the *Let It Be Naked* album. The orchestration and choir have been removed, and you can hear the Beatles playing the complex, striking ballad as they meant it to be. John's six string Fender bass, almost inaudible on *Let It Be* turns out to be subtle, nicely done and apparent for the space he leaves between notes. He does a nifty little rhythm walk on the bridges. George's heavily tremelo'd and phased Telecaster guitar acts as a nice counter-point to the piano (the instrumental leader of the recording) and you can see in the movie that he is dedicated to the task. John and Ringo, on the other hand, look as if they'd rather be somewhere else, which is probably true. After all, this is the last day of the band's month-long, heavily filmed venture into trying to be Beatles again.

There are subtle moments when you can hear what sounds almost like a "spector" of Spector's Wall Of Sound Orchestra, especially during certain walk-ups from chord to chord. The solo at 2:30, played by Billy Preston on his ever-faithful Hammond organ must explain the cause of these subtle musical shifts. It is him who is filling in the gaps, playing beautiful little fills in little places and then falling back out of the scene again. The best example of what I'm getting at here is the "orchestration" at 3:02 just after Paul sings "A long long time ago." Nice job.

I recommend heading over to youtube and comparing the two versions of the song *(Let It Be* and *Let It Be Naked*. But, in the end, the Beatles just sound tired on this song. It's unfortunate that it wasn't done at some other point in their story.

"'The Long and Winding Road' reminds me of a trip to Yellowstone National Park. The drive seemed to take years, and the road was not straight, lots of curves. For some reason, that song also made me cry. Even at 12 years old, the lyrics

'The wild and windy night, that the rain washed away. Has left a pool of tears crying for the day. Why leave me standing here? Let me know the way' broke my heart. And the way Paul sang it!! You could almost feel his pain and want to fix it."

~ Dawn Carlson-Kingsley

(*email*, 2013)

Let It Be (track listing)

Side One	Side Two
1. "Two of Us"	1. "I've Got a Feeling"
2. "Dig a Pony"	2. "The One After 909"
3. "Across the Universe"	3. "The Long and Winding Road"
4. "I Me Mine"	4. "For You Blue"
5. "Dig It"	5. "Get Back"
6. "Let It Be"	
7. "Maggie Mae"	

"Get Back" (Single)
"Don't Let Me Down" (B-side)
(Released 11 April 1969)

The two songs on this single, "Get Back" and "Don't Let Me Down" show Paul and John at their best as songwriters during early 1969. The recordings for both sides of the single were done in the studio on January 28th. [1]

Paul played through a Fender Bassman amplifier during the making of *Let It Be*, which gave the sound a slightly raunchy, barely distorted sound he did not get at any other time. The best example of this is heard on "Don't Let Me Down."

"Don't Let Me Down" is a Lennon classic and one that he was looking forward to singing when they eventually got to whatever live show they were to put on. The released version (recorded in the studio) has an appealing tug to it. The song itself is bluesy and powerfully woeful. And yet the feel of the song is one of a live, happy feel.

"'Don't Let Me Down' is arguably about as archetypal and emblematic of the *Get Back / Let It Be* Era as either of one the latter's alternating 'title' tracks. Nevertheless, 'Don't Let Me Down' curiously failed to make the cut for the 'Let It Be' album. It appears in official release only as a lowly single B-side, taken no less, from a take that sounds peculiarly muddy, and in my humble opinion is not necessarily the best take that was available to them."

~ Alan W. Pollack

(*Notes on . . . Series*, 1989-2000)

[Note: This single was the first commercial release from the *Let It Be* sessions.]

"The Ballad of John and Yoko" (Single)
"Old Brown Shoe" (B-side)
(Released May 30, 1969)

"The Ballad of John and Yoko" was recorded by John and Paul. John, freshly returned from his whirlwind marriage and honeymoon with Yoko, had written a song about his adventures and was hot to record. Both Ringo and George were unavailable, so the ol' John/Paul duo put their next record together on April 14. Paul played drums and bass while John played acoustic and electric guitar. Both sang on the song.

Did John and Paul have fun doing this?

"A study of the original session tape provides an amusing insight into the session and clearly reveals that despite the wranglings, arguments and bitter business squabbles so widely reported of them in 1969, John Lennon and Paul McCartney's great talent, humour, musical understanding and togetherness shone through from start to finish."

~ Mark Lewisohn

(*The Beatles Recording Sessions*, 1990)

"Beyond technique, you don't need to read Lewisohn to tell with your own ears how urgent a sense of creative fun and collaborative byplay was shared by John and Paul in this April 1969 recording session, in spite of the overtly John and Yoko focus of the narrative. It forces you to question the well worn conventional wisdom that insists their musical relationship had manifestly gone bust by the previous January . . ."

~ Alan W. Pollack

(*Notes on . . . Series*, 1989-2000)

That, readers, is the John and Paul that I love to read about. They joked with each other all through the session and had a great time. Makes you sort of wonder, what if they had just kept it going. The two of them.

The flip side to "The Ballad of John and Yoko" was a brilliantly played song, "Old Brown Shoe." It is one of the Beatles' songs that is rarely mentioned. But to me it is one of their better ones. There it is, sadly languishing its life away as a flip side on a single (on the other hand, being the flip side of a Beatles single is not exactly languishing). Anyway, it is not brought up in Beatle discussions, and it was gratifying to hear it on George's *Live in Japan* album. Listen to the bass and guitar doublets on the bridge ("if I grow up . . ."). Some very fast playing, indeed! The whole song, in fact, is super-fast, and if it turns out that it was not sped up during the recording process, then it's really impressive. Well, you might say that's a mighty wicked bass part Paul is playing but if you did you'd be happily wrong. That's George Harrison showing how it can be done.

"I've tried to convince others that George played bass on 'Old Brown Shoe.' It became obvious to me after *Anthology 3* came out, because of the liner notes. The notes state that George did the demos for OBS and Something on his own that day in the studio, and the 'bass' line on OBS is exactly the same as the final version (well, 99% the same). Figuring he dubbed it on the demo himself, it would have been very hard to get Paul to play

something *George* dictated, so I surmised George played it
himself. (clever little detective, ain't I?)"

~ Michael Kimsal

(email, 2007)

George himself has admitted to that bit of insanity.

"Let It Be" (Single)
"You Know My Name (Look Up the Number)"
(B-side)
(Released March 6, 1970)

John Lennon was the bass player on the song, "Let It Be" and he, as
always, did a good job of it. The song was the Beatles only excursion
into a gospel mode and did it in true Beatles style.

"'Let It Be' is the song I hear in my head and heart when I feel
troubled. There is a lot of wisdom and truth in that song. It
reminds me to let life unfold the way it needs to. I need to just
be, to live in the moment. Sounds very simplistic but not necessarily easy to do. And for some reason, that song plays whenever
I need to hear it."

~ Priscilla T. Gomez

(email, 2013)

The instrumentation for the flip side to "Let It Be" was actually
recorded back in 1967. "You Know My Name (Look Up the Number)"
was put together two years before and, now that the B-side to a single
was needed, John and Paul (that good ol' duo) pulled the tape out of
the library and added all of the vocals you hear today.

"John and Paul weren't always getting on that well at this time,
but for that song they went onto the studio floor and sang

together around one microphone. Even at that time I was thinking 'What are they doing with this old four-track tape, recording these funny bits onto this quaint song?' But it was a fun track to do."

~ Nick Webb (*Second Engineer*)

(*The Beatles Recording Sessions*, 1990)

John and Paul having fun together in the absence of the other two Beatles seems to have had a bit of a trend during those troubled times. Listening to the record today, the fun shines through and to know it was mostly ad-libbed just makes it all the better.

The title of the song was the cause of a moment of embarrassment for me some years after its release. I was at Tower Records looking at the 45s and heard two younger guys talking to each other. "Hey, what song was the flip side of 'Let It Be'?"

I tried to resist the urge to be the know-it-all, but I turned around and said "You Know My Name."

They looked perplexed. "Ummm . . . we . . . do?"

It took me a minute to try to explain.

Final Notes on the Let It Be Sessions

As the month of January, and the end of the recording of their album came to a close, the Beatles got hot. On January 28, they recorded "Get Back" and "Don't Let Me Down" that was to become the single (session produced by George Martin). On the 29th, they recorded their first version of "I Want You (She's So Heavy)." On the 30th, they went up to the rooftop and recorded their set up there (produced by George Martin).[2]

As for that unforgettable rooftop concert:

"That was one of the greatest and most exciting days of my life. To see the Beatles playing together and getting an instant feedback from the people around them, five cameras on the roof, cameras across the road, in the road, it was just unbelievable . . . a magic, magic day."

~ Alan Parsons

(*The Beatles Recordings Sessions*, 1989)

"There were people hanging off balconies and out of every office window all around. The police were knocking on the door—George Martin went white! We really wanted to stop the traffic, we wanted to blast out the entire West End."

~ David Harries

(*The Beatles Recording Sessions*, 1990)

The recordings, proper, on the sessions that ended up producing the *Let It Be* LP effectively ended on January 31st. The songs recorded that day are a feature point in the movie: "The Long and Winding Road," "Let It Be" and "Two of Us." The first of those two feature Paul as the prominent performer on the piano with the other Beatles sitting around him looking a bit glum. The recordings from that day were produced by George Martin with Glyn Johns as 1st engineer and Alan Parsons as 2nd engineer.

If forced to pick a day when the sessions for what was to become the *Abbey Road* LP, it would be almost a month after the previous sessions ended, February 22, when the Beatles began recording "I Want You (She's So Heavy)." So, as was so often the case during the recording of Beatles albums, it was a strong John Lennon song that started things off. In the case of this first venture into the recording of the song, *Let It Be* "producer" Glyn Johns was at the helm for this session.

Abbey Road (LP)

Released
September 26, 1969

Cover Notes
On August 8, 1969, the Beatles arrived early at EMI studios (Abbey Road) to have their photograph taken. Photographer Iain Macmillan is the one who took what has become the most recognized album cover in history (the possible exception of their own *Sgt. Pepper*). He stood on a step-ladder in the middle of the road while the four Beatles walked across the street and back just in front of the recording studio.

The Beatles had broken the rules with the *Rubber Soul* album cover by leaving the name of the band off of the cover. With *Abbey Road* they went the full route and had no print on the cover at all.

Peak Position
Number 1

Number of Weeks on the Chart
129

Number of Days in the Studio
47

First Song Recorded for the Album
"I Want You (She's So Heavy)" on February 22, 1969

or

"You Never Give Me Your Money" on July 1, 1969

1969 was a jumble between *Let It Be* and *Abbey Road*.

It should be mentioned again that even though the Beatles were clearly going through hard times, they seemed to (for whatever reason) have a real need to keep recording music together. As I've picked my way through their history to write this book, it has become evident that no matter what the hard times were, when it was time to strap on and start rolling tape, these guys enjoyed playing with each other. It's possible then, that as issues outside of their music got worse, their desire to keep their musical camaraderie alive grew even stronger.

Every album they made sounds and feels so different from all the others. They seemed to re-invent themselves for each album. For *Let It Be* they decided to "return to their roots" and go for their good old live sound (a sound that was circumvented by later Phil Spector orchestration). Now, for *Abbey Road*, they were going to go back to being a studio band and spend a lot of time doing it.

The starkness so evident on *The White Album* was now replaced by lushness. It's difficult to find a classier album. The Beatles, produced again by George Martin, and engineered once again by Geoff Emerick, seemed to be back into playing songs as a cohesive unit.

Notes on the Bass Playing on Abbey Road

McCartney's bass on the white album may have been his most influential, but his playing on this album clearly stands up to his best ever. It's solid and heavy when it needs to be. Then (especially on John and George's songs) it is freewheelin' and fun. Right in the middle of those two sides is what might be the best known bass line ever recorded.

"Come Together"

The song that opens the *Abbey Road* LP is one of the most powerful the Beatles recorded. That's not to say that it was their heaviest (that distinction lies with "Helter Skelter") but for power that is sometimes subtle and sometimes not so subtle—as in the opening moments of the song.

There are many factors at work to make "Come Together" such a balanced song. The Beatles had long before learned how to shift that balance of power amongst their instruments. The first two notes of that bass line is the first thing you hear and it virtually shoves its way to the listener. As the bass line rolls up the neck, the drums set up a counter-dynamic cymbal/tom roll that is relaxed. This trade-off is played four times before John's super-cool voice begins telling the tale.

As the song rolls along, Paul's nice Fender Rhodes piano part becomes evident. "Swampy" is what John wanted, and Paul delivered.

The driving force in the song, by both the playing and the level in the mix, is the bass guitar. Good studio bass players learn that they hold so much power, defined in what they play, when they don't play and how long they hold their notes. McCartney gives us a clinic in all three aspects here. Once you start noticing these aspects of his playing on the song, it's hard not to find yourself listening to the bass as the prime instrument with the other instruments and voice riding somewhere over the top.

Note that each time the song stops at the end of John's verses (i.e., "got to be good looking cause he's so hard to see") Paul holds the bass note for varying lengths of time, each time somehow perfect for the moment in the song. It becomes addicting to hear the bass with it's ultra low end on those notes.

In fact, it occurs to me that we can only be glad that it was recorded by the Beatles. Lennon, in his solo career (not including the brilliant bass playing by Tony Levin on *Double Fantasy*) clearly called for "less is more" from his bass players. Had "Come Together" been on, say, *The Plastic Ono Band*, the song would have been a very different thing.

I think that since the Beatles were basically a "vocal" band, the vocals or melody, usually came first and the chords seemed to have been fit in to support them. Since Paul was originally a guitar player I feel that both of these things have influenced his bass playing style. For example, to be able to start on a low note and then shoot up the neck to play a slow, almost a chord-like trill as in the song "Come Together" shows something that maybe a guitarist would do in a completely different song. Paul, of course, still keeps the bass in its rightful context of the song.

"The first refrain doesn't appear until 1:10, and the extended and harmonically static outro occupies a virtually equivalent amount of time at the end. In the meanwhile that intro recurs over and over. As a result, the mood is one of having all the time in the world, in spite of the fact that both tempo and backbeat are moderately driving. (By the same token, you'll note the detail-sweating wisdom exercised by shortening some of those intro reprises in the second half of the song.)"

~ Alan W. Pollack

(*Notes on . . . Series*, 1989-2000)

It's interesting to note that by the time the Beatles came around to recording "Come Together" (July 21st), the Beatles had already record-ed quite a few songs. Geoff Emerick, who had been 1st engineer on *Revolver*, *Sgt. Pepper* and part of *The White Album* came back for this ses-sion. The old team of George Martin/Geoff Emerick, which would last for decades, was back together again.

Also note that, as a shadowy portent of things to happen 11 years later, John Lennon sings "shoot me" throughout the song. It's difficult to hear, but it's there.

"On the finished record you can really only hear the word 'shoot.' The bass guitar note falls where the 'me' is."

~ Geoff Emerick

(*The Beatles Recording Sessions*, 1990)

The other Beatles showed great skill in what they did not play. They are very restrained. The electric piano on the song, played almost out of a Quaalude-type fog, set a nice tone for the record.

"Whenever he [John] did praise any of us, it was great praise, indeed, because he didn't dish it out much. If ever you got a speck or crumb of it, you were grateful. With 'Come Together,' for instance, he wanted a piano lick to be very swampy and smoky, and I played it that way and he liked it a lot. I was quite pleased with that."

~ Paul McCartney

(*The Beatles Recording Sessions*, 1990)

"Something"

If you had not gotten enough of the McCartney touch on his Rickenbacker bass during the album opener, all you had to do was stay tuned for the next song on the album, George's beautiful song, "Something."

Here the Beatles are playing with the same confidence, poise and fun that they exhibited on "Hey Jude" from the year before. The song rolls nicely. While it is known for one of the sweetest guitar solos George had ever played, it is also known by we bass playing fans for being one of his more adventurous bass lines. And yet, as much as he plays on the track, he manages to stay out of the way of the melody; in fact, he enhances it from beginning to it's ending. In fact, you could say that it's the bass guitar that makes the ending such a moving section of the song. The bass line he plays during the final chords makes it appear that he is not going to make it through on time, but of course he does!

"Something," even with some of its lyrics lifted directly from a James Taylor song "Something In The Way She Moves," is a great song and the second most recorded song of all time; second only of course to Yesterday.

"Something was the first Beatles song I ever heard. I love how Ringo's lunky drum rolls straight into George's distinct guitar motif within the first 5 seconds of the song. That guitar owns the song but I don't think it'd be as effective without Paul's bass almost playfully plodding along. And the subtle staccato organ that holds the rhythm is such an effective texture."

~ Darrin Carlson "DC" (*Disk Jockey*)

(*email*, 2013)

"Maxwell's Silver Hammer"
"Oh! Darling"
"Octopus' Garden"
Even the greatest albums of all time, of which *Abbey Road* is certainly one, have their low moments. For me, those moments are the next three songs on the album (listed above) so we'll skip directly to one of my favorite all-time Beatles tracks . . .

"I Want You (She's So Heavy)"
"I remember that the simplicity on the new album was evident on the Beatles double album. It was evident in 'She's So Heavy,' in fact a reviewer wrote of 'She's So Heavy': 'He seems to have lost his talent for lyrics, it's so simple and boring.'

'She's So Heavy' was about Yoko. When it gets down to it, like she said, when you're drowning you don't say 'I would be incredibly pleased if someone would have the foresight to notice me drowning and come and help me,' you just scream. And in 'She's So Heavy,' I just sang 'I want you, I want you so bad, she's so heavy, I want you,' like that. I started simplifying my lyrics then, on the double album.**"**

~ John Lennon

(*Rolling Stone Interview*, 1971)

The first comment to make about this song is a recommendation to find the Beatles' *Love* CD and listen to what they did to the ending of this song. You can hear the instruments better, including the unusually heavy Hammond organ and, of course, the massive bass guitar playing by Paul McCartney.

Side one of *Abbey Road* opens with the restrained power of "Come Together." Then come the poppier songs all in a row. The closer of the side is John Lennon's second song of the album. He's back again and at his best, this time without the subtlety of his earlier song.

The recording is a study in tension and how it can be used to keep us in our seat and listening. There is that all-powerful, all enveloping opening guitar riff. That riff acts as a monster that is unleashed now and then throughout the song, and then pulled back in. In between, John leads the Beatles through various blues tempos and styles while singing his heart out. He backs his vocals up with an effective, matching guitar part. There are moments, most noticeable in the guitar solo, when the recording becomes extremely nice to listen to. As each twist and turn in the song comes about there is the sure knowledge that the guitar monster riff is right around the corner, waiting to wreak havoc on the city of our consciousness.

The sound of the guitar riff was created by John and George, apparently as a shot at Paul, recording the line over and over again, trying (successfully) to develop the thickest, rockiest guitar sound they could evolve.

The ending is mammoth and, interestingly, when the full monster is unleashed at last, it's Paul who creates the perfect backdrop with some of the wildest bass guitar this side of John Entwhistle. He goes completely haywire as the song moves along like giant alien robots tramping across the earth and bringing on the judgment day.

That section plays fifteen times and fifteen times the bass part perfectly loses all sight of reality. And then, it suddenly ends! This was in the days when albums had two sides, and when the song ended, it was followed by the record player's arm lifting and then silence in whatever house you were in at the time. The CD, almost unlawfully, goes right into the opening song on side two, "Here Comes the Sun." Not so in the record days.

But, they must have been some sessions, those that produced this stunning song.

> "This is guts Lennon R&R and all I can say is that McCartney plays his guts out too. A must listen."
> ~ John Martin
>
> *(email*, 2008)

> "'I Want You (Shess So Heavy).' I think it's first Beatles song I heard that for the first time, actually made me pay attention,

verses simply loving it just because it was the Beatles. It was kinda my first WTF moment, and a music impetus that made me want to play. As a result, I went back and started listening to the Beatles with a naive, critical ear, and wondered how I missed so much of what they did on my first go-around."

~ Todd Morrison

(*email*, 2013)

What were the discussions like when it was being determined which song would end the Beatles' last album? At first, what is now side one was to be side two (and, naturally, vice-versa). Did John fight for "I Want You (She's So Heavy)" while Paul countered with "The End"? Both songs are full of power, but I've come to think (especially with the advent of the CD) that maybe John's song would have been an equally interesting finale.

"I Want You (She's So Heavy)" ends with that sudden break and, after you've pulled yourself out of your seat and turned the album over, we have the complete opposite. It's morning time, and here comes the sun.

"Here Comes the Sun"

The song is a nice one, one of George's all-time best. But if you're a fan of rhythm sections, and if you're reading this book you probably are, you get the feeling that it is Paul and Ringo who carry the day for George. The bass and drum styles are very similar to their backing of George's "Savoy Truffle" from *The White Album*. The song needed a powerful groove and they were just the two to provide it.

I saw George perform the song with Paul Simon on *Saturday Night Live* once and found myself waiting for the drums and bass to smash their way in all through the song.

According to George, Ringo had a tough time with the rhythms, especially the triplets between the verses, but it's impossible to tell that listening to the finished recording.

All that said, I'll claim this as Paul and Ringo at their best. Well, maybe except for "Polythene Pam" . . . or "Come Together" . . . or maybe "Taxman" . . .

"Because"

Bass, by itself, is rarely engaging. But bass, playing in the background and just filling in at perfect parts, is invigorating to me. Examples of excellent bass mood setting are Woody Herman's "Bijou," Percy Faith's "Theme For A Summer Place," and maybe the best of them all: Simon & Garfunkel's "Scarborough Fair." McCartney has his moment with the next track on the album, Lennon's beautiful ballad, "Because." It fills up some of the vocal lines and walks down with little three run lines that don't just fill in gaps, but keep the song set in the right direction. Without the bass, the song is beautiful. With it, we get a lesson in tasteful playing.

"You Never Give Me Your Money"

"'You Never Give Me Your Money.' Another song framed by 3 different sections that come together as an amazing whole. It's almost a mini symphony. I love how Paul's voice changes at the 'Out of college, money spent . . . see no future . . . pay no rent' part. Same voice he uses in Lady Madonna. Then the build up of 'aaahhs' and guitar part that keeps climbing higher and higher then settles into the 'one sweet dream' part . . . then out into the '1-2-3-4-5-6-7 all good children go to heaven' fade into Sun King. It's an amazing composition."

~ Darrin Carlson "DC" (*Disk Jockey*)

(*email*, 2013)

"Sun King"

"Sun King" provided the Beatles with the opportunity, for the second time, on side two of *Abbey Road* to create the sound of morning and the sun rising. This time they pulled out all of the aural stops and created true morning. The lazy guitar and bass provide the perfect backdrop. And what about that gibberish at the end, so beautifully sung?

"for the listener who understands neither Spanish nor Italian, the question of whether or not the words make sense in literal or even figurative translation is moot and meaningless. John's fortuitous grasp of some of the rhythm of the two languages, the lilt of their vowel sounds, and even a couple of real vocabulary words thrown in for good measure, works just as well; even if it doesn't really make 'sense.' Because (and here's the kicker) in the context of a song like this, 'making sense' per se is much less important than sounding convincingly as though you do."

~ Alan W. Pollack

(*Notes on . . . Series*, 1989-2000)

"Mean Mr. Mustard"

Fuzz bass, on the lefty Fender Jazz bass, was employed on "Mean Mr. Mustard," employed over the standard bass sound. The rhythm moves in and out of 3/4 time. Then it's onward and upward to some more classic rock sounds.

"The two songs ('Mean Mr. Mustard' and 'Polythene Pam') are musical portraits of individuals who are blood-related but otherwise very different personality types, not to mention separate genders."

~ Alan W. Pollack

(*Notes on . . . Series*, 1989-2000)

I include Mr. Pollack's comment here because, embarrassed as I am to admit it, it had never in all these years occurred to me, "his sister Pam" was indeed Polythene Pam.

"Polythene Pam"

Ringo, engineered again by Emerick, never sounded better in his Beatles days than he did on this album, and this song is evidence for that. Where the drumming sounded a bit thin at times on *The White Album*, it was round and full on *Abbey Road*. There's some aggressive playing by both Ringo and Paul on this song, especially when they bring each verse line back home with that eighth note slam.

The intro line, repeated throughout the song, has an excellent stumble in it that was well contrived by Paul and Ringo. There are the three guitar chords (D A E) and then the four beats on bass and drums. Then Paul sounds as if he's trying to find his way back up to E, stops for a moment at D and finally gets up top. He may have added this little bit on accident and decided to leave it in.

Whatever, it works.

"She Came In Through the Bathroom Window"
If there's one thing that made The Beatles likable, it was their unbridled enthusiasm. Even when they weren't getting along, they always sounded like they loved what they were doing. He'd probably have denied it, but it honestly does sound like John had fun recording the acoustic guitar track on this song. Once again, Ringo and Paul work like . . . like they'd been playing together for years.

"Golden Slumbers"
"Carry That Weight"
The bass playing is deep, rich, extremely tasteful, and beautiful. With a sound system that can carry bottom end, "Golden Slumbers" comes across like a symphony. The bass, which sounds slightly out of tune to the strings, was a Fender played with power and taste by George!

"The End"
Put tastefulness aside and play some rock solid bottom end. Really set up a foundation that the guitar players can trade solos atop. That's what Paul and Ringo did for this song. The sound of the drums is good, especially the toms as Geoff Emerick had mastered the fine art of drum recording. He'd mastered bass recording some years back and took care to make sure it was done right for "The End." They laid the rhythm down like there's no tomorrow, and in their case, it was just about true.

It was the Beatles last recorded album and "The End" was, after all, an excellent way to say goodbye to their listening and buying public. Everyone gets their shot at stardom in it. Ringo gets a drum solo (his only one to this day), and along with Paul's bass, lays down a killer groove for George, Paul and John (in that order, done three times through) to play lead guitar over.

This side two of *Abbey Road* has a lot more going on for it than might meet the ear. Paul and George Martin wanted an almost symphonic movement with melodies repeated ("You Never Give Me Your Money" and "Golden Slumbers"), book-ended songs ("Mean Mr. Mustard" and "Polythene Pam") all with a lot of care. George Martin says that side one, with its shorter rock songs, was for John while side two with its anthems and medleys was for Paul.

While listening to various Beatle songs over the past years as I prepared for this book, time and time again I found myself wondering if they were just lucky and fell into these fantastic arrangements, with happenings much deeper than I felt free to go into in a book like this (and the medley is a perfect example). The structure of the chords Paul uses to begin "You Never Give Me Your Money" (A minor 7 with the 7th at the bottom of the chord, i.e., G A C E) and the piano chord structuring on "Golden Slumbers" point to some serious musical knowledge with the ever sharp ear for catchiness.[3] At times, I wondered if McCartney worked with an arranger to create these great piano sounds. But by now he has shown time after time that he just has a good head for how to make music sound good and appear to be simple.

"Her Majesty"

Have you ever wondered what the big sounding chord is that comes at the start of "Her Majesty"? Wonder no more! The original running order was "Mean Mr. Mustard," "Her Majesty," "Polythene Pam," "She Came In Through the Bathroom Window." The chord that begins "Her Majesty" was the last chord of "Mean Mr. Mustard." This explains also why the ending of "Her Majesty" seems to end in mid chord. The final note of the song was to be immediately followed by "Polythene Pam."

It was decided one day to remove "Her Majesty" from the medley, probably because it slowed the energy of the events. Paul instructed 2nd engineer John Kurtlander to throw the song away. Kurtlander, who had been scolded against ever throwing away a Beatles' recording, cut it from the tape and attached it to the end of the tape after adding about 20 seconds of leader tape. Malcom Davies' task was to cut a playback lacquer of the medley. He, also concerned about tossing out Beatles' material, left "Her Majesty" right where it was. The Beatles must have liked it because the song stayed on the album, with no final mix given to it.

That is how an accident became the final song on the final recorded Beatles' album.

During the *Abbey Road* sessions, on April 26, 1969, the Beatles were recording "Oh! Darling" and having a lot of fun at it. Producer George Martin could not be there for the day and left Chris Thomas in charge.

> "I was really thrown in at the deep end. George Martin informed me that he wouldn't be available. I can't remember word for word what he said to me, but it was something like 'There will be one Beatle there, fine. Two Beatles, great. Three Beatles, fantastic. But the minute the four of them are there that is when the inexplicable charismatic thing happens, the special magic no one has been able to explain. It will be very friendly between you and them but you'll be aware of this inexplicable presence.' Sure enough, that's exactly the way it happened. I've never felt it in any other circumstances, it was the special chemistry of the four of them which nobody since has ever had."
>
> ~ Chris Thomas (*Beatles producer*)
>
> (*The Beatles Recording Sessions*, 1990)

Abbey Road (track listing)

Side One

1. "Come Together"
2. "Something"
3. "Maxwell's Silver Hammer"
4. "Oh! Darling"
5. "Octopus's Garden"
6. "I Want You (She's So Heavy)"

Side Two

1. "Here Comes the Sun"
2. "Because"
3. "You Never Give Me Your Money"
4. "Sun King"
5. "Mean Mr. Mustard"
6. "Polythene Pam"
7. "She Came In Through the Bathroom Window"
8. "Golden Slumbers"
9. "Carry That Weight"
10. "The End"
11. "Her Majesty"

Notes

1. The version of "Get Back" on the *Let It Be* LP sounds like a live performance. Interestingly, that is a studio version, recorded on January 27th, 3 days before the rooftop performance. The comments from Paul ("Thanks, Mo" to Maureen Starkey) and John ("I'd like to thank you on behalf of the group and myself . . .") were cross faded onto the album version from the rooftop session to make it sound live. Tricky!

2. The set included an edit of 2 versions of "Get Back" that ended up in the film; "Don't Let Me Down"(the films); "I've Got a Feeling" (film and LP); "The One After 909" (film and LP); "Dig a Pony" (with Ringo's nose-blowing false start (film and LP) and, after a few other non-used songs were recorded, the final version of "Get Back" that was to make it into the film. This is the one where the police have made it to the rooftop. Ringo's wish was that they'd drag him off of the drums . . . which would have been a great dramatic effect.

3. To play "Golden Slumbers" strike the middle C and the G above, alternating it with a lower A note. It's an interesting and subtle way to play the chord because the C and G sound like a C major while the A brings it to the relative A minor. This simple effect causes a bittersweet sound, alternating between the happy major and the sadder minor. The next chord is a series of two note D minor chords. D with F, D with G, D with A and back down again.

Crossing Abbey Road

Here's the apartment building seen on
the right side of the *Abbey Road* cover.

This is EMI studios as it looked the
day my brothers and I paid a visit.

And here is the result of our effort: a blurry photo.
Left to right: my brother Gary, me and my brother Mike.

In 1970, EMI studios was wisely renamed Abbey Road Studios. Their website proclaims "welcome to the most famous studios in the world" and they are not stretching any truths. You could say that, and also claim that the road itself is amongst the most famous in the world *and* that the album cover *is* the most famous ever.

You can go to that famous crosswalk. My brothers and I did back in the '90s. While we were all in London, I hit upon the brilliant and (so I thought) altogether unique idea of heading there and having our picture taken while crossing the road in single file.

My brothers and I stood in silent awe for a while, looking at the building where the music that changed our lives was recorded. And then, it was back to my unique and original idea.

"Which one of us is going to take his shoes off?" one of us asked. I was a bit embarrassed to do that. After all this isn't something that people do every day. I realized that an elderly woman was standing watching us with what could only be described as a bemused expression.

She was very friendly, but spoke to us in almost a sing-song voice that indicated we should just get on with what we came to do. "You put your camera over there, the three of you cross the road, you get your picture and you're done."

"What?" we asked, amazed that she had somehow figured out what we were there to do. We looked around and there, not far away, was a group of four guys, one of whom was taking off his socks, waiting their turn.

"So, this . . . happens a lot?" one of us asked, still stunned.

"All day. Every day. Have fun, boys."

It was late afternoon and we took our (blurry) photo. Waiting for us to cross was a man in a car, and I'll never forget him. He had a look that I've only ever seen on the faces of British people. You'll never see it on French, German or Italians. If you've seen this look, you'll recognize what I'm talking about. The expression is friendly indeed. But behind that charming friendliness there's something in the posture that says "Right. I've been through this one too many times in my life." I could imagine the poor guy getting home, taking off his coat and saying to the wife, "Why . . . WHY do I drive down Abbey Road every day?

More people in the crosswalk, dear?"

"Americans again. And behind them were a group of Italians. I curse the day the Beatles put that photo on an album cover."

Tourist Information: Get on the Tube and follow the maps to make your way to Kilburn High Road station. Exit the station and turn to the right on Belsize Road. In a very short time you will see the street sign that lets you know you're almost there. Turn right on Abbey Road and get ready for a nice little walk. Before too long puzzle pieces will start falling into place. Look up to the left and, hey, there's that tall brown building that appears from behind the trees on the right side of the album cover. So that's what it looks like! It's a very nice neighborhood. Up ahead, there's a crosswalk. Could it be? To verify we need to see the building itself. Turn to the right, and there it is. There isn't a whole lot of signage on the building, but there doesn't need to be. And so, that is the crosswalk!

EPILOGUE

The Best is Yet to Come
(1970s and Beyond)

It is impossible for us to imagine what it would be like to have been a part of the greatest show on earth; to have been a vital member of the most popular and influential group of musicians ever to live, and then to have it fall apart.

We all expected the Beatles to shoot right into their solo careers with blinders on, but that would have been an impossible task. Interestingly, it was George Harrison, the man who had always had to wait his turn, who made the biggest post-Beatles splash with his *All Things Must Pass* and his concert and album dedicated to the people of Bangladesh. And Ringo! He started popping out the hits.

McCartney went through a rough period. His first album, recorded haphazardly at home, was popular but a critical failure. He was advised to make his next album in a much more *professional manner*. So he came back with *Ram*, full of top-notch McCartney songs and done with top-notch musicians. When that, too, was roasted by the critics, he decided to form a band and build a new career.

Wings became his central focus, and I must admit that I was not a fan of most of what I heard. Having only heard it on cheap car radios and juke boxes, I disliked "Listen to What the Man Said," until I heard it on a stereo.

In 1975-76 he took the band around the world. I was fortunate to see them in San Francisco on June 14th, 1976. It was the first time I'd seen a Beatle and, though I've seen him 3 times since, I count this one as my favorite.

There are various reasons, but the over-riding cause is that McCartney clearly wanted to tell a whole lot of his critics to shut the hell up. Perfect. With that in his mind, he wanted these shows to hit us right in the gut. He succeeded masterfully. The energy came in mountainous waves, not watered down by the screams during vital moments.

It's time to throw all restraint out and talk about one thing that pounded itself into my brain that night. It was that Paul McCartney's bass guitar playing was exactly how I wanted a bass to be, never having known it before. With his instrument, he expressed an incredible mix of coolness and mile-high flashiness that I'll never forget.

As a bass player, I had been coached through the years to stay firmly in the background. I never did like that and generally ignored the advice, but here was the preeminent bass player of us all leading the way down a new highway.

He would run up the neck, hold down the bottom end: his bass was in control of the show. Yes! "Take that, guitar players of the world," I shouted into space, but was drowned out by the full force of the crowd who was on its feet and loving it all.

Later, when I heard that the full show was coming out as an album, I couldn't wait to pick it up and listen to it. Had I been mistaken? Did I hear what I wanted to hear, but not reality? Only this album would tell. I was not disappointed.

I include this small discussion of the album because the bass playing here is what was the most-ever influential for me. I can't speak for others, but there must be many of us.

Wings Over America (LP)

Paul McCartney, working with a sound company from Texas, obviously spent a lot of time and money getting a proper sound for his tour of the states. Many that saw the show, such as the concert given at San Francisco's Cow Palace were amazed at the ability of the bass to cut through the sound. Many a bass player had died a death in that huge building. This sound comes through well on the record, put well to the fore in the mix. One aspect of McCartney's bass playing that impresses a lot of musicians is his ability to play difficult lines and sing at the same time. There is no doubt that he puts considerable effort into preparing for his performances.

The final effect of the playing and mix on the record makes the first focal point the bass and drums, with the extraneous instruments and voice almost secondary—even if this is in your subconscious. The rhythm section constantly pulls you in and then when you do break away and listen to the other instruments, it's an added treat. It is safe to say that this is the Paul McCartney people had been waiting for, hard-driving and rocking.

"Rock Show"

Is it possible for two versions of the same song to be as different as are the studio and live versions of "Rock Show"? The studio version is schmaltzy—the McCartney I was not fond of at the time. The live version is out and out hard-driving rock and roll. He played his bass with a plodding thunderous style that required him to remain rooted within himself. Every note is played from the guts, where bass playing needs to come from.

"Jet"

At the show, when the blaring horns of "Jet" filled the air, a wave of screams, such as I've never heard since, began at the front and whipped its way back. "Jet" was always a good song, but never more so than it was that night.

"Rock Show" is plodding along at a high rate of speed, the bass and drums pumping rhythm. Then, suddenly, it ended and there was a moment of almost nonchalance. The beat was taken away, and then brought back again with the beginning of "Jet."

Various Notes

Paul had by now developed a new style of bass playing. This style had showed some evidence of itself on the *Band On The Run* LP, furthered itself on *Venus and Mars* and *Speed of Sound*. The style is completely evident throughout the *Wings Over America* album and, in my opinion, stands up to anything he's ever done—including *The White Album*.

The best way to define it is that he'd genuinely solidified—obviously through countless hours of practice—his left wrist. If you watch the video you can see a very stiff left picking hand. In those days, he held his pick directly underneath his hand.

Also, for the purpose of adding to the show, he pulled off some pretty flashy bass runs. "Time To Hide" had Paul playing as if he were sitting on a burning kettle. He'd lock in with drummer Joe English and then, every so often, stick his Rickenbacker out and leap way up the neck and flash for a moment. But, and fledgling bass players take heart, his high bass runs are done with solid rhythm. There was no need whatsoever for speed just for the sake of speed, with one awe-inspiring exception.

"Soily"

This song is mentioned specifically for the silencing any possible naysayers as to his technical ability to play. To achieve a Tommy gun effect, he builds to that vocal line and then sprays—right in the middle of the drums—a chromatic run that darned few could duplicate. Many may play a chromatic run of that many notes, and many may do it with speed, but not many will do it at that speed and with perfect tempo.

Time had him on the front cover of one of their '76 magazines. "Paul Comes Back," said the caption. They were right, he was back. It's an amazing album, in spite of the fact that much of the harmony vocals were reproduced in the studio. Paul was back, if he'd ever truly left.

"Silly Love Songs"

The following note from a reader is regarding "Silly Love Songs."

> "'Silly Love Songs' is not just a silly love song. Using the compartmental song writing he really developed during the *Abbey Road* period, the use of themes and variations that all meet up in the end are all driven by separate bass lines while singing lead, really makes this one of Paul's all around best songs he ever wrote."
>
> ~ Christopher P. "Duffy" Hughes
>
> (*email*, 2007)

McCartney was, from the start, very skilled at playing his bass and singing at the same time. And, it is not easy to play a driving rhythmic instrument while singing melody. McCartney was my inspiration when I first learned to sing and play bass at the same time. I knew how well he did it, and it is the standard by which I graded myself. But then, who can sing as good as McCartney? Certainly not me! As Sting says, "Paul McCartney is the guv'nor."

When John Lennon died, the world fell out of kilter. It became flat for a while. How could a Beatle be dead? We all dealt with it in our own ways, but within each fan the lingering thought "Could the Beatles get back together?" began to die as well. As George Harrison said, "the Beatles will never get back together as long as John Lennon remains dead." It was a cold-blooded statement, but just the thing we needed to hear to get our head out of the clouds.

Then, in the mid 90s, the Beatles did get back together.

"Free as a Bird"

Realizing they wanted to record a new song for the upcoming *Anthology*, the surviving Beatles asked Yoko if there were any recordings John had around. It turns out he had quite a few. After inducting John into the rock and roll hall of fame, he went to Yoko's house to listen to the songs.

"She was there with Sean . . . and she played us a couple of tracks. There were two newies on mono cassettes which he did at home . . . [s]o I checked it out with Sean, because I didn't want him to have a problem with it. He said, 'Well, it'll be weird hearing a dead guy on lead vocal. But give it a try.' I said to them both, If it doesn't work out, you can veto it. When I told George and Ringo I'd agreed to that they were going, 'What? What if we love it?' It didn't come to that, luckily. I said to Yoko, 'Don't impose too many conditions on us, it's really difficult to do this, spiritually. We don't know, we may hate each other after two hours in the studio and just walk out. So don't put any conditions, it's tough enough."
~ Paul McCartney

(*Q magazine*, 1995)

George Martin was approached about producing the song but deferred due to his hearing loss. Then, along with producer Jeff Lynne, they did their best to turn that into a top-flight recording. It was an extremely difficult task.

"Free as a Bird" was recorded by Lennon on a cassette tape in 1977. The piano and vocal were, of course, all on the same track and so impossible to separate.

"Lynne had to produce the track with voice and piano together, but commented that it was good for the integrity of the project, as Lennon was not only singing occasional lines, but also playing on the song."

(*Wikipedia*)

It took a year and a half to get it done, but thankfully they did it and then—Holy Cow—a new Beatles' single came out. There was, of course, so much hype and publicity leading up to the first airing of the song when the *Anthology* played on television. What kind of song would this new Beatles record be? The video started at last, and there was that bird flapping around a room made up to look like Aunt Mimi's front parlor. When would the song start? I doubt if any of us, other than those who had heard Lennon's taped demo, had any idea it would be anything like it actually was.

I recall being excited about it and then when I heard it on the radio the next day was surprised that the disk jockey thought it was a big let-down. Was I, once again, gob-smacked by the Beatles into thinking se-cond-rate stuff was better than it was. Turns out, no. I think people probably wanted the second coming of "She Loves You."

Instead, we got what we've come to expect: fascinating chord pro-gressions, key changes, whooops and roller-coaster moments all based around the plodding rhythm of the song. Most of all, the Beatles are back and breaking the rules!

> "here, as always, they throw in these mold-breaking variations so effortlessly and casual like; more often than not, serving sub-tly expressive, not merely clever, ends. The form is capacious: The intro is the length of a complete verse. The verse sections are thrice doubled up; something I don't think you ever find before now in a Beatles' song.
>
> It is also somewhat complex:The bridge is halved in its se-cond appearance (George's vocal). The guitar solo appears so late in the proceedings that many other songs would be starting to pack it in by that point."
>
> ~ Alan W. Pollack
>
> (*Notes on . . . Series*, 1989-2000)

The chord progression during the introduction (as well as the vers-es) is worth taking some time to ponder. The song is in the key of A major and the verse progresses as follows: A |: F#m Dm E :| A F#m Dm G C Am Esus4 E.

The A F#m Dm E is very close to what's called, incorrectly, a circle of fifths. A whole lotta songs from the 50s, if played in A, would be A F#m Bm E or A F#m D E. John's shift to a D minor (instead of the usual major) brings a somewhat melancholy atmosphere to the sound.[1]

That sequence is followed by A F#m Dm "G C" Am and Esus4 and E.

The melancholy feel of the Dm is supplanted neatly by the G C run which brightens the mood considerably. As Mr. Pollack points out, the introduction is extremely long (about 50 seconds). With the steadfast pop-music rule being to get to the hook as quickly as possible, this is almost heretical.

When John's voice begins at last, one is struck by the (seeming lack of) quality. It seems to waver. All due to the situation of the original recording as described above.

The background music, with the mood set by the chord progression and George's pleasant sounding slide guitar, provides the perfect cushion for the song.

All three surviving Beatles had a strong influence on the recording and arrangement. It was not a simple process of playing along with whatever John had recorded. The key changes and much of the arrangement was done in the studio.

"Real Love," however, was a different story. While "Free as a Bird" was a very unfinished Lennon song, "Real Love" did not require a lot of input. For this reason, it was not as pleasurable to Paul, George and Ringo to record.

Final Notes . . . on the Beatles

Looking back over the Beatles' recordings, the thing that stands out is how quickly they grew. Step by step, they went from Liverpool lads who had a vision but not yet incredible talent to gaining that record contract to having number one hits in England to having a world-wide fame that has never been equaled.

Not satisfied with that, along the way they became masters at taking a song idea and making it sound incredible to our ears. When it came to making music, the song was always the thing. The question was, "What can we do to make this song sound as good as possible?" (Even if it was at the expense of the feelings of various people involved with their projects.) The song was the thing, and as the years went by they grew exceptionally talented at making the song the best thing you could hear.

And now, ironically, it's the songs that remain. Two of the Beatles are gone. The movies are enjoyable, but growing older all the time. Our memories of those fantastic days may fade to the background of our consciousness, but the songs still sound as impressive as they always did - and that is thanks to the tireless and endless efforts of John, Paul, George and Ringo as they worked to fulfill their end of the bargain they struck with us when we gave them our hearts and the world.

So, please! Go back and listen to those songs again; maybe with a new ear for what was going on in the background. There will always be new ways to listen to the music of the Beatles.

. . . on Paul McCartney as a bass player

Had there been no Paul McCartney to influence us, the bass-playing world would sure be a different place than it is. We went through the mill with him on the instrument, from the early years ensemble playing, through the mid-late Beatle period of flashier melodic playing and on into his solo years. He alone took the bass from the back of the band to the front. He was the first front man/bass player and the first in pop/rock to use chords. The Höfner viola shaped bass is instantly recognizable because he used it. He inspired us all and thank heavens he came around!

Notes

1. And if it sounded vaguely familiar to you, there is one precedence that occurs to me. Orbison's classic "Pretty Woman," also in the key of A major, goes through a number of key changes until it reaches the point where he pleads "Pretty woman look my way, pretty woman say you'll stay with meeeeee . . . I'll treat you right." The key has shifted back to A major and follows the A F#m Dm E progression.

The Beatles in the Studio, 1967

The Beatles never talked much about the goings-on in the studio. There were monumental efforts being made but between they certainly decided to let the music speak for itself. When you add John Lennon's demand that we stop *dreaming* about the Beatles, discussion of their studio times—the very aspect of their story that has become the most important—it became a taboo subject. So, when Mark Lewishohn was given full access to the Beatles' recording tapes and released *The Beatles Recording Sessions* in 1989, it was as if a dam had burst. It's a book you can't help but be completely soaked into. Beatle fans refer to it as "The Bible" and I've read it, cover to cover, many times. It was from his book that I discovered that Lennon almost always started the recording process for a new album with one of his stronger songs. It was through the pages of this book that we learned of the different approaches John and Paul took to turning their songs into records. Paul knew exactly what he wanted even before the session began. He worked to get others to play the parts as he had created them in his head. John was less technically savvy than Paul about recording. He'd give George Martin vague references to what he wanted and expect results.

"If I get down to the nitty gritty, it would drive me mad . . ."
~ John Lennon

(Rolling Stone Interview, 1971)

Both approaches created magic in the studio, and it is from *The Beatles Recording Sessions* we can read the story of how all of their songs were recorded. For the purposes of this book, I'll paraphrase (and quote when necessary) from Lewisohn's book to tell the story of the recording of "Strawberry Fields Forever."

Some Technical Tidbits on Recording in 1967

The Beatles style of recording by this time was to lay down rhythm tracks (no vocals) until they had a perfected, numbered, "take." It was on this take that they would add vocals and other instrumentation, piling it on until they were finished.

There were only four tracks available to them when recording during this period. This means there were four separate recordings that were bound together. Though the Beatles preferred a mono mix, in the end they needed to mix down to two tracks to allow for a stereo release. When all four tracks were filled, the engineer would perform a "reduction mix," meaning he would copy the four tracks onto one or two tracks of a new tape. This would mean that on the new four-track tape there would be two tracks filled and two available. This task required skill and technical knowledge because the sounds on each track on the old tape had to be balanced just right as it was transferred onto the new tape. The mix on the new tape was assigned a new track number.

A lot of the Beatles sounds during these days (instrumentals and vocals) were recorded slow and then sped up (for the best example, listen to McCartney's sped up voice in "When I'm Sixty-Four"). This is referred to as "vari-speed."

ADT is Automatic Double Tracking, invented by EMI head-technician Ken Townshend. It gives the voice a sound of being out of phase with itself as if the singer had sung the part twice in unison.

"Strawberry Fields Forever"

In late 1966, the Beatles convened to begin recording the album that was to become *Sgt. Pepper's Lonely Hearts Club Band.*. They were free at last to cast aside the shackles of schedules and dates and touring and playing shabby music on the road. They wanted to do what they did best: record great music and they were—at last—going to take their time doing it.

There was a theme developing for their new project. John and Paul had both written songs that were reminiscent of their Liverpool childhood, and this was to carry throughout the album. Sadly, the songs ("Strawberry Fields Forever" and "Penny Lane") never made it on the album.

> "'Strawberry Fields Forever' captured in one song everything the Beatles had learned in the four years spent inside recording studios, especially 1966, with its backwards tapes, its use of vari-speed and its use of uncommon musical instruments and it could only have been born of a mind (John Lennon's) under the influence of outlawed chemicals."
>
> ~ Mark Lewisohn
>
> (*The Beatles Recording Sessions,* 1990)

> "Before the very first recording of 'Strawberry Fields Forever,' John stood opposite me in the studio and played me the song on his acoustic guitar. It was absolutely lovely."
>
> ~ George Martin
>
> (*The Beatles Recording Sessions,* 1990)

It was to become the most complicated and difficult song they ever recorded.

November 24th They recorded a first take this night that was, according to Lewisohn, "magnificent but as far removed from the final version as possible."

In this early stage, the song began with verse instead of chorus. It included McCartney playing the flute-sounding mellotron (the first time the instrument was used in this way) and John's first attempt at the vocal. Added afterwards were a rhythm guitar (John), bass (Paul), a slide guitar (George, played onto track 4 with the vocal) Ringo's drums and maracas. Take one is a very lightly brushed attempt at the song.

> "I think that version is very charming. A very simple version of a very simple song. But, in fact, it never appeared like that and no one's ever heard that one since."
>
> ~ George Martin
>
> (*The Beatles Recording Sessions*, 1990)

Over the weekend, John and Paul thought about the simple recording they'd made and decided to heavy it up. John wanted it in a lower key.

November 28th So they decided to start over with a whole new rhythm track and tape. They tried four new takes before they found the one they wanted to work with, take 4. Track 1 contained all of the rhythm tracks (bass, guitar, mellotron and drums). The slide guitar (over "cause I'm going to") was much further back in the mix. Tracks 3 and 4 were John's double-tracked voice at the lower, and more familiar, key. Though it was faster than take 1, take 4 was still fairly restrained and somewhat simple sounding.

November 29th New takes were created (5 and 6), six being best. With each take, the song was being played faster. All four tracks were now full, so a reduction mix was made to create take 7. Onto this take ADT was added to Lennon's voice along with piano and bass.

The Beatles took a few days off to record their Christmas song and begin "When I'm Sixty-Four."

December 8th

> "John thought about it and said 'I think we can do it better. I think I want to have a bit more bite in it. Brass! Strings!' So I said 'okay, let's give it a whirl'"
>
> ~ George Martin
>
> (*The Beatles Recording Sessions*, 1990)

John wanted more than more bite. He wanted the song to be a powerful expression. Skipping take 8, they recorded 15 takes of the new version (9-24) in a new key. In the end, they decided to combine the first part of take 15 with the last part of take 24 (both incomplete takes). Being 3:40 a.m., you can't blame the engineer for putting the task off for the night. With the key raised again and sped up. The instrumentation was heavier.

December 9th Takes 15 and 24 were mixed down to one track to create take 25. Onto the now vacant track 2, Ringo added percussion and heavy drums, George added a swarmandal (the harp sounding instrument on the record), more backward cymbals, a tricky process.

December 15th George Martin recorded the three cellos and four trumpets he had scored for the new version (listening to these instruments separately from the recording shows the brilliance of his score). John's double-tracked voice was on tracks 3 and 4 along with percussion on track 3. George's very effective swarmandal (the Indian harp-sounding instrument) was also on track 3.

All four tracks now full, a new reduction mix was made, called take 26, tracks one and two. John added manic, fast vocals to the two vacant tracks (including the "cranberry sauce" comment heard at the very end). With heavy rhythm, strings and trumpets, the song had, according to Lewisohn, "taken on an intensity of almost frightening proportion." Take 26 was now best.

The rhythm instruments, including the cellos and brass were on tracks 1 and 2. Backwards cymbal and a nine or ten-piece percussion section (Beatles recording over and over on earlier takes) were on track 1.

December 21st Another piano track and more vocals by John Lennon and the song, under the guise of take 26, begun on November 24th and with countless hours put into it (no Beatle song had taken nearly so long), was finished. Or so everybody thought.

"John Lennon told me that he liked both versions of 'Strawberry Fields Forever,' the original lighter song and the intense, scored version."

~ George Martin

(*The Beatles Recording Sessions*, 1990)

John, happily bereft of technical studio knowledge, requested that Martin figured out how to join the two versions together. The problem was that they were in different keys and different tempos. Absolutely impossible. "Fine," said John, "you can fix it."

December 22nd The words "absolutely impossible" were words the Beatles did not understand, so George Martin and engineer Emerick came into the studio to see if the impossible could be done. George Martin said it was done by the grace of God and a bit of luck. They gradually sped up the remix of the slower take 7 and slowed down the faster take 26 and the miracle happened. The two mixes were matched, and the result of the technical prowess of these two men is that you would never know where the weld-point is.

"For those who want to know, the edit can be found precisely 60 seconds into the released version of the single, after one of the 'let me take you down' lines. But seek it out at your own peril: if you hear it once you might never hear the song the same way again."

~ Mark Lewisohn

(*The Beatles Recording Sessions*, 1990)

Bibliography

Cynthia Lennon, *A Twist of Lennon* (Avon Books, 1980).

George Martin and Jeremy Hornsby, *All You Need Is Ears: The inside personal story of the genius who created The Beatles* (St. Martin's Griffin; Reprint edition, 1994).

Beatles Bible, "All You Need Is Love" <http://www.beatlesbible.com/songs/all-you-need-is-love/page/2>, 2009.

David Sheff, "An Exclusive Interview: John Lennon And Yoko Ono on Love, Sex, Money, Fame and ALL ABOUT THE BEATLES." *Playboy*, January 1981.

"Drive My Car" <http://www.beatlesinterviews.org/dba06soul.html>, 1977.

Noise Addicts, "'Hard Day's Night' Mystery chord solved using math." <http://www.noiseaddicts.com/2008/11/beatles-hard-days-night-mystery-chord-solved/>, 2008.

Geoff Emerick and Howard Massey, *Here, There and Everywhere: My Life Recording the Music of the Beatles* (Gotham, 2006).

George Harrison, *I, Me, Mine* (Chronicle Books, 2002).

Derek Taylor, *It Was Twenty Years Ago Today* (New York: Fireside, First Printing 1987).

Norman "Hurricane" Smith, *John Lennon Called Me Normal* (Self pub, 2008).

Beatles Bible, "Kansas City/Hey-Hey-Hey-Hey!" <http://www. beatlesbible.com /songs/kansas-city-hey-hey-hey-hey>, 2009.

Beatles Bible, "Leave My Kitten Alone" <http://www.beatlesbible.com/songs/leave-my-kitten-alone>, 2009.

Chris Salewicz, *McCartney* (St Martins, 1987).

Alan W. Pollack, *Notes on . . . Series* <http://www.icce.rug.nl/~soundscapes/ DATABASES/AWP/awp-notes_on.shtml>, 1989-2000.

Jann S Wenner, ed., "Paul McCartney and his excellent adventure." *Rolling Stone*, January 1, 2005.

Tony Bacon, *Paul McCartney - Bass Master - Playing the Great Beatles Basslines* (Backbeat Books, 2006).

Barry Miles, *Paul McCartney: Many Years From Now* (Holt Paperbacks, 1998).

Beatles Bible, "Revolver" <http://www.beatlesbible.com/albums/revolver>, 1966.

Beatles Interviews, "She Loves You" <http://www.beatlesinterviews.org/db63.html>, 1963.

Tim Riley, *Tell Me Why* (Da Capo Press, 2002).

Tim Riley, *Tell Me Why: a Beatles Commentary* (Alfred A Knopf Inc., 1988).

Geoffrey Stokes, *The Beatles* (Rolling Stone Press - Times Books, First Edition edition 1980).

Tim Riley, *The Beatles: Album By Album, Song By Song, the Sixties and After* (Cambridge, MA: Da Capo Press, 2002).

Walter Everett, *The Beatles As Musicians, The Quarry Men through Rubber Soul* (Oxford University Press, 2001).

Mark Lewisohn, *The Beatles Recording Sessions* (Harmony Books, 1990).

Bruce Spizer , *The Beatles' Story on Capitol Records, Part One : Beatlemania & The Singles Hardcover* (Four Ninety-Eight Productions, 2000).

Max Weinberg and Robert Santelli, T*he Big Beat: Conversations with Rock's Great Drummers* (Billboard Books,1991).

Mark Lewisohn, *The Complete Beatles Recording Sessions: The Official Story of the Abbey Road Years 1962-1970* (Bounty Books, 2005).

Jerry Naylor and Steve Halliday, *The Rockabilly Legends: They Called It Rockabilly Long Before They Called It Rock and Roll* (Hal Leonard Corporation, 2007).

George Martin and William Pearson, *With a Little Help from My Friends: The Making of Sgt. Pepper* (Little Brown & Co, 1995).

Song Index

About the Author

Dennis Alstrand started playing a Kent bass his mother bought for him in 1969. It was an intense but easy experience to become adept at the instrument, especially with heroes such as Paul McCartney, Jack Bruce and Chris Squire as role models.

He still plays to this day (along with guitar and piano) and lives with his wife Sandi in the Puna district of the Big Island of Hawai'i.

As can be surmised by the frequent inclusions in this book, he loves to converse with fellow Beatles' fans and can be contacted at dennis@alstrand.com

http://dennisalstrand.com